To Kyle —

TO THE
MOON

Enjoy going to the
moon + back and
all my adventures!
Follow your destiny —

Rosemary D. Roosa

An Autobiography of an Apollo Astronaut's Daughter

ROSEMARY ROOSA

Printed in the United States of America

Library of Congress Cataloging-in-Publication data

ISBN: 978-1-072206-47-7

Published under contract with
The Nautilus Publishing Company
426 South Lamar Blvd., Suite 16
Oxford, MS 38655
Tel: 662-513-0159 • nautiluspublishing.com

To Mama and Daddy, who taught me that love endures
through the ebbs and flows

Author's Note

Life is an adventure. Particularly when it is going to the moon and back. I was born and raised during the space race between the two superpowers of the former Soviet Union and the United States. This is the first autobiography written by a child of an Apollo astronaut. It is about my life growing up in the space race, the Apollo program, and witnessing the changes in America's space program and NASA, while living my own adventures with my parents and friends. It is a book about love, change, and how, every once in a while, only a glass of champagne will do.

- Rosemary Roosa

INTRODUCTION

BY CHARLIE DUKE, APOLLO 16 ASTRONAUT

"Tranquility Base here, the Eagle has landed."

When Neil Armstrong uttered those immortal words, I was the sole voice on earth communicating with the first humans to arrive on another celestial body.

"Roger, Twang-quility," I said, stumbling over the words, "we copy you down . . ."

We were all so nervous. The lunar lander had almost run out of fuel trying to find a smooth area to land. I regained my composure and added, "… there are a bunch of guys about to turn blue. We're breathing again."

And with that, history was made.

The Apollo program was a great and challenging time, and I am proud that I am one of twelve men to have traversed the distant place called the moon. But I could not have done it without the support of family and friends.

One of my best friends was Stu Roosa. We called ourselves the Dynamic Duo. We met in 1964 at Edwards Air Force Base where we were students in the same class in test pilot school. Then we were both selected by NASA to be astronauts.

My journey in life has been one of exploration. Not only of the moon, but spiritually as well. I have been blessed. We all have a path and journey, and Rosemary, Stu's only daughter, tells her story in the pages ahead. I believe you will find it fascinating and interesting as Rosemary tells what it was like to be a child of a famous father, to work together in business, and then after the death of her dad, to sacrifice her life to be her mother's companion and caregiver.

Travel with Rosemary on her adventures in life. It is the story of a daughter who deeply loved both her parents. This book is delightful, daring, and well worth the read.

TABLE OF CONTENTS

Apollo 14 on the crawler-transporter from the NASA Vehicle
Assembly Building (VAB) to Launch Complex 39, moving at 1 mph.

Chapter 1

Preparing for the Mission

Ten. Nine. Eight. Seven. Six…

With the advent of the space program, Americans and the world counted backward with every launch as they waited with bated breath to hear the words, "…Zero. We have liftoff!"

Everybody shared in the excitement and anticipation of launches, particularly moon launches. Yet on the afternoon of Sunday, January 31, 1971, the countdown for Apollo 14 was on hold. An unexpected hold. With only 8 minutes to go before launch, the news blasted over the loudspeaker: there would be a 40-minute weather delay. The first for an Apollo launch. A small storm cloud drifted by. Flashes of Apollo 12 being struck by lightning 36 seconds into the flight came to mind. A nervous energy heightened in the crowd at Cape Kennedy as the skies darkened, but NASA wasn't taking any chances. After the near-fatal flight of Apollo 13, NASA could not afford to take any more chances.

All I could think about was that my father, Stuart "Stu" Roosa, rather Daddy, was sitting in the middle seat at the top of a 36-story-high rocket. He was 37 years old. I was 7. This was not my first Apollo launch to witness. Daddy had wanted me to see the enormity of the rocket and what he was going to experience, starting with the historic mission of Apollo 11, which in 1969 put Americans on the moon for the first time. Now it was time for my father's mission. As the crowd stared anxiously at the clock on hold, the astronauts on top knew there was only a small window of opportunity to launch this day, or the mission would be scrubbed for a month. As with all Apollo moon missions, there was only a certain amount of time to launch a Saturn V rocket. The earth was moving. The moon was moving. Delay a flight too long, and the moon would orbit past the three-day rendezvous point, putting the rocket on a trajectory to fly behind it. The launch would then have to wait another month to intercept the path of the moon. On January 31, the window of opportunity was less than three hours. We had no choice but to wait as the countdown stopped.

In the distance, we could see the large Saturn V next to a massive tower with steel arms stretched out and latched to the rocket. It was mostly white with black bands, with U.S.A. in red and the American flag painted on the side. The Saturn V rocket was a mixture of majestic beast and new-age sophistication. There was something magical about it. It looked sleek and beautiful. The rocket was designed with five bell-shaped engines and three stages, with the Command Service Module and its escape tower at the top. Venting for pressure build-up caused white "smoke" to exhale from the stages. The crystals that formed outside the fuel tanks from the liquid oxygen and hydrogen made it sparkle like it was dipped in diamonds. It was alive and waiting for its deep-space journey. All in all, the Saturn V totaled 363 feet high. The Statue of Liberty is 305 feet tall from the ground to the tip of the flame. Since Daddy did not know if this was going to be his one and only mission, he wanted as many family and friends as possible in Florida to see him blast off. But now the crew was just sitting there, in three small seats side-by-side no longer than an average sofa, not knowing if the count would continue within the launch window.

The VIP viewing area simply had bleachers and rope around a grassy area a few miles from the Saturn V rocket and launchpad. There was a small make-shift structure built of wood and plastic for some relief from the weather. No telling how many dignitaries or celebrities were there, but King Juan Carlos and Queen Sophia of Spain were in attendance, as well as politicians and military leaders. Everyone from the family was in the area, including aunts, uncles, cousins, brothers, and many close family friends. My mother, Joan Roosa, or Mama, was near my side. I was never

The astronaut wives during a press conference, with Mama (center) flanked by Louise Mitchell (right) and Louise Shepard (left), holding her hand-painted purse

The crew of Apollo 14 training in the command module simulator, with Daddy (center), Edgar Mitchell (right), and Alan Shepard (left)

too far from Mama, for in all the unknowns, she was my known. Although concerned that her husband might not lift off from the earth that day, fear was not on her face. Fear was not an emotion that my parents expressed in "The Program" – which is what the Apollo moon missions were called. All in attendance that day wanted to see that baby fly.

I wore a black and maroon pantsuit and an Apollo 14 necklace. Mama wore a red, white, and blue outfit. She had painted a square wooden purse with the Apollo 14 emblem and carried it with her on launch day. A reporter made a comment about how amateur her purse looked, but my Mama was proud to display it. Apollo 14 was the first launch to have all the wives present, although the other two wives chose a more private viewing area reserved for only family and close friends. NASA did not encourage the wives or families to attend launches, just in case the rocket blew up. Rocketry was a dangerous business. Dealing with wives and families during a potential disaster might complicate the entire situation. If wives were in Houston, at least a support system was in place.

Houston, Texas, was home base for Mission Control and the astronaut families. Our house was in a neighborhood called El Lago, "The Lake" in Spanish, which was a subdivision in Seabrook, Texas. It was a small community developed for the emerging space program. Our house was at 506 Cedar Lane and located at a bend in the lane, like the elbow of an "L", with a long straight road heading towards the community pool and the elementary school. Other astronaut families, including Neil Armstrong's, lived in El Lago. The subdivision was typical middle-class and nice, but home to some unique and talented families who were changing history.

Our home was decorated '70s modern, for my mother liked to be on the cutting edge of fashion and style. The house was a one-story ranch, with a formal living area that had a large stereo console for record playing, an upright Yamaha piano, and a black leather sofa, which was one of the first of its time. Neiman Marcus, the premier haute-couture store in Houston, shocked the furniture world in the early '70s by featuring a black leather sofa. Mama bought one, and to make it her own, she laid two bobcat-skin rugs on top of the couch, with the heads facing each other. Animal heads, mostly deer, hung here and there in the home. The dining room linked to the living room and was decorated with square tiled smoky mirrors on one wall, similar to the walls at Graceland, Elvis's home in Memphis. There was a large family room and kitchen, four bedrooms and two baths. My bedroom was also used as the guest room and was decorated with thick, dark red shag carpet and pink walls, *très* groovy. The large family room was the main room, decorated with a colorful floral carpet and a multi-colored striped couch. There was a wooden bar in the corner with three bamboo swivel stools, and all along the wood-paneled walls were Air Force plaques and photos of jet planes and rockets. The chairs and coffee table were also of bamboo and were bought when Daddy and Mama were stationed in Japan in the early 1960s. The family room also had a large, furniture-style TV positioned on four prongs. This was pre-remote control days - if one wanted to change the channel, one had to get up to do it.

The Vietnam War was showing most of the time on the TV, but it was another world to me, for we were immersed in the world of NASA and the space race with the Soviet Union. NASA, National Aeronautics & Space Administration, was formed in 1958 as an independent agency from the military to be responsible for the civilian space program. In only 11 years since inception, on July 20, 1969, NASA successfully landed on the moon. Apollo 12 followed in November and also landed successfully. My father was originally assigned to Apollo 13, but was switched to the Apollo 14 crew after NASA headquarters had vetoed the crew assignments, stating that Alan Shepard needed more time to train and that he had chosen a rookie crew. There were also rumors that the switch occurred because the crew assignment had been leaked to the media prior to the official NASA announcement, and this upset NASA, so to show that NASA was in control and did not have a media leak problem, it switched the crews. Either way, the crews were changed, and unfortunately, Apollo 13 had an oxygen tank explosion on its way to the moon, and the crew had to use the lunar module as a lifeboat until time for re-entry. I personally felt that a higher power must have been watching out for my father, for Daddy became instrumental in getting the Apollo 13 crew home safely, thanks to his training in the command module simulator for years. I also became superstitious of the number 13, for Apollo 13 launched at 13:13, and the explosion occurred on April 13. Apollo 13 was a near-fatal flight, but after the famous words, "Failure is not an option," promoted by Gene Kranz, a Mission Control Flight Director, the crew successfully splashed down in the Pacific Ocean in April 1970. Apollo 14 was put on hold to sort out any problems, but not for long.

Daddy knew the dangers involved with his job. He had already seen several of his fellow pilots die in test flights and accidents. He used to say, "If I die doing what I love to do, then know that I died happy." I grew up around the sound of supersonic jets and going to Saturn V launches. Being at NASA and around spacemen was "normal." The kids in the neighborhood attended Ed White Elementary School, named for the first American astronaut to walk in space, which was during the Gemini program. So even my school was part of The Program.

Unfortunately, Ed White died in a fire on the launch pad during the Apollo 1 full-up simulation. With him were "Gus" Grissom, one of the original seven Mercury astronauts, and Roger Chaffee, whose crew was scheduled to conduct the first moon landing. On January 27, 1967, Grissom, White, and Chaffee were participating in a "plugs-out" countdown test at Cape Kennedy for the planned February 21 launch when a fire broke out in the cabin. Some believe Chaffee's was the first cockpit voice to report the fire to ground controllers. My father was in the "blockhouse," the concrete communications room near the launch pad, and was talking with them when suddenly a voice screamed out, "Fire! ... We're burning up!" The fire raged for seventeen seconds and was fed by 100% pure oxygen. Chaffee stayed strapped in the right-hand seat, as it was his job to maintain communications in an emergency, while White in the center seat apparently tried in vain to open the hatch. The pressure build-up burst the inner cabin wall, and the surrounding air quickly decreased the intensity of the fire but produced large amounts of smoke. Daddy, along with Deke Slayton, scrambled to the Command Module as quickly as possible. But it was too late. My father said they did not burn to death but died of asphyxiation.

He used to have nightmares about the horrible accident, not only from the screams he heard, but from his own reaction. As a fighter and test pilot, a first instinct was to never panic in an emergency. Years later Daddy told me he felt guilty because his first thoughts were that they were going to regret the next day having screamed in such a way. I remember telling Daddy that he was just trained that way, but he could not get over his sense of remorse for his thoughts, and it weighed heavily on his soul, along with the loss of life of his fellow astronauts.

Despite the setbacks, Daddy planned to be ready for the Apollo 14 mission. In 1970 as the designers, engineers, and NASA reviewed the Apollo 13 oxygen-tank explosion, my father made sure the family had full-court access to NASA facilities, training, and his mission – just in case. The astronauts enjoyed playing squash to improve eye-hand coordination, and rope climbing to build upper-body strength. I was in the second grade and thought it was fun to watch the men in the scuba tank, the centrifuge, and to play in the capsule simulators.

Mama told me years later that she had been called to a second-grade teacher's conference, and the teacher showed her a drawing I made of my father apparently in a "coffin." The teacher suggested that I must be having bad thoughts about my father going into space. The teacher told Mama that for my psychological benefit, that he should not fly.

My mother laughed and told the teacher, "Rosemary is just a bad artist! And my husband is not going to stop his mission over a drawing from a 7-year-old! Besides, that's a spaceship, not a coffin! Can't you tell?" And Mama stormed out.

I do not recall the drawing, but to this day, I practically draw stick figures for people. What I do remember is that I was not in class much. We had a hectic schedule. NASA was on an aggressive pace, and Apollo 14 was scheduled for the end of January 1971. There was a lot of controversy about the assignment of Apollo 14, for it was referred to in the media as "the retread and the rookies." Alan Shepard was the first American in space in 1961, and with Shepard's historic 15-minute flight, President John F. Kennedy committed America to going to the moon and back by the end of the decade… "not because it is easy, but because it is hard." It began an all-out space race between the United States and the Soviet Union.

It was a tense time between the two superpowers, for it was believed that the country that dominated space would dominate the world. When Sputnik was launched by the Soviets in October 1957, the United States was in fear, almost panic. There was this tiny satellite flying right over our country, going "beep, beep, beep…" Kids and parents would go out at night and try to see it circling overhead. Sputnik was being controlled by the Evil Empire, our sworn enemy, for these people were "damn pinko commies!" The Soviet Union did not believe in God or freedoms. As Americans, we wondered: if they could send a satellite over us, could they wipe us out too? It was not only a battle of who controlled the sky, but our ideology and culture were at stake, too. Going into space was critical to our nation's success, if not survival.

In April 1961, Yuri Gagarin - a Russian - was the first man in space. He was a brave fellow who at the age of 34 died in a plane accident. It was rumored he got into the vodka and decided to go flying in his jet. The rule of "eight hours between the bottle and throttle" may not have applied to a man who just hurtled himself into the earth's atmosphere and whose name was now catapulted into history forever. A later inquiry into his death surmised he went into a rapid tailspin due to the backwash of a heavier test airplane that passed too close. Despite the sad circumstances, Gagarin is still one of the most beloved heroes of Russia, and his widow has a revered status. Next came the first spacewalk in March 1965 by Alexei Leonov, a gregarious, quick-witted, short and squatty cosmonaut. He left the safety of the spacecraft in zero gravity and moved around in space, and it was supposed to look like a walk in the park, but stories later revealed these "walks" were harrowing and dangerous. In zero-g, once in motion, always in motion, until acted on by an equal and opposite force. Maneuvering in space was difficult, for there was nothing to latch onto for stability. When a spacewalker twisted a latch, he would also turn with the latch and keep going in circles until he could figure out how to stop the movement. It was not like being in water, although in both environments, man cannot survive without protection and oxygen. But space was a new frontier, and both superpowers wanted to show they could master it.

Then Russia had a huge and sudden setback. Its heavy-lift rocket blew up in the late 1960s and there was a massive fire. The details were unclear, as Russia's space program operated in secret, unlike the United States, who showed its program's activities live for the world to see. The Soviet Union was at square one. The U.S. passed them up and landed on the moon by the end of the decade as boldly stated by President John Kennedy. Most people who were a part of that era can tell you exactly where they were when Neil Armstrong stepped out onto the moon for the first time and famously said, "That's one small step for man, one giant leap for mankind." In a sense, Neil Armstrong united the entire world on that historic day. However, that sense of beating communism was not far from my father's mind. He had friends flying in Vietnam, and he wanted the ideals of freedom and democracy to prevail. Daddy was patriotic and was led by simple beliefs – love of God, country, family - and planting U.S. flags on the moon.

· · ·

Stu Roosa was a talented and skilled pilot. He knew as a young boy that he wanted to be a pilot. He used to tell people what he was going to do, but my father said they would pat him on his head, and say, "Well maybe one day if you are good in school, you can work at an aircraft manufacturing company." As he got older, Daddy quit telling people about his dream, but he kept up his studies and interest in flying. He got straight A's and would ask for extra math homework from Ms. Gassett, the hardest and most feared teacher at his small high school. He built model airplanes, which he hung from the ceiling in his family's small house in Claremore, Oklahoma. Daddy loved to play marbles with the other kids on the playground and with his good eye-hand coordination would win the marbles from most of them. His pants would be dragging from all the marbles in his pockets when walking home from school. Daddy's favorite marble was an extra-large blue one. He placed his winning marbles in a large pickle jar but kept that special blue marble near him at all times.

Daddy grew up poor in the 1940s and did not have running water in the house, only an outhouse and a well. His shoes and clothes were hand-me-downs. One day while giving a book report in front of the class, Daddy looked down and noticed a hole on top of his shoe, with his big toe hanging out. He was so embarrassed that he stumbled over his report. He made an A but wanted to sit down as soon as possible. The other kids probably did not notice, for he was not alone. Claremore was a rural community, and many families were in the same economic condition. No one truly thought of themselves as poor, but they struggled along together and debated such things as which truck, a Ford or Chevy, would drive better in the mud.

My father must have thought Chevy trucks were just fine, for when Chevrolet gave each astronaut his choice of an automobile to drive, most astronauts chose the sleek Corvette. Daddy picked a Blazer. It was a simple truck and great for the outdoors and hunting, and Daddy loved to hunt. At a duck hunt one weekend, Daddy met Bob Jamison, a man who liked to hunt and fish too. Bob was a tall, lanky fellow, quick with a laugh and joke. He was the president of a small local bank in Dayton, Texas, which catered to the rice farmers in the area. In Bob's office, behind his desk, was a stuffed bobcat poised in a stalking position. "A bob for Bob," my young mind thought. When not at the bank, Bob was in blue jeans and a baseball cap, covering up his balding head. Together our families bought 100 acres just outside of Houston, near Dayton, and built a weekend home called "The Place." My mother had dreamed the home's design in her sleep and told Bob about it. While she was describing it, Bob took out a white envelope, sketched the design, and gave it to a contractor, who built the home.

The Place was not fancy but had a large center room with a circular brick fireplace, a kitchen that stretched along one wall, two bathrooms, and five bedrooms. It was just the right-sized home for a weekend getaway, except that my mother forgot to dream closets, so there were none in the bedrooms. Total cost to build: $5,000. While at The Place, my father used to love to take the Blazer into the mud and would often come back to work on Monday with mud on the tires, gun shells on top of the dashboard, and blood on the bumper from frog-giggin'. The muddier, the better. He would line up his Blazer right next to the polished Corvettes of the other astronauts. One day NASA security called Daddy with an urgent request to go to his Blazer. Security was worried one of the shotgun shells in the dashboard would blow up from the heat build-up in the truck. My father informed them that a shell explodes when a lever pushed against the back of the shell pushes against the gun powder, which then triggers the pellets being forced out of the casing. Daddy shook his head as if to say, "you should know this." My father could not tolerate stupidity. He thought security personnel should have known better. Perhaps they did and just wanted to meet the astronaut who drove a muddy truck.

To keep astronauts' flying skills sharp, NASA gave the men full access to supersonic T-38 jets. These sleek white jets painted with a streak of blue could travel over 800 mph, and Daddy loved to buzz The Place in them, coming in right over the tree tops with no warning – fast and loud. He used to fly so low that we laughed that he would have grass stains on the bottom of his jet when he landed. One time he buzzed a local crop-duster, and someone got so excited that he ran out on the grass strip to watch him. Daddy came back for a second pass and was so low over the strip that he made the guy duck.

He was proudly chuckling about it later to my mother when she simply asked, "What would have happened if he had not ducked?"

"I would have hit him!" my father said matter-of-factly.

Bob Jamison was also a pilot and had a Piper Cub that he used to let Daddy fly for fun. The J-3 Cub was a tail-dragger, with one wheel at the tail of the airplane and two wheels in front, which made the airplane sit with its nose high to the sky. Bob also had access to a Citabria, which had two seats, one in the front and one behind. The pilot generally sat in the back seat. The plane flew by a center stick, and my father was known to be a great "stick and rudder man." Often times while at The Place, Daddy used to take me up and do aerobatics, including spins and stalls. I loved stalls, and as we would steeply climb into the sky, pointing up to the moon, the plane would slowly lose its momentum. Just as we would crest, a small fishing weight which was

Stu Roosa training for weightlessness in the KC-135
Stratotanker called the "Vomit Comet"

Official NASA photo of Astronaut Stuart "Stu" Roosa

tied to a nylon string would start to rise. We were in zero-g for a few seconds, and I felt like I was floating in space. Then the ground would start to appear as we started downward, and I could hear my father push in the throttle, and we would start to rise again until the plane slowly lost its momentum, and then went into another stall. We would do this several times in a row, like the astronauts did when training in something called the "Vomit Comet." The Vomit Comet was a Boeing KC-135 Stratotanker that was hollowed out and padded and was used to conduct roller-coaster maneuvers called parabolas, a bell-curve shaped maneuver that would give the astronauts about 25 seconds of weightlessness. When Daddy flew those stalls in the Citabria, I, too, felt like an astronaut in training – minus the vomit.

· · ·

My father was unique; he had a personality one could never pigeon-hole. At 5'11" with red hair and blue eyes, he had a James Bond-like air about him, and was cool, calm and collected under pressure. He was slim and athletic, but Stu Roosa also had a sensitive side that he did not show to many. One day another astronaut, Bill Pogue, was talking about his interest in hand-writing analysis. Pogue asked some astronauts to write a few words and let him have a go at trying to analyze their personalities. Daddy said he wrote something, and after a few moments, Bill looked up with a surprised expression and said, "Hey Stu, I didn't know you were the sensitive type!" Daddy grabbed the piece of paper from him, put it in his mouth, and chewed it up! He did not want that kind of reputation around the office, for astronauts were tough and showed no fear or vulnerability. But it was this sensitivity that kept the respect between my parents. My mother said each avoided hurting the other's feelings, and I cannot remember one "down-and-out" argument between my parents. I am sure they had their disagreements, but theirs was a marriage that I truly admired. It seemed about as close to a 50/50 partnership as it comes. My mother was just as dedicated to The Program as my father, and each respected and understood the other's role and commitment.

While Daddy was training for Apollo 14, my mother was taking care of the family. I was the youngest and only girl, and my mother loved having a daughter. She had four children in four years with no twins, thus we were all born about a year apart. My mother said she was willing to have up to six boys before stopping to try for a girl, but I came along in 1963, and was born in Starkville, Mississippi. My brothers generally did their own thing and were usually out doing what boys do, picking on each other and fighting. And when they got tired of picking on others, I was usually the target. When they did pick on me, I would scream for help, and my father would wonder how so much noise could come out of such a little mouth, but it was my only defense against the three of them. Since Daddy was not always around, my mother became the disciplinarian, and she tried her best to keep order. She did not want to make the proverbial threat, "Wait till your father gets home!" She wanted Daddy to enjoy his moments with his children.

My mother, Joan Barrett, was a dynamic Southern belle. A buxom brunette with green eyes, she grew up in Tupelo, Mississippi, and went to grade school with Elvis Presley from the sixth to the eighth grades. Elvis moved to Memphis in high school, where he started his famous singing career that relied heavily on his upbringing of listening to good ol' Southern blues and gospel. My mother was youngest of three sisters and a brother, whose father was a veterinarian of large farm animals and wild creatures. People around town called my grandfather "Doc," and my grandmother was referred to as "Mammy." They were a striking couple, well-known and well-to-do. Mammy made sure my mother was versed in all ways Southern, and I, as a good Southern daughter, also learned the rules of etiquette and polite ways. My mother grew up in wealth and would regale me with stories about going to school dances that included formal gowns and dance cards. By high school graduation, she had over 20 ball gowns. I could never quite understand the concept of dance cards, but she said it was a card with a small pencil attached and worn on the wrists of the girls. The boys would write their name on the card to request dances. The protocol dictated that the boy who brought you to the dance would have the first and last dances. Other boys were allowed in-between dances, and cut-ins were acceptable.

ASTRONAUT'S WIFE — Mrs. Joan Roosa, wife of Apollo 14 command module pilot Stuart Roosa, (right), chats with her sister, Mrs. Jack Reese and mother, Mrs. J. T. Barrett of Sessums. An MSCW graduate, the former Miss Joan Barrett is visiting relatives in Oktibbeha County awaiting the wedding of her niece.

ASTRONAUT'S WIFE

Her Big Moment Will Be When He Gets Safely Back

By JESSE HILLMAN

SESSUMS — The December 1 flight of Apollo 14 should take on special significance for residents of the Golden Triangle area, since an Oktibbeha County native who graduated from MSCW will be among the millions who will wait expectantly for her husband to return from his trip around the moon.

The former Miss Joan Barrett of Sessums, now married to Major Stuart Roosa, veteran Air Force test pilot slated to be the command module pilot for the next moon mission, says she met her husband while teaching school in Virginia. She first started dating him when he was stationed at Langley Air Force Base.

Mrs. Roosa is visiting with her mother, the wife of the late Dr. J. T. Barrett of Sessums, and will stay here for the upcoming wedding of one of her nieces. With her are her four children, Chris, 11, Jack, 9, Allen, 8, and Rosemary, 4.

Mrs. Roosa states her husband was a fighter pilot and experimental test pilot before becoming a member of the Astronaut program four years ago.

"The first time he was eligible to apply, well, he applied," she states matter-of-factly. "I was happy to get what he wants."

Major Roosa, according to his wife, is a man of many talents.

Not only is he a pilot, but also has an aeronautical degree and has "what amounts to a degree" in geology — training he has received in anticipation of setting foot on the moon.

The personable Mrs. Roosa learned to hunt from her husband, and now owns a 20 gauge shotgun she uses for bobcat and deer. She also shoots "pistols, rifles... whatever I'm hunting demands."

The only complaint she voices about the astronaut program is the fact that she has little time to spend with her husband. She seems somewhat resigned to this, however, noting Major Roosa is part of a "fascinating era."

When he was assigned to a crew, she says, it was no great shock. "It wasn't a sudden thing — you learn to live with it."

Mrs. Roosa will be at Cape Kennedy for the blastoff of Apollo 14, journeying afterward to the Houston Space Center in Texas to wait out the days long flight which will once again put man on the moon.

Apollo 14, according to Mrs. Roosa, has set a new record. "It's been 33 months from launch three times," she laughs.

How does she feel about her husband going to the moon?

"I'll be glad he's fulfilled his lifelong dream," she concludes, adding that "my big moment will be when those parachutes open."

Miss Crumby Is Crowned Miss Chickasaw County

OKOLONA — Miss Margie Nell Crumby, 18-year old daughter of Mr. and Mrs. Garth Crumby of Woodland, was crowned Miss Chickasaw County in the annual pageant sponsored by the Houston Jaycees and Jaycettes. She will represent this county in the Miss Mississippi contest in July when she will vie for the title of Miss Mississippi and the opportunity to compete in the Miss America pageant.

The blonde Miss Crumby, a graduate of the Woodland High

placed first in talent and bathing suit competition. Her talent number was reading and her hobbies are reading, piano, swimming and hiking. She was crowned by Miss Barbara Webber, Miss Houston of 1969.

First alternate was Miss Lura Sharon Beasley, daughter of Mr. and Mrs. Otis Beasley Jr. of Houston, who presented an original skit. She is 18 and a sophomore at the University of Mississippi.

Named second alternate and selected Miss Congeniality by

My mother had a vivacious personality, and she smiled at everyone because she could not see well and did not want to offend anyone by not greeting them in a friendly manner. Her dance card was always full, and she laughed that she never had a moment to stop for a rest or to have a glass of punch or visit with her girlfriends. She was also a good dancer, having learned rhythm and music, like Elvis, from a mixture of Southern culture and rock & roll roots. Mama used to say she was an "original rock & roller" — and she could boogie like no other.

Mama was also the politician in the family. While at NASA, Mama understood the need to work the social networks to help her husband advance his career. She was an active member in the Astronaut Wives Club, the Officers' Wives Club, and volunteered for major charity events in Houston. The socialite of the time in Houston was Miss Ima Hogg, who had great wealth, power, and prestige. She adored Mama, and one time at a large charity event, a few years before my father's flight, Daddy was checking the seating chart and saw that he and Mama were to sit next to Ima Hogg at Table #1. Alan Shepard, who had already flown in space, was seated at Table #2 along with his wife, Louise. My father kept thinking it was a mistake, for in his mind Shepard outranked him, but there was no mistake, and the next day in the *Houston Chronicle* there was a large picture of Daddy listed as "the famous astronaut" sitting next to Ima Hogg. Alan Shepard took notice, and along with my father's flying skills and dedication to The Program, it probably helped Daddy get recognized early on by the first American in space.

Once while flying back to Houston from the Cape, Alan Shepard flew lead while Daddy flew in formation. It was a rough flight, for Alan Shepard was all over the sky, and it took skill and concentration to fly in a tight formation off his wing.

When they landed, Daddy said, "Al, you were a terrible lead! That's one of the most difficult flights I've had from the Cape!"

Shepard fired back, "Sounds like a personal problem," and shrugged it off.

Daddy said later that Al was probably testing his flying skills.

• • •

Astronaut selection for a mission was competitive and its process a bit of a mystery. Daddy would say, "You knew who you needed to impress, you just didn't know how!" Out of the hundreds, if not thousands, of applicants for my father's class, only 19 were chosen. My father's group was the fifth astronaut selection that NASA conducted. The first was for the "Original 7" chosen for the Mercury program. The Mercury program was in the late 1950s /early 1960s, and each flight was with one man. On May 5, 1961, Alan Shepard was the first to fly with a 15-minute sub-orbital mission. Gus Grissom was second in July, with his spacecraft being lost at sea when the hatch accidentally blew open. In 1962 John Glenn was the third, and the first American to orbit the earth. In time, the other Mercury astronauts had their missions, too.

After Mercury was the Gemini program, which had two men per flight. These missions were critical for the development of space travel techniques in support of Apollo, including orbital maneuvers necessary to achieve rendezvous and docking. A highlight of this program was on June 3, 1965, when Ed White performed the first American spacewalk for 20 minutes while he was in orbit. "This is fun," he reported back to Mission Control. On the ground, he told reporters that he felt "red, white, and blue all over" during his spacewalk. Also in 1965, there was a selection of scientists in the fourth group. And finally, in April 1966, NASA announced the largest class ever chosen, the "Original 19" as they called themselves, a parody of the "Original 7." These men were selected for future space flights, including Apollo, which were comprised of three men per crew whose goal was to step foot on the moon.

All astronauts selected for NASA had to meet certain requirements. At the time, they were male, under 6 feet, and had test-pilot experience. And all wanted a mission. They would volunteer for just about anything to show their "right stuff." My father was determined and driven and was working hard to get on a crew assignment. Once, at the Cape, he volunteered to be the first human subject for the slide-wire from the escape tower on top of the Saturn V rocket. All the test dummies had crashed and been ripped apart. My father strapped himself to the wire and miraculously made it to the bottom unscathed. Or if he was hurt, he was not going to show it. The brave maneuver got his name buzzing. He also volunteered, along with two other astronauts, to sit out at sea in the command module capsule for three days to see how the spacecraft would hold up if lost in the ocean for not re-entering on target. The capsule did great. The astronauts were terribly seasick from bobbing around in a closed structure for 72 hours, but not one of them complained.

In March 1969, Daddy was CAPCOM (capsule communicator) on Apollo 9. CAPCOMs were astronauts, whether they had flown a mission or not. Astronauts trusted each other when it came to crucial communication, and it was decided early on at NASA that only astronauts would talk to each other on the "earth-space" communications link. Information was generally relayed from the flight controllers to the flight director to the CAPCOM and vice-versa. Apollo 9 was the first mission to test the docking procedure and the first time the lunar module was tested in space. The crew consisted of Commander Jim McDivitt, Command Module Pilot Dave Scott, and Lunar Module Pilot Rusty Schweickart, the other red-headed astronaut. The mission was an important one and lasted 10 days in space. Daddy knew the checklist and flight plan like the back of his hand. It was a difficult mission, and my father was key in assisting the crew from the ground. The Flight Director, Chris Kraft, said, "Stu, you seem to know this flight better than the crew!" It got the attention of those in the NASA hierarchy, and I believe put him on the fast-track. He was voted MVP "Most Valuable Player" for the mission, and thus the one chosen to hang the Apollo 9 plaque at Mission Control in Houston.

The Chief of the Astronaut Office was Alan Shepard, and after correction of an inner ear problem, he was put back on flying status. He had been grounded for five years. He placed himself as Commander of the next unassigned Apollo mission and hand-picked his crew. He was known as either "Smilin' Al" or the "Icy Commander" – depending on his mood.

Stu Roosa as CAPCOM (Capsule Communicator) during an Apollo
flight, for only astronauts spoke with astronauts in the
Earth-space communication link

Apollo 14 crew on the lunar lander with Edgar Mitchell (top), Stu Roosa
(center, on last rung of ladder), and Alan Shepard
(bottom, as if "on the moon")

His secretary used to put a picture outside his office so that a person would know what kind of mood Al was in that day. He was feared by most of the new astronauts, and if Daddy saw Alan Shepard walking down the hall, he would duck into another hallway just to avoid him. Then one day Alan Shepard asked Daddy and Edgar Mitchell into his office.

Shepard said, "If you don't mind flying with an old retread, then I'd like you to fly with me as the prime crew on the next Apollo mission."

Daddy had not yet served on a back-up crew and said to him, "Did you say prime?"

The Icy Commander flatly said, "You heard me."

That day, my father became the first and only Apollo astronaut to be placed on a prime crew without having first served on a back-up crew. It sent a few shock waves through the astronaut corps, and some were not happy with Roosa's new assignment. One veteran astronaut of high rank started to fight the selection, pushing T.K. "Ken" Mattingly to fly as the Command Module Pilot, since Ken had been replaced on Apollo 13 due to exposure to the measles virus. Daddy started to get nervous that he might get bumped due to politics. He finally went to Alan Shepard and told him his concerns, and without saying a word, Al got up and marched out of the office. Alan Shepard sent a message to the other astronauts: "Do not mess with my crew."

• • •

In preparing for the mission, the Apollo 14 crew was placed in quarantine for several weeks prior to the flight to protect against germs from the outside world, and to ready themselves mentally and physically for the mission. We would visit Daddy through a thick pane of glass that had a speaker below. I would tap on the glass and wave and talk like I was at a bank window. Since I was only 7 years old and in the second grade, these strange proceedings seemed normal, and I knew my daddy was to be launched into space soon. A few days before launch, we traveled to Florida on a private jet and stayed at the most famous hotel in the area, the

Holiday Inn. Mercedes Benz had shipped a bus over from Germany with a driver to take the Mississippi contingency to Florida. There were all kinds of parties prior to launch, and the "Space Coast" was jammed with RVs, Volkswagen buses, and people – lots of people – who ranged from the elite to the beachgoer.

Finally on Sunday, January 31, it was launch day. We went to a private Mass at the local Catholic church, which was in a beautiful palm tree setting off A-1A. We said our prayers, paused in the gravity of the moment, and then with a police escort headed for the VIP area. NASA security was tight, so we had to be in place hours ahead of launch time. The priest headed to the crew quarters to the staff, doctors, and astronauts. The priest conducted another private Mass for Daddy inside the quarantined area, prior to the men suiting up.

The countdown had been going perfectly... until the afternoon storm clouds had built up and caused the delay. Delays were something Mama often encountered being married to an astronaut. But not these kinds of delays. Daddy was generally running late due to his need to complete "just one more thing."

She used to poke a friendly jab at him and say in a slightly irritated tone, "Stuart, you might even be late to your launch!"

Daddy would counter in a consoling tone, "Now, Joan, you know I can't be late to that... there will be a cast of thousands making sure we are on schedule."

Mama was thinking about that banter and how technically, her husband was now late to his own launch, although this time it was due to Mother Nature.

Mama had visited the Apollo 14 Saturn V rocket the night before as it was lit up brightly by the arc lights. She never got accustomed to seeing a rocket in all its glory. As it glistened in the crisp night air, Mama looked up and saw the moon. She thought about how this magnificent vehicle was about to leave and go there the next day. Or was it?

Suddenly, the storm cloud dissipated. The 40-minute hold ended. As a murmur started building around us, everyone was staring at the sky and rocket. Venting stopped from the Saturn V, which meant the system was going into internal controls. The count was back on. The crowd went still and quiet. The minutes counted down to seconds. Mama's green eyes were focused on the Saturn V. Finally, from Pad A, Launch Complex 39, at 4:03 p.m. (EST), Apollo 14 hit zero in the countdown.

Mama and me in the VIP viewing area, waiting for lift-off

Apollo 14 launches January 31, 1971

CHAPTER 2

To the Moon and Back

The fire from the five large engines spewed out and went as far to each side as the rocket was high. The distance from the launch pad to the VIP viewing area was over two miles, so at first all we could see was gigantic flames of red, yellow, and white. Then we heard a loud, deep growl, and the ground began to shake as it would in an earthquake. For a split second no one breathed as eyes strained to see if the rocket was going to take off or blow up. The Saturn V was so big and heavy that even with fuel burning at 3,357 gallons per second, it sat on the launch pad for a few moments before gaining momentum. At the time, it was classified information that the rocket was fastened down with steel rods to help eliminate oscillations. The fire had to burn through steel fasteners before allowing the Saturn V to lift off. This was a brilliant solution by the rocket engineers to prevent gyrations and allowed for a straight trajectory. Yet nothing was ever certain with launches, and a myriad of things could go wrong in a split second. If the rocket slightly leaned to one side and hit part of the tower during lift off, the ripping and tearing of the metal with the fire below would certainly have assured an explosion. The crew was ready to use the escape tower if necessary, but even this was a risky and tricky maneuver, so lives were on the line from the get-go.

We all jumped to our feet when we saw the flames. Excited screams filled the air over the massive rumble of the rocket taking off for deep space. The ground shook as the sound of the crackling fire reverberated in our ears. The tremendous energy hit our bodies, and our hearts were pounding. I heard voices shouting, "Go, baby, go!" The rocket began to slowly lift off, and the crowd roared over the popping of the fiery mixture of thousands of pounds of liquid hydrogen and oxygen burning together in a great propellant symphony. Mama blurted out, "God Speed, Stuart!" Water jets spraying to keep the launch pad from burning up caused a misty bright white smoke to surround the area. This sophisticated fiery beast was alive and on its own to start the journey to another world. As the massive rocket cleared the tower, a slight gasp of relief was heard as prayers were answered. The first stage of the Saturn V propelled the vehicle to 42 miles high in a mere two and half minutes, traveling at a speed of 6,164 miles per hour. Due to the clouds in the area, we soon lost sight of the rocket.

As the white smoke lingered in the air around the launch pad, the crowd quieted down as everyone's adrenaline diminished. Apollo launches were spectacular events — a feast for the senses. Apollo 14 did not disappoint. Now it was on its way to the moon for America's third attempt to land successfully on the lunar surface. The crew journeyed on as we earthlings packed up for the trip home to wait out the mission. The astronaut families were escorted to the airport to head back to Houston, Texas. We boarded the plane in Florida thinking this was going to be a successful mission.

But back on Apollo 14, trouble was brewing. Barely three hours into the flight, the Command Service Module (CSM) was to dock with the Lunar Module (LM, pronounced "lem"). Since my father was the Command Module Pilot, he moved to the left seat shortly after take-off and was responsible for docking the CSM with the LM. Stu's sharp piloting skills were honed and ready, and Daddy hit the docking probe dead-on. But the latches did not catch. Daddy tried it again, coming in fast and hard. No capture. Ed Mitchell made the comment, "Stu, don't run through it!"

Daddy made the call to Mission Control: "Let's back off and think about this for awhile." As Houston and the experts were working on the problem, Alan Shepard was kicking around the idea among the three of them that he might conduct an unauthorized spacewalk – just suit up, go out, and pull the two spacecrafts together while manually connecting the

Apollo Crew Overcomes Docking Problem

Antares, Kitty Hawk Finally Lock On Sixth Try

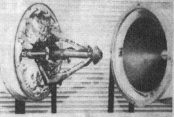

FAMILIAR VOICE FROM SPACE

Pioneer Shepard Still Enthusiastic

SHEPARD 'LEAVING TOWN'

Astronauts' Wives Are Confident

latches. This would have been a dangerous, unpracticed maneuver, but these guys were used to handling quick-thinking "do-or-die" issues.

The world was on edge after Apollo 13's flight, and as soon as our family arrived in Houston the reporters were already at the airport, asking Mama how she felt about Apollo 14 having trouble. She had not yet heard the news, but like Daddy, was cool, calm, and collected. She said she had faith and confidence in her husband and the entire NASA team, and that she had no doubt the problem would be resolved. Daddy later told me that he was praying hard to Mother Mary. While verbally communicating with NASA, he silently kept the prayers up. An in-flight televised inspection of the docking mechanism revealed no apparent reason for the malfunction. The system appeared to be functioning normally, yet the latches were not holding. Daddy made several attempts. Still no capture. On the sixth try and approximately two hours later, the latches finally took hold. Apollo 14 was about 23,800 miles from earth. They had a hard dock. Daddy's prayers were answered. This was not the first time Daddy had prayed for divine assistance in a critical situation. One time while flying an experimental jet, the fuel feed from one of the engines quit working. In an incident such as this, a pilot would have no choice but to eject and bail out. Daddy, a quiet and devout man, said he prayed to Mother Mary and somehow "dead-sticked" the jet to a safe landing. The mechanics afterwards said it was a miracle that he was able to keep flying with no fuel feed. But losing an airplane might have meant losing a career, and Daddy was destined to fly.

During the mission, the reporters buzzed 24 hours a day. My mother had warned us that we would be in the spotlight while Daddy was flying and that once his flight was over, so would be the attention from the reporters. Another astronaut's wife, Sue Bean, married to Alan Bean from Apollo 12, gave Mama some good advice. Sue told Mama to go out each morning and give a statement, be positive, and let the reporters take a few pictures of the kids, the dog, or of her going to the grocery store – just something to give the reporters a story for the day. And sure enough, once they had a story, they would back off a bit. For me, the mission was a bit of a blur, for we continued riding our bikes to school and back, then waking up

Mama posing for the daily picture during the mission for the photographers outside our home in El Lago with our dog, Beau

sometimes at night to visit Daddy on the big screen at Mission Control. My young brain did not comprehend why the astronauts were not on the same schedule as we were, and I wondered sometimes why they weren't sleeping. There was no fear in the air, or that anything was abnormal with our lives. Daddy was just flying to the moon and back.

As the men did their job in space, the family went live with an interview with Walter Cronkite on the CBS Evening News. My mother said that was the most nervous she was in the mission, for she did not want us to mess up in front of all America. We got dressed and drove to the gates outside of NASA. The camera crew set up near a cement bench, where we sat with a fountain as the backdrop. The reporter seemed nice, but I was so painfully shy that I hoped he would not ask me anything. The crew fit my mother with an earpiece so she could hear Walter Cronkite directly, but we were in the dark. My mother put me on her right side and the boys to her left, lined up from oldest to youngest. We seemed to instinctively know to convey a positive attitude for the cameras, and when the reporter shoved the microphone at us and asked how we felt about our Daddy going to the moon, we said it was "just great!" However, with our Texas drawls, we laughingly made "It's greaaaat" the running line. It sounded a bit like Tony the Tiger from the mornings we'd eat our cereal and drink Tang - the official "orange juice" of the astronauts. Tang was an orange-flavored powder that the astronauts mixed with water in flight to cover up the taste of minerals and vitamins that NASA wanted the men to have to ensure their health in space. It also became a hit drink with kids on earth.

At the house, NASA had placed a small white voice transmitter, called a squawk box, near the family room so that we could listen to the communication between the Apollo 14 crew and Mission Control. Mama used to laugh and say she was one of only a few women in the world who heard everything her husband said for nine days straight! We could not communicate back, but when we had our scheduled family visits to Mission Control, our fathers knew we were there and watching them. At one point, Daddy asked what we were having for dinner, and Mama was able to send through CAPCOM: "Lasagna." It was one of Daddy's favorites. Mama, a gourmet cook who loved to read cookbooks, had adapted the recipe from Julia Child's cookbook. He must have felt very far from home and missing earth and those dinners.

At night, the moon was about three-fourths full, and we started calling it a "Fra Mauro Moon" based on the landing site. It was a strange feeling looking up and knowing that Daddy was at the moon. Even as a young child, I felt the connection. In space, the earth view is reversed to the moon, so the crew was looking back at a one-fourth full earth. There was not a lot to see from 240,000 miles away, but Daddy said there was no denying which object in the blackness of space was earth. It was like a bright blue marble, just like the blue marble that was his favorite as a child.

It took approximately three days to reach the moon, traveling up to 25,000 miles per hour – which is roughly 10 times faster than a speeding bullet shot from a high-powered rifle. Faster than Superman, my father used to say. The personalities of the Apollo 14 crew were diverse. My father described their crew as professional and the best at what they did in terms of intelligence, skill, and precision. Shepard told his crew that they were going to be the best-trained, for the Icy Commander expected perfection. Alan Shepard did not micromanage his crew and allowed my father to name the Command Module, since it was "his baby to fly." My father named it *Kitty Hawk* in honor of America's first flight by the Wright Brothers at Kitty Hawk, North Carolina, in 1903. Ed Mitchell named the LM, calling it *Antares*, the brightest star in the constellation Scorpius.

• • •

When the crew approached the moon, the earth got smaller and smaller, while the moon got bigger and bigger in the capsule window. After a critical burn to slow the spacecraft down, they entered into lunar orbit. The crew of Apollo 14 had arrived at their new "home" with nothing to see but gray rocks and a desolate landscape. It was a lonely and unforgiving place. At the appropriate time, Alan Shepard and Ed Mitchell moved to the LM and closed the hatch door to the Command Module. Soon they would be unlatching to land on the moon. The unspoken question that hung in the air was whether the latches would work again upon return.

The first two moon landings were in the "mares" or seas – which were known to be smooth. Fra Mauro was in the "highlands" or mountains of the moon, and it was a risky landing spot. As Alan Shepard guided the LM towards the surface with limited fuel and time, an on-board guidance and altimeter reading suddenly malfunctioned. Flight procedures dictated to abort the mission and rendezvous with the Command Module. The moon landing was in jeopardy of being lost again. My father called Alan Shepard "Oh, Fearless One" and instinctively knew that Al would not abort; he would land it without the computer if necessary. However, one bright young man working with Mission Control figured out the altimeter was set on infinity and relayed to the LM via CAPCOM to simply recycle the program and turn it off and on. This did the trick.

Alan Shepard and Ed Mitchell descended to the lunar surface for Apollo 14's historic landing on February 5, 1971. *Antares* made the most precise landing to date, approximately 87 feet from the targeted landing point. Daddy was left alone to fly solo in *Kitty Hawk* around the moon in a lunar orbit about 60 miles high, orbiting to the back side of the moon every couple of hours. Because the moon has no atmosphere, there is no dawn or dusk as on earth. The Command Module would instantly go dark on the back side and start to cool. Then condensation would start to form on the instrument panel, and communication with earth was lost. Although my father was not an outwardly emotional man, I could tell by his voice when he recounted losing sight and sound of earth, that these moments were heady, and a time for pause and reflection. After a while, and without any warning, the spacecraft would instantly hit sunlight again, communication with Mission Control would crackle back to life, and he could see the earth – shining bright against the blackness of space. He could hold up his thumb and completely cover the view of this magnificent planet, and in one instant wipe out his world, his country, his home, and his family.

On one particularly lonely orbit, Daddy turned on the cassette recorder that was floating nearby. A few Country & Western singers had made a

NASA rendering of the Command Module circling the moon with the
Lunar Module landing on the surface

special recording for him, and Sonny James was singing *How Great Thou Art*. Just as the earth came back into view, he heard those beautiful lines, *"… in awesome wonder, consider all the worlds Thy hands have made. I see the stars, and hear the rolling thunder… Thy power throughout, the universe displayed…,"* and it gave him an immense sense of comfort. He was a small blip in a vast universe far from home, circling around the moon with country music as his companion.

• • •

My father was trained by one of the world's leading lunar geologists at the time, Farouk El-Baz. Originally from Egypt, Farouk was well-liked and had an engaging personality. One of my father's main objectives was to take pictures of future landing sites. On the first day in lunar orbit, he experienced problems with the Hasselblad camera. After trying to fix it for Farouk's sake, and going on almost 24 hours of no sleep, Daddy finally gave up and tried to take a sleep break. My father was exhausted. However, sleep was difficult in near weightlessness, and Daddy liked to sleep with a pillow over his head – which was impossible floating in space. He got only a few hours before the checklist began again. Using another camera, Daddy was successful in mapping out the areas for Apollo 16 and 17. While circling in orbit, he could see the lunar module on the surface of the moon. He described it as a "foreign object" that did not fit in the dull gray starkness. It was a small speck but definitely recognizable as something that did not belong on the surface. Daddy communicated to Mission Control that he could see *Antares*, and Alan Shepard responded with a slight sigh of relief knowing Stu had an eye on them.

A goal of Apollo 14 was to show the world that spaceflight could become "routine." Moon landings were not achieved by mere luck, but could be successfully performed over and over. Since Apollo 14's landing site was the first in this dangerous area of the moon, another goal was to traverse to Cone Crater to pick up lunar samples to see if the rocks were different from those collected on the previous two missions. Yet the lunar maps did not clearly show the degree of undulations in the surface. It's like when watching golf on TV, the commentators talk about the slight slopes of the green, but on TV it looks flat. Although Cone Crater looked close on the map, Shepard and Mitchell soon found themselves hiking up one hill and then into a valley, then up another hill, and back into a valley. Every time they reached a top of a ridge and thought it was the edge of Cone Crater, they would see another hill to traverse – all in one-sixth gravity and spacesuits, which made walking difficult. Most astronauts developed their own technique of "hopping" on the moon, thus falling and tearing open their spacesuit was a real concern. With time and oxygen also a concern, Mission Control finally ordered the Apollo 14 crew back to *Antares*. As studies showed later, the astronauts were closer to Cone Crater than they thought. It was a huge disappointment not to have made it to the ridge.

Shepard and Mitchell set up some important experiments, one being the ALSEP – Apollo Lunar Surface Experiments Package. This package was designed to run autonomously to relay data about the moon's environment back to the earth for years to come. After planting the United States flag, which was 3 by 5 feet and hung on aluminum tubes, Alan Shepard conducted one final "maneuver." He dropped two golf balls on the moon. He had a special club head made to adapt to one of the rock pickers, and to NASA's chagrin, since this was being broadcast live, Shepard hit a ball. CAPCOM commented, "Looks like a slice to me, Al." Since the moon's gravity allowed the ball to travel much farther than on earth, Shepard said with a bit of mischievous sarcasm in his voice, … "miles and miles and miles…" At least he did not have to worry about any water hazards. My father had a friend who loved golf and gave Al the balls, so everyone wanted to know what brand they were… but some things are just kept secret. The truth is the company that made them was no longer in business, so no company could capitalize on it.

After 33½ hours on the lunar surface and two moon walks totaling 9½ hours, it was time for the crew to be reunited and start the journey home. There must have been thoughts of what would happen if the crew could not make it off the moon, for going down and picking them up was not an option. These types of scenarios were not openly discussed, but I once heard my father say that if there had been a failure of the LM, it would have been a lonely ride home. Daddy would have exhausted all efforts and stayed in orbit for as long as possible if there had been a problem before starting back to earth.

On February 6, *Antares* launched from the moon, never to return. As the Lunar Module came closer and closer into view, my father called out, "What are you doing way down there, Oh, Fearless One?!" There was jubilation in his voice, but he was privately wondering if the latches were going to work. After a perfect rotation and inspection of the Command Module, *Antares* and *Kitty Hawk* connected. The latches worked without a hitch. As happy as he was to be united with his crew, my father was now worried about lunar dust and the effect it could have on his controls. He made Al and Ed vacuum their suits, the spacecraft, equipment, and everything else multiple times until the Commander finally said, "Come on, Stu, let us in!"

The hatch opened, and a joyous reunion occurred. In interviews on the way home, the three astronauts could hardly restrain the smiles on their faces, very different from their usually stoic public personas. One reporter was urging my father to send his love or a message to his family, but my father finally said, "We'll talk about that later" – meaning, "I am not going to share these emotional moments and personal feelings with the world! We are professional astronauts." However, privately, as the moon started to get smaller and smaller in the spacecraft window, my father turned to Shepard and said, "Al, do you have anything prophetic to say?" Al said, "Stu, you know me better than that!" and just smiled. Sometimes silence says it all.

• • •

Back on earth, as reporters continued to camp out at the house, my mother provided daily coffee for them in the garage. Soon it was time for splashdown, and the house filled with close friends, family, other astronaut wives, and a few select reporters. We all gathered in the family room, and

Roosa checks his flight plan
while in space

Apollo 14 plants the U.S.
flag at Fra Mauro

Apollo 14 crew
reunited and
returning to Earth

Splashdown 0.6 nautical miles from the targeted point near the USS New Orleans

Frogmen secure the Apollo 14 capsule as Daddy (center) and Shepard (right) look back at the charbroiled spacecraft (masks were worn by the astronauts so as not to release any "space germs" into the atmosphere)

Watching the splashdown at our home in El Lago

I sat next to Mama on the couch. We stared at the TV console, waiting for Daddy and crew to return from space. Re-entry had to be precise, for if the Command Module came in too shallow, it would skip off the earth's atmosphere and head into deep space — forever. There would have been no fuel or power to stop its permanent thrust into the unknown. If the spacecraft came in too steeply, it would burn up, like what happens with meteors and other space debris. The angle of attack had to be just right. Communication with Mission Control during this time was non-existent; the "blackout" period was between three to four minutes.

As we sat on the couch at our home in El Lago, once again a nervous excitement filled the air. As the newsmen announced from the TV console that reentry was about to occur, the room went quiet. The blackout period began and time ticked by. Everyone was still and barely breathing. Then we saw them - the parachutes! Three beautiful red and white striped parachutes, and Mama started to cry. I was so young that I did not understand the concept of tears of joy and was wondering if something was wrong. I kept asking Mama, "Why are you crying?" And as the group cheered and clapped, Mama turned to me and said, "Because I'm so happy!" Suddenly, I started to cry too. On February 9, Apollo 14 splashed down in the Pacific Ocean at 4:05 p.m. (EST), exactly nine days and two minutes after launch.

Daddy liked precision, and he was able to time the release of the parachutes so that the Command Module did not flip over. Since the spacecraft was bottom heavy, the cone of the CM would generally go under water due to the weight of the parachutes pulling it down. If the parachutes were released at just the right time, and the angle of splashdown was correct, then the Command Module remained upright. If not, then small balloons that looked like honeycombs would deploy and turn the capsule upright. Daddy did not like the looks of these small balloons and made it a personal goal to not have to deploy them. He wanted the Apollo 14 photo shots to be of the charbroiled spacecraft, not of the distracting yellow and white balloons on top. Not only did Apollo 14 release the parachutes at the precise moment, but it also splashed down closer to its projected landing spot than any other Apollo mission, only 0.6 nautical miles from the target point and 3.8 nautical miles from the recovery ship USS New Orleans. Ed made the comment, "Good thing you didn't land on the carrier's deck, Stu." Commander Alan Shepard achieved his goal of flying one of the best missions on record, and this success put The Program back on track. America would be heading back to the moon in less than 6 months with Apollo 15, with one new item — a moon rover.

It was unknown if space contained some type of "Andromeda Strain." *The Andromeda Strain* was a 1969 novel that in 1971 became a sci-fi movie about a mysterious space germ that contaminated the human race. This issue was a real concern of NASA's, and after returning to earth, the Apollo 14 crew was placed in quarantine once again. This time it was to protect the entire human species from the astronauts. Apollo 14 holds the record for being the longest in quarantine, and for the next three weeks, the families once again had to view the crew through thick panes of glass. A joke went around about "lunarticks." Mama used to say she wondered what would have happened if NASA had found something — would they have kept them quarantined forever? On Valentine's Day, February 14, to show my love and happiness, I pulled out my crayon set and construction paper and sent homemade cards with candy to the crew trapped behind the glass wall. Finally, on February 27, the crew was released. Daddy wanted to be surrounded by his family, so we were all there. Each astronaut gave a short speech about the flight, and Daddy was happy to be "free."

While in quarantine, Daddy told Mama that on his first night home, he wanted a huge party to thank key NASA personnel and everyone at Mission Control, so a party was had. It was jammed with people, but nobody cared if it was a bit crowded. Everyone was jubilant. On the second night, Mama cooked him lasagna. But staying at home had to wait, for the parties and celebrations had just begun.

· · ·

NASA sent the crew on publicity tours. We were flown to Washington, D.C., on the Presidential airplane, Air Force One, – although if the

President is not on it, then technically "One" is dropped from the name. We left Ellington Air Force Base and landed at Andrews Air Force Base outside of D.C. The families were then whisked off to the White House to take a tour and meet President Nixon. An official State Dinner honoring the crew was scheduled for later that evening. To attend a State Dinner, a person had to be 18 years or older, but one of Alan Shepard's daughters was close to that age, and he asked if she could attend. At first, we children were to meet President Nixon and then go back to the hotel, but while we were in the Oval Office and talking to the President, he wound up inviting all us children to attend the State Dinner. This was unexpected and sent the White House into a scramble to rearrange seating and other details.

When we arrived at the hotel in Georgetown to get ready, there was no luggage – and suddenly Mama had to dress not only herself, but her four children too. Mama said in exasperation, "How could Air Force One lose our luggage?!" White House personnel were on the phones and asking Mama her dress size as the finest department store in D.C. was hastily trying to find long gowns, tuxedos, and appropriate children's clothing. Then someone had the bright idea to call NASA Headquarters, and sure enough, they had the luggage. For security reasons, the flight personnel were not told where the astronauts were staying, so, logically, someone dropped the luggage off at NASA Headquarters.

There was not much time for Mama to get all of us and herself ready, and there was a sense of frenzy in the room. The only calm person was Daddy. He was slowly and meticulously putting on his tuxedo when he pulled out a box with a new tie and cummerbund that Mama had purchased prior to the trip. The cummerbund had been mistakenly sewn with two hooks and no catch, so suddenly, even Daddy needed assistance getting dressed. There was a sewing kit in the hotel, so Mama had to quickly sew Daddy into his formal wear. But soon we were ready, and the limousines picked us up for the White House. We pulled into the gates and underneath the portico with the iconic brass lantern suspended above, and even though I was young, I did not mistake the significance of the evening. The astronauts and wives were taken on a private tour of the living area on the second floor

The President and Mrs. Nixon

request the pleasure of the company of

Miss Roosa

at dinner

on Monday evening, March 1, 1971

at eight o'clock

Black Tie

DINNER

Suprême of Striped Bass Commodore

Johannisberger
Klaus
1969

Roast Rib of Beef au Jus
Pommes Mascotte

Louis Martini
Cabernet
Sauvignon

Fresh Asparagus au Beurre

Hearts of Palm Vinaigrette
Porte de Salut Cheese

Louis Roederer
Cristal
1964

Soufflé au Grand Marnier
Sauce Sabayon

The White House
Monday, March 1, 1971

QC

Miss Rosemary D. Roosa

will please present this card at
THE SOUTHWEST GATE
The White House
Monday, March 1, 1971
at 8:00 o'clock
NOT TRANSFERABLE

Table

1

as we gathered near a piano at the base of the stairs. A short while later, the Presidential Anthem "Hail to the Chief" started playing, and we heard the familiar "don, don, ta don…", and down the red carpet came President and Mrs. Nixon, Vice President and Mrs. Spiro Agnew, and the Apollo 14 crew and wives. In one of the official White House photos, Mama was looking over at us kids and smiling, but I believe she was making sure no one was acting up. Since the party was so large, we were escorted into the main room at one wing instead of the traditional dining room. We sat at the "kiddie table" with Tricia Nixon, President Nixon's 25-year-old daughter. We learned a White House rule is that one may begin eating when he or she is served and isn't required to wait until all are served, as typical etiquette dictates. Thereafter, Mama would say at dinner parties, "White House Rule! Eat when you are served!"

I gazed at the old-world splendor and elegance of the room, but Mama and Daddy's table was too far away for me to see them. The room was full of people in tuxedos and beautiful gowns. There were white linens, porcelain plates, crystal glasses, chandeliers, and gold — from Jackie Kennedy's remodeling of the White House in the '60s. The Apollo 14 crew and wives were seated with the President, and when it came time to be seated, President Nixon held the chair for Mrs. Joan Barrett Roosa. Mama was in mid-squat when she paused for a moment. She was thinking about how far she had come — from being a young girl in small-town Mississippi, dreaming about going places and doing things, to now having the President of the United States hold her chair. She said later she wondered what the President was thinking… something like, "Go ahead and sit… I'm not going to pull the chair out from underneath you!" But he was patient and gracious and waited for her to sit down. At some point during the dinner, Vice President Agnew walked over and said hello to me. I don't know why he picked me, but he said he wanted to give me something. He held out his hand and gave me a golf ball with the Presidential seal on it. I thanked him, and he moved on. I later learned that I was the youngest person ever to attend a State Dinner. I don't know if that was the reason, or because Alan Shepard had hit a golf ball on the moon, but it was a nice gesture. Although my demeanor did not show a lot of emotion on the outside, I was beaming on the inside with my new ball.

. . .

The next day, the Apollo 14 crew was invited to give a speech on the House Floor in Congress. The U.S. flag hung proudly behind the chair of the Speaker of the House, and there was a crowd of people to see the famous astronauts. Once again, I could sense the history being made. After all the pomp and circumstance in D.C., the families were then invited to Camp David, about 60 miles outside of D.C., for some rest and relaxation. We flew on "Marine One" – the Presidential helicopter. It was my first time in a helicopter. As the whirling props lifted us into the air, we kids found something more interesting than the view - M&Ms with the Presidential seal on the package. We were constantly surrounded by Secret Service, but they were discreet, sharply dressed, nice, and accommodating. They politely made sure we remained secured in our seats after the initial giddiness of being in the helicopter and finding candy.

We soon arrived at Camp David, and each family was assigned a cabin. Camp David is surrounded by deep woods but has all the amenities of a first-class resort. Daddy went snowmobiling one day and veered off the beaten path to explore the woods. He soon regretted that decision, for he got tangled up in wires from the trees. The trees were wired down to make sure they grew straight, for Camp David was pristine and visually perfect. Camp David, named in honor of Dwight D. Eisenhower's grandson, was originally built as a retreat for federal government agents and their families. It was made for relaxation in all forms, and besides pools and tennis courts, it had a bowling alley, another great amusement to us kids. One of the boys dropped a bowling ball on his pinky finger. The Secret Service agent assigned to us was petrified his career would be in jeopardy for allowing an astronaut's child to get hurt while on his watch. But it was all okay after a few bandages. Career saved, and we kept on playing and exploring.

Later that night, the families gathered for dinner. The atmosphere was relaxed and comfy, and we were told that while at Camp David, we could order anything that we liked, 24 hours a day, as a chef was on hand to accommodate us. For fun, Daddy asked if the chef could make a S.O.S. – a sandwich that Daddy had created. It consisted of two pieces of white bread, sausage patties, and onions – a Sausage Onion Sandwich. This sandwich was a favorite of Daddy's while he was in quarantine, and Alan Shepard thought it was so funny that he had one enshrined in acrylic for posterity. Daddy wound up not forcing the chef to make him one, but Al got a kick at the request. We were also told that we could watch any movie that we liked on demand. This was a big deal in the early 1970s, as on-demand services were not commercially prevalent. Daddy wanted to watch the movie, *Tora! Tora! Tora!*, so we did. Daddy loved WWII flying movies. I must say at 7 years old, I would not have chosen this movie, but those old flying movies that pit pilot against pilot in a dogfight were his favorite. It was dark in the theater room, and I am not sure who was left after it ended, but one of the Shepard girls suggested showing a newer, more risqué movie. Some of us kids moved to the floor and nestled in as the movie started. We were not 10 minutes into the film when suddenly the door swung open and there was Mama. She shouted, "Roosa kids, out! Now!" As the disciplinarian, she meant business. We jumped up obediently and went to bed.

• • •

Post-flight was a blur as NASA sent the crew and families on publicity tours. While in Houston one evening, the astronauts and families were the stars of the Houston rodeo. Growing up, we often went to the rodeo, for this was a major part of the culture and entertainment around Houston. The arena had a dirt floor, cages, and chutes where the bulls and cattle would huddle. Horses felt right at home in this large, covered, circular arena called the Astrodome. But before the barrel races began and the cowboys proved their salt on the bucking broncos, we were placed in cute little wagons and led out one by one as if we were heading West in a wagon train. As kids, we were used to sitting in the stands watching Evel Knievel wipe out on his motorcycle in the Astrodome, but this time we were the ones in the arena with the smell of manure permeating the air and the bright lights shining down on us. It amused me as we started the slow trot around the large dome that the crowd was sitting in the dark, so although I knew they were there, I could not see them due to the spotlights. Mama was by my side, and as I heard the crowd roar, I didn't know what to do. My shyness swept over me. I was ready to retreat when Mama gently grabbed my arm and said in her Mississippi Southern drawl, "Start waving, Sugar, they are looking at you!"

Next stop was a big trip to Chicago. Richard J. Daley was the mayor, and he ruled the town. He made sure we were treated like royalty. We had the entire top floor of the Palmer House, the premier and oldest hotel in Chicago. It was elegant with a rich history and a long list of who's who in the registry, from presidents to top entertainers. Since we were kids, we wound up running and playing up and down the halls - with no retribution since there were no other guests. As my parents were wined and dined, we children were given Cubs jackets and a grand tour of the Chicago museums. I was more impressed with the large souvenir pencils than anything else.

Then it was on to Las Vegas, where children were rarely welcomed. It was an adult town for boozing, gambling, and enjoying first-class entertainment. As my parents hit the town, we were treated to a special showing of *Circus Circus*, the animal and big-top show. And when I mean special, it was for us astronaut children only. No tickets were sold, but the trapeze artists, performers, and animals did their show as if it were a sold-out crowd. One day as we were heading out to see the sights, there was a huge slot machine by the elevator doors. My father said without fanfare, "I am going to teach you kids a lesson about gambling. When you gamble, it is just like throwing your money away…" as he placed a quarter in the slot machine and pulled down the gigantic handle. As the cherries and oranges spun around, it hit on Bar, Bar, Bar. Quarters started filling up the silver slot tray with a loud ching, ching, ching, ching as the lights flashed that he was a winner! We jumped with delight as my father scooped up the quarters and put them in his pockets without saying a word. The rest of the day he had these quarters bulging from his pockets, with the weight of them pulling his

Mayor Daley welcomes us to Chicago

Ticker tape parade for the Apollo 14 astronauts

pants down on his hips, almost to the point of indecency. We chided him, saying that he really taught us a lesson.

Later that night, we dressed up for the Debbie Reynolds show. As the spotlights came on, this beautiful curvy blonde wowed the crowd. Debbie Reynolds started her show by talking to the audience and moving her way through the tables, sitting on men's laps and making them quite nervous with her seductive moves and comments. The Roosa family was seated about midway in the crowd in a booth that made a half moon. Mama was on one side, and Daddy was on the other, sandwiching us kids in the middle for no escaping. As Ms. Reynolds made her way through the crowd, she stopped by our table. Kids were a rare sight, especially at a Vegas show where the opening act featured scantily-clad dancers with large feather headdresses, sparkly sequins, and bare breasts. Debbie Reynolds looked at my father and said, "What, is the television set broken in the room?" She delivered a few more lines about my parents having so many kids, and I started feeling embarrassed. My father must have given her an "I am not amused" look, for she moved on, and definitely did not try to sit on his lap. After "warming up" the room, she proceeded on stage and was about to start into her act when she pulled a piece of paper from her bra. She said, "I must recognize someone in the audience tonight. He is just back from THE MOON, and what a great hero he is! Please help me give a warm welcome to Astronaut Stu Roosa and his family!" The spotlight descended upon our table as Daddy got up and waved. A horrified look came over Ms. Reynolds as the crowd cheered and clapped, for she realized she had just given us such a hard time. But as the consummate performer, she raised her shoulders in a shrug, smiled, and began her act.

Being around celebrities, politicians, and social elites was now the "new normal" for the astronauts. And there was traveling. It went with the territory of being a famous astronaut. There were "groupies," and they could be celebrities or famous in their own right, too. Somehow, we found out our parents had been to a party with Barbara Eden, another famous blonde bombshell of the day who starred in a sitcom, *I Dream of Jeannie.* Although it was a family show, she broke television ground by dressing in a bikini top and low-waisted loose-fitting pink pants. The TV executives had forbidden the exposure of her belly-button. She portrayed a fun-loving, faithful genie who had been let out of the bottle by an adventurous astronaut who was stranded on a desert island when his space capsule malfunctioned on re-entry. The astronaut actor was Larry Hagman, who later garnered more fame by playing the calculating character J.R. Ewing on the TV drama *Dallas.* But on *I Dream of Jeannie,* Hagman was an Air Force Captain who got himself into predicaments because of his genie's innocent mishaps. Barbara Eden must have wanted a real astronaut, though, for she chased my father around a room one evening, liking his looks and personality. From then on, when the show would come on at our house, we would gleefully say, "There is your girlfriend, Daddy!" He was not amused.

Europe was also on the agenda, and soon my parents were whisking off to France for parties and to attend the Paris Air Show as celebrity and VIP guests. My mother recounted going to the Palace of Versailles, the magnificent chateau expanded by Louis XIV when he moved the Royal Court there in 1682. Mama, the history major, once recounted how Louis XIV would have chefs prepare 100 dishes each night, and the King would take a bite out of each dish, sampling and trying new and different things. As a gourmet cook, Mama would have been in heaven. She loved to experiment with sauces and French cuisine. On this night at Versailles, they were treated like the royal court. Mama recounted riding up to the entrance with men lined up backward on the horses, trumpeting their arrival. She had come a long way, baby.

• • •

As for me, it was back to school. And for Daddy, soon it was back to NASA. Since I was a child, I did not realize that moon missions were being cut, and although my father was in line to be a Commander and walk on the moon in a future mission (Apollo 20), this would not come to pass. Yet his dedication to The Program was true, and although other astronauts were leaving to find corporate jobs with contracting companies, enter politics, or

64-C Class at Edwards Air Force Base with signature of each pilot

"The Original 19" selection of NASA astronauts in 1966

pursue business ventures, my father agreed to be back-up crew on Apollo 16 and 17.

Daddy's best friend in the astronaut corps was Charlie Duke, a fellow pilot who was tall, thin, with dark hair and handsome features. They met at Edwards Air Force Base. Charlie and Daddy had both been part of the class at Edwards called 64-C or as they called it in aviation terms, 64-Charlie. A = Alpha, B = Bravo, C = Charlie, and so on. My father used to say that this was the class the stars fell on. They were a talented bunch. Every single one of them was already a top-notch pilot when they arrived at Edwards, with many being the first of their class during pilot training. They had learned to push the outer envelope, and when flying fighter test planes, they would push the jet to its limits. The pilots would call out their numbers to record the jet's maximum capability. Daddy loved to push his flying skills by dogfighting. Charlie and Daddy would start their dogfights by speeding towards each other in their supersonic jets, head to head. Once they passed each other, it was game on to see who could "shoot down" whom. Out of their class of only 12 men, four of them got to fly in space, and three of them got to go to the moon. Charlie was selected for NASA at the same time as Daddy in 1966 as part of the "Original 19." Charlie was CAPCOM when Apollo 11 landed on the moon, and soon it was his turn to fly in space on Apollo 16 as the Lunar Module Pilot, same position that Ed Mitchell had held. The Commander was John Young. The Command Module Pilot was Ken Mattingly — the one who had gotten bumped from Apollo 13 because of having been exposed to the measles. We flew to the Cape a few days before the flight, and then on April 16, 1972, the family witnessed another spectacular launch of a Saturn V rocket. Daddy was happy to see his best friend fly, and I was excited to see another launch. Apollo 16 became the fifth successful mission to the moon.

Then in December 1972, the family headed back to the Cape for the only scheduled night launch, that of Apollo 17. The flight was commanded by Gene Cernan, who seemed to have a rivalry with Daddy. Gene was a bit of flirt, and the women liked him a lot. I gathered that Gene would flirt with my mother, and Daddy was a jealous man. Gene had been back-up on Apollo 14 and the crew rode the Apollo 14 crew hard. The back-up crew — Gene Cernan, Joe Engle, and Ron Evans — even had their own patches made depicting a coyote circling the earth to find a roadrunner already standing on the moon, going, "Beep-Beep." This was a parody of the official Apollo 14 patch, which showed an astronaut pin circling the earth and heading towards the moon. During Daddy's mission, the roadrunner patches found their way into everything on the Apollo 14 flight and this irritated Daddy to no end.

Paybacks can be hell, and Gene got his prior to launch. Months earlier, while jogging around the track at the lunar geology training grounds behind the simulators at the Cape, Daddy heard a rattling sound. He suddenly saw the largest rattlesnake he had ever seen and quickly maneuvered away. The sheer width of it was as large as a man's fist. It was as thick-as-a-forearm big. The snake was curled up and ready to strike. My father happened to be jogging with Charlie Duke, and together, they threw rocks at the snake until it was dead. Daddy said the snake seemed to say, "I'm a mean ol' bad ass; bring it on" and struck at the rocks as the astronauts flung small boulders at it. It took some work, but the snake finally caved to the determination of men who would not be defeated in a man vs. nature battle. My father cut off the head with a ragged edge of a rock, for even in death, a venomous snake can release its poison. The snake's body was almost six feet long. Stu Roosa knew just what to do with it. Back at the astronauts' office, the snake was curled up tightly underneath the desk of one Gene Cernan. Gene loved to talk on the phone, working this deal or that. As Gene rushed in, and hearing he had an important phone call, he quickly plopped in the wheeled chair and pushed himself towards the square desk. Other astronauts knew of the visitor now "sleeping peacefully" underneath the desk, and they waited in the wings. Gene was reaching for the phone when he looked down and saw 16 rattles from a tail sticking up from this curled body. He suddenly went flying up in the air as he pushed the chair back with such a great force that it dented the strong metal chair when it hit the wall. Gotcha! Over the years, John Young loved to tell that story and describe how the blood rushed from Gene's face in horror when confronted with this huge monster of a snake. Even Gene said it almost gave him a heart attack. Astronaut pranks were frowned upon by the higher ups, but it was a way of defusing tensions and evening up the score. The acts were harmless in the end.

However, prior to the Apollo 17 launch, a real threat was occurring. The '60s and early '70s were a time of protests, and not just against the Vietnam War. A militant group called the Black September was also bringing attention to their cause. Beginning on September 16, 1970, when thousands of Palestinian fighters were killed and expelled from Jordan after attempting to seize the kingdom, the group wanted revenge. High profile acts of crime were their way of getting attention. Black September murdered a number of Israeli athletes at the Summer Olympics in Munich 1972. Now astronaut kids, a high profile but soft target, were in their sights. Being only 9 years old, I was not aware of the threat. When we flew to the Cape, instead of staying at the Holiday Inn, we stayed at Patrick Air Force Base near Cocoa Beach and were assigned Secret Service agents. I was told only that they were there for assistance. Once again, the agents were polite, well dressed, and kind.

In the past, the pre-launch parties were big events, but with the final flight to the moon, the parties were huge. Since Daddy was on the back-up crew, he stayed in quarantine at the Cape, ready at a moment's notice to step in as a replacement if needed. Mama was assigned a Secret Service agent to escort her to the parties, and at one party, Farouk El-Baz, the Egyptian lunar geologist, grabbed Mama's arm and was whisking her away to meet someone when Mama realized her Secret Service agent didn't know him and may think he was trying to kidnap her. She was right, for the agent said later he was reaching for his gun and trying to figure out how to shoot in the packed crowd of party-goers. From then on out, the Secret Service agent stayed close to Mama. Apparently he was quite the handsome man, and talk of his looks reached Daddy. Daddy was not happy, and the other astronauts started ribbing him about it. Unaware of this, all I knew was that for entertainment, our "babysitting" Secret Service agents took us to Disney World. The lines were long, but somehow a badge would be discreetly flashed at the rides, and *voila*, we would be climbing on board.

It was great, and spoiled future trips to Disney World when I was a "mere mortal" tourist.

Finally it was time for the launch. The launch pad was a strange sight, for the rocket was surrounded by darkness with only floodlights to show its lone massive figure. Then shortly after midnight on December 7, the countdown hit zero. The flames were so vibrant against the blackness that my brain was not sure if the launch was normal or not. The white fire against the black sky was intense. The ground shook and the popping sound from the fuel igniting roared in my ears once more. I witnessed the last of the great rockets to be propelled into another world. I wasn't even 10 years old but had already seen and experienced a lot of history. And the next 10 years were going to be life-changing as well.

Blast off at night of Apollo 17

CHAPTER 3

Destiny

Of the many things that I admired about my parents, being genuine was at the top. Mama and Daddy were from the "opposite side of the tracks," but they were bonded by the spirit of adventure. Mama loved to read, and as a young girl in the fourth grade, she read *Richard Halliburton's Complete Book of Marvels*. Printed in 1941, it was a book that chronicled a man's adventures around the world, starting with the bridges in San Francisco and ending with Mount Fuji. The book included black and white photographs and writings about places and wondrous structures — such as Mount St. Michael, the Kremlin, the ancient Pyramids, and Greek ruins. The Halliburton book broadened her world view, and she knew she did not want to spend the rest of her life in only the social circles of Tupelo, Mississippi. After graduating from college, she and a group of her lifelong best friends applied for teaching jobs, destination: unknown

One evening they pulled out a map of the United States, blind-folded one in the group and told her to throw a dart at the map. They said wherever it landed, they would move. The dart hit Newport News, Virginia, close to the water. One friend said, "Any farther and it would have been in the ocean!" They all applied for teaching jobs and were accepted. Next was finding a place to live, and they chose Hampton, Virginia – renting a beach house on the water. Mama said it was the best summer ever… having three girlfriends living in a beach house with nothing to do until the fall but relax and play. At that time, the beach in front of homes was considered private property, so public beach areas were few and far between. Needless to say, the girls were very popular with the boys. Nearby was a beach house with three men in the military, and the party grew. One of the roommates had a nephew stationed at Langley Air Force Base. One evening for a birthday party, the young women were invited to the Officers' Club at Langley. Langley was the location for the new hot fighter jets, and my father, stationed there, had just received one of the first "Purple Tails" – an F-100 jet. Daddy said he saw Mama at the Officers' Club and said to the bartender, "See that woman over there? I am going to marry her!" And thus began his courtship of Miss Joan Barrett, whom he decided to woo with his jet.

Mama was supposed to marry a man back in Mississippi. Everyone just expected her and Van Chaney to get engaged. He was handsome and had the proper education, family, and other Southern credentials to marry Miss Joan. However, the two agreed before she moved that they would socialize with other people, so my father approached this beautiful brunette at the Officers' Club and asked if she had ever tried champagne and beer. She smiled and said, "no," but liked his opening line. He asked for her number, and they went on a date. Mama explained to him that she was to return and marry a boy from Mississippi and to not get serious with her, but by the third date, Daddy was ready to ask her to marry him. One evening Mama was casually recounting a tale when she looked up and saw a look of lost enchantment in Daddy's eyes. She thought to herself, "Oh no, what do I do now?" She was, in essence, "torn between two lovers."

Daddy respected Mama's need to figure things out, but he continued trying to win her love, and she was starting to like this red-headed boy from Oklahoma. My father did not make much money as a young officer, but he knew this woman he had quickly fallen in love with needed a proper, and expensive, courtship. To take Miss Joan on proper dates, Daddy wound up getting money from a shady loan shark who charged 20% interest. Mama and Daddy's first date was to an expensive restaurant where they both ordered lamb. Neither one knew that the other had never tried lamb before, but both were curious about the taste, and neither mentioned it was a first. This would be one of many firsts they would experience together.

Mama's mother: Mary Ethel Falls Barrett (Mammy)

Mama's father: Dr. John Thomas Barrett (Doc)

• • •

Mama's parents, Mary Ethel (Mammy) and John Thomas (Doc) Barrett were the quintessential Southern couple. Mammy had seen Doc through the post office window and told her mother that she was going to marry him. With love at first sight, they did marry, and soon became a prominent family. Doc was easygoing and jovial and loved to tell stories, mostly of his mischievous childhood and teenage years. He had a daring spirit. His family came from Ireland during the Great Potato Famine and started settling land in Mississippi. Doc always had a cigar in his mouth, gnawing at the end, whether it was lit or not. The only time he took it out was to shower. He would often fall asleep with it dangling from the side of his mouth. Besides taking care of animals, Doc had a garden, which he loved to attend. There were rows of fresh corn, tomato vines, black-eyed peas, and string beans growing. Every week Mammy would go to the butcher shop and spend about 20 to 30 minutes discussing the fresh cuts of meat, ordering only the finest beef. Then Mammy would cook the hell out of it. It was always tough. Mama started taking over some of the cooking, which was just fine with Mammy.

Mama started experimenting with cooking when she was about 8 years old, having received an Easy Bake-type oven for Christmas. One day her oven broke and she called the local repairman to say the stove was out and that it needed fixing (or as Southerners say, fixin'). The man came over and started to walk into the kitchen. Mama yelled, "Wait! It's right here!" and promptly held up her small oven. Mama was a bold and bodacious little girl, a little like Shirley Temple. The repairman smiled and decided it was easier to fix it than have a disappointed little girl on his hands, so he did. He was starting to leave when Mama said, "How much?" He said, "Nothing." And she quickly fired back, "Here is a nickel. I know you cannot stay in business working for free!" He took the nickel, chuckled, and told her to call back if she had any more problems.

Mama grew up understanding how to cook vegetables, how to properly season foods, and how to make a plate look presentable. As she got a bit older, Mama started doing most of the cooking and would help fix the wild game that was shot. She started to read cookbooks and experiment with seasoning and sauces. Mama's parents did not mind her cooking, as Mammy preferred sewing, and Doc loved to piddle in the garden or read the newspaper when he was home.

· · ·

When courting Mama, Daddy instinctively knew he could not let her see his financial struggles, or she might choose the comfortable life with Van Chaney in Mississippi. Daddy's paychecks would immediately go to pay back the loan shark, and then he would borrow more money to take Mama out again. Mama and Daddy had met in October 1956, and hunting season was approaching. He had to figure out some way to break the cycle of the loan shark and expensive restaurants. He and a few buddies went on a turkey hunt, and Daddy, always a good shot, bagged a big turkey. With Thanksgiving approaching, he asked Mama if she knew how to cook a turkey. To his surprise, she said "yes," so Thanksgiving would be a date. Mama cooked that turkey perfectly, and Daddy was quite impressed. Mama once said that a way to catch a man is to aim a bit higher than where you would expect… and go for the stomach. My mother also impressed my father with her confidence. At some point in the dinner, Mama was drinking champagne near the fireplace. My father came up from behind and said with a twinkle in his eye, "Ya know, a real fighter pilot throws his glass in the fireplace when he is done with his drink." Without a word, my mother saw that she only had a sip left. She raised the champagne flute to her mouth, took the sip, and without warning, hurled it into the fireplace with a great SMASH! Daddy was shocked! This was no ordinary girl.

Mama and Daddy were now going out regularly, and he often drove her to Catholic Mass on Sunday, even though he grew up Baptist. Then Mama received a letter from Van. Van said he did not mind her going out on dates but to stay away from that Roosa fella. I guess he could tell from her letters that she was intrigued. Daddy came by one day as the Christmas holidays were approaching and saw a man in a convertible car. He had his arm around Mama. Daddy's heart sank. Van had come to town to visit. Daddy resolved right then and there that he would do whatever it took to win over this woman, or he would lose his true love forever.

One evening Daddy was scheduled for night flying. He was jealous because Mama and her friends were entertaining the neighboring boys that night. Back in the day, a pilot could call in his coordinates to the tower but could physically be somewhere else… and that's exactly what Daddy did. He was flying the F-100, and there was a delay between reaching full throttle and the afterburner kicking in. He was good at picking out landmarks from the air and soon found his way to the beach, towards the house where Mama was entertaining. He called in his false coordinates over the water and started down low. He turned off all the exterior and interior lights and went by moonlight and instincts. He identified the house and judged his closure rate, going hundreds of miles per hour. He started counting in his head and came in low, really low… he pushed in the throttle… "one, two…" and the jet came within feet of the roof of the house… BOOM! The afterburner kicked in just over the house, and my father went straight up in a vertical climb. He reached altitude and quickly headed out to the flight practice area, turning on the lights and calling the tower again with his proper coordinates.

Down on the ground, the party at Mama's house had been in full swing. The BOOM blasted right over their heads, and one of the boys hit the deck spread eagle on the floor! Drinks went flying, and the women shrieked. Everyone was stunned, not knowing whether a bomb had gone off or an earthquake had happened. Then one of the men yelled, "That's that damn Roosa! I know it is!" Of course, Daddy denied it all with a sly smile and a muffled chortle. Many years later he told me it was one of his finest moments and that he timed it just perfectly, getting the afterburner to kick in just *feet* over the roof of the house.

Christmas came, and Daddy gave Mama a turquoise cashmere sweater. He also started converting to the Catholic faith, telling no one, not even Miss Joan. In the spring, Mama's sister, Patti, and brother-in-law, Knox, came up from Mississippi for a visit, and they met this hot-shot talented

Miss Joan Barrett with Daddy's jet at Langley Air Force Base

pilot named Stuart. Patti and Knox said they liked him right away and gave their approval. Now Mama was truly in a dilemma. Daddy kept asking Mama to marry him, and she was no longer saying no, but she was not saying yes, either. Van was waiting back in Tupelo. Mama started to pray hard. She did not know whom she should marry. Then one night after a date, she and Daddy went to the beach house, where a party was in full swing. Daddy told everyone he had an announcement. The room quieted as all eyes turned to Stuart and Joan. He declared in front of everyone: "Joan has agreed to marry me!" Cheers roared. Mama said she did not recall ever saying yes, but that she did not want to embarrass Daddy in front of all their friends by saying, "No I didn't!" — and in her heart she felt like her prayers had been answered and that the decision had been made. The wedding date was set for September 21, 1957, less than a year after they started going out. Now she had the hard part of telling Van.

For spring break, Mama returned to Mississippi, but this time to Sessums, a small agricultural area outside of Starkville. Her parents had moved there to start a dairy farm in the rolling hills and peaceful countryside due south of Tupelo. Mama was happy to be in Mississippi but dreaded telling her soon-to-be-ex beau that she was going to marry another man. Mammy and Doc's house in Sessums was a large, two-story white antebellum-style home with a wrap-around porch that extended on the front and both sides. On one side of the porch was a swing that hung from the ceiling by two chains. Mama called Van to drive over and visit. When he arrived, the two sat on the porch swing, slowly moving the swing back and forth with their feet. Mammy and Mama's older sister, Gloria, crouched on the couch just inside a window. Mama, with her heart beating, told Van that she was going to marry Stuart Roosa… and then waited for his reaction. He paused, and then started yelling, "NO, NO! I'm going to kill myself… NO, NO, this can't be! I'm going to kill myself!" He took off running and jumped straight off the porch and over the hedges onto the road. He frantically got into his car and sped off. Gloria ran for her car and sped off after him. Mama ran into the house and into Mammy's arms. She didn't know what to do, but she knew she had made her decision. Gloria caught up to Van and motioned for him to pull over. He was sobbing uncontrollably. She consoled him and talked to him for hours. He wound up not killing himself, although it was many years before he would happily marry, remaining in Tupelo.

After school was out for the summer in Virginia, Mama returned to her parents to plan a wedding for the fall. Mammy was a great seamstress and made many of Mama's clothes. When Mama was in college, she stopped by a dress shop, and the clerk asked her size. She had no idea, as her clothes were tailor-made by her mother. Mama had a great figure and was known as "the bod" in her high school and college years. Mammy started making her a beautiful white dress that went to her mid-calves. All was proceeding well except for one big detail that needed to be handled soon.

Joan told Stuart that he would have to come down and properly ask for her hand in marriage. So as Daddy flew down South in his jet, he took out a road map and decided to buzz the big white house in Sessums before landing at Columbus Air Force Base. Once again, he was proud of his instincts and skill, and he found the house without ever having been there. And he made quite an impression. The one and only country store in this tiny area usually had locals playing checkers on the rickety front porch. Some were playing when Daddy buzzed the area. He descended to treetop level and came in out of the blue at a high rate of speed. As before, he was only feet above the rooftops, and all the checker players hit the deck and scrambled underneath the porch in fear. From that moment on the locals called him "Mr. Lieutenant with the Big Shoes!" He was not sure why, except that his flying boots were big.

As he landed, Daddy wasn't sure if he had done the right thing by buzzing his future in-laws without meeting them first. When Daddy arrived in Sessums, Doc was tending to his garden. Daddy went out to ask for Joan's hand, which he did. But Doc just strolled about his garden and talked. Daddy followed him around as Doc spoke about the corn ears, how big his tomato plants were, and how to grow this and that… and finally, when Daddy walked back inside, Mama said excitedly, "What did he say?" Daddy said, "I don't know! He just talked!" Mama said, "Well, you would have known if he had said no – so, I guess you have his approval!"

Secretly, Doc had liked Daddy even before meeting him. Doc loved all things related to aviation. When Mama was around the age of 5, a barnstormer came to town for an airshow. Unbeknownst to Mammy, Doc paid the pilot to take Mama up during the show. As the pilot performed loops and spins and waved the plane's wings over the crowd, Mammy exclaimed, "Thank goodness no one I know is up in that airplane! I'd have a heart attack if there was!" When the pilot landed, out jumped Mama, and Mammy nearly fainted.

The wedding was in the one and only Catholic church in Starkville, Mississippi. On Mama's wedding day, Mammy and Doc met Daddy's parents and brother for the first time. Daddy's family had a chicken farm outside of Tulsa, Oklahoma, with a sign that read, "Roosa Poultry Farm – We feed and recommend Purina Poultry Chow." Daddy's father, Dewey, was ahead of his time and tried to accomplish what Tyson did later, but at the time, the Oklahoma Roosa family struggled financially with indoor chicken farming. Moving in the right social circles was not as important. Mammy was not impressed with Daddy's family and told Mama at the back of the church on her wedding day, "It's not too late… if you want to back out!" My father's mother, Lorine, had an eighth-grade education and was a bit prejudiced. She thought all Catholics were Mexican, and although Mama was not, the two families looked down their noses at each other at the wedding. Mama walked down the aisle anyway. She had no doubt. As soon as the reception was over, she and Daddy jumped into the car for the honeymoon – literally. The two virgins, or at least my mother claimed Daddy told her he was a virgin, consummated their marriage in the back seat just a few miles out of town in a romantic little spot off the road. They were in love and happy to be with each other.

Not too long after Mama and Daddy were married, Mama discovered that an Air Force lieutenant did not make that much money and that the high society scene that Mama grew up in was no longer a part of her life. They rented a small furnished house with velvet paintings and "nudie girls" in the ashtrays. Mama knew their deployment would be soon, so she tried her best in the temporary tacky rental. Just one catch: Mama did not know how to clean house, for she'd grown up with maids. She watched the kitchen floor get dirtier and dirtier. One day it dawned on her that it was up to her to mop it! She did so, and Daddy came in from flying that day and said, "Thank goodness, Joan. I was wondering if you were going to ever mop it!" Mama said, "Don't let that ever happen again, and when you feel that something needs cleaning, then do it!" Throughout the years, Mama tried her best to clean, but eventually took on the philosophy, "If you can't see it from a galloping horse, then it's clean enough." Mama and Daddy agreed that a housekeeper was a necessity and not a luxury, and rarely did they not have some help from then on out.

Mama wanted an adventure, and she was about to get it. For their first Christmas as man and wife, her husband gave her a rifle, a pair of hunting boots, and a down jacket. Although Mama grew up around hunting, only the men hunted. Daddy taught her gun safety and how to shoot. Mama liked it. Mama gave Daddy a scrapbook and wrote on the front "General Roosa." She knew Daddy was going to do well in his career. A few months after their marriage, Daddy received orders to fly a jet to a squadron in Europe. Mama was to sail over on the *Queen Elizabeth* and share a cabin with another female traveler. Early one morning Mama watched Daddy take off right at sunrise, thinking that the next time she saw her husband, it would be in Europe. Daddy did not have much more than an ADF (Automatic Direction Finder) – basically, a needle and compass, and was told to pretty much head east, and when he saw land, he'd be there. He checked a Fodor's book on Europe out of the library. It was cheaper to pay the overdue fees than to buy the book.

Mama's roommate was seasick for most of the trip, and the cabin was cramped. So Mama started getting out and about on the ship. She had a great optimistic aura about her and soon became a hit. Her being newly married did not keep the men away. She met a German man who stood and clicked his heels when she passed by, and a French pilot who spoke of a family chateau. She would smile and be friendly, like at the school dances, but she let the men know their bounds. Mama and the other young ladies organized a hat contest and played bridge for hours. Anything to entertain themselves and have fun. The plan was for Mama to meet Daddy at the port in Le Harve, France. While on the ship, she was told that no one got off at the port and stayed, and that a train would take all the passengers to Paris. Mama had no way of contacting Daddy, but she knew if he said he would meet her at that port, then that's where she was staying — she trusted Daddy. After a few days at sea, she received a telegram to meet Daddy in Paris, so she did. Happily reunited again, they were off... on their own Richard Halliburton's travel adventure. They considered this to be their true honeymoon. One evening while driving in Italy, they noticed the moon was full and shining brightly as they entered a small town. They were lost and just looking for a place to spend the night. Suddenly Mama looked up and saw a leaning tower. They were in Pisa! The trip was enchanting from start to finish. Instead of saving for new furniture, they spent their money on food, drink, and traveling. Adventure was their bond. Later in life, Daddy once commented that he had taken Mama to almost every place that she had read about when she was in the fourth grade. He was proud of that.

• • •

As Daddy went through life, he used to say, "I won, I won." He had won Mama's heart, and thus did not cheat on her. He had fought too hard. She was independent, and although she never said it, she might have retaliated with an affair of her own if he had ever cheated. Theirs was one of the most equal partnerships I have seen. They demonstrated respect, communication, and most importantly, love. Daddy used to call Mama "The Perfect Snob" – but she took offense to that because she was fun and likable. She was not catty, callous, or mean. He used to say that's what made her the perfect snob, that because she did not act like a snob, she was perfect! Mama still did not cotton to the name. Daddy also knew that he wanted to get her back into all the right circles. Part of why he worked so hard was so that he could take care of Joan Barrett, the high society girl of Tupelo. Stuart Roosa may not have had the pedigree, but he had the talent and ambition to take both of them to new heights. Yet their destiny might

Their Worlds Have Changed

Louise Shepard Is Disciplined
And Poised, Wears Chic Clothes

MRS. ALAN SHEPARD

> 'I had a great childhood'

> 'I didn't take him seriously'

Joan Roosa Bagged A Turkey
For Family's Holiday Dinner

Colorful Plan

Louise Mitchell Is
Shy And Softspoken

> 'Ladies do not raise their voices'

never have been realized if it hadn't been for the foresight and instincts of an Air Force man whose name my father could not remember.

After my father's first flight as an aviation cadet, he promptly left the airplane, went behind the hanger, and threw up. The flight instructor tore up the paperwork and told him to come back the next day and start again. Daddy could have been washed out from the beginning, his destiny gone, but the instructor saw potential. My father returned and flew well enough to pass. Off Stu Roosa went into the wild blue yonder and an Air Force career. The instructor also gave some invaluable advice. He advised Daddy to check "no" to every medical question on any form he was required to complete. The docs could ground a pilot at the drop of a hat. And flying was what it was all about for a hot-shot up-and-coming pilot. He needed flight hours to get ahead, and staying on the ground due to health reasons didn't cut it.

Destiny is something to ponder. What would have happened if Joan Barrett and her friends had not hit that dart close to Langley? For in the end, my parents seemed destined for each other. She supported him, and he appreciated it and respected her. And destiny played a part in my being the offspring, the only daughter, of their union. I have oftentimes thanked the good Lord for putting me in such a family, for I could have just as easily been born in the barrios of some foreign land, poor and without many options. My blessings have been immense, and growing up during the Apollo program was fascinating.

It seems all the astronauts followed their destinies. Most of the Apollo astronauts came from humble beginnings, but each had a drive to succeed. In the early days of NASA, the astronauts ruled the roost. An Apollo astronaut was like a rock star – he called the shots, was allowed to break the rules, and led a celebrity life. Groupies, women, CEOs, and politicians wanted to have them in their presence for bragging rights. But it was more than that to the astronauts — space wasn't there to be explored; it was there to be conquered. And they were the ones who could do it. All were test pilots and wanted to be the first at something related to flying. An astronaut was courageous, pushed the envelope, and lived life to the fullest. The astronauts were competitive and liked to play practical jokes on each other. They were bonded, no doubt about it. No one but each other could corral them.

And even though personalities differed, there was great respect among the men. While being in the presence of these elite few at private functions, the moonwalkers and the command module pilots were treated the same among them. The media and the public seemed to think that the men who flew solo while the other two walked on the lunar surface were shortchanged. But in order of rotation, the Command Module Pilot would rotate to Commander before the Lunar Module Pilot would. The Command Module Pilot was in charge of getting the crew to the moon and back, and after launch, the CMP would rotate to the left seat. Each had an important role on the flight, and they trusted each other to accomplish their respective tasks. And they kept each other's secrets. After a mission, only the astronauts were allowed to attend the "pin party." Generally thrown by the back-up crew, it was the party in which the prime crew received their astronaut pins. It was like a secret society, and the public was not allowed, nor were NASA administrators and directors. The specifics of what occurred were not disclosed, but what I did pick up on is that astronauts would rib and roast one another as way of keeping each other grounded and humble.

There have been fewer astronauts to the moon than there have been Presidents of the United States, by almost half. Twenty-four men went to the moon. Twelve men walked on the moon. And only six soloed while the others walked on the moon. It is a small fraternity. Years later, my father wanted to go back and thank that instructor who tore up his initial paperwork on his first flight in Aviation Cadets, but he couldn't remember his name. The cast of thousands were out there who made each mission possible, and my father appreciated every one of them.

• • •

After the cancellation of future moon landings, my father, along with most of the other Apollo astronauts, had to face up to the fact that they'd hit their peaks in their flying careers. NASA offered astronauts an opportunity to attend the Harvard Business School to adjust to life outside the military and to transition into the civilian world. The Harvard Business School executive education course was called AMP, Advanced Management Program. The course was several months, and my parents debated whether to move the family to the Boston area. They decided that Daddy would go alone. To me, it was just another long stint of Daddy being gone.

The Harvard program was uplifting to my father. He enjoyed the intellectual interaction and the case-study method. He described the living situation of four rooms, with a bathroom in the center for all to use. Thus, the dormitory area was referred to as "The Can." It was customary to ask each other which "Can" they lived in while at HBS. Shortly after graduation from the Harvard program, Daddy was scheduled to interview for a position as Undersecretary of the Interior. The Department of Interior encompassed the U.S. Forest Service, so it was a department that was near and dear to my father's heart. Nixon was gone due to the Watergate scandal, and President Ford was in the White House.

During this time, my stomach had been giving me fits, but every time Mama took me to see the NASA doc, he would poke on my stomach, and I would giggle from being tickled. My skin was sensitive to the touch — so sensitive that tickling me too hard would hurt. My parents took it seriously, and if the brothers tried to hold me down and tickle me, it was a belt-on-the-behind offense. But the NASA doctor thought I was just trying to skip school when I complained, until one day after poking on me, my laughing turned into throwing up on him. The doc immediately sent me to the emergency room at the local hospital. The hospital doctor said he needed to take my appendix out right away and started prepping me for surgery. My father had left earlier that day in his T-38 for Washington, D.C., for the interview with the Department of Interior. As soon as he landed at Andrews Air Force Base, word got to him of my surgery. Daddy refueled, turned the jet around, and headed back to Ellington. He missed his interview and spent the night by my side. The job went to someone else.

As the astronauts were learning how to become leaders in other fields, they were also learning about how to adjust mentally. Achieving travel to the moon was the goal. Now that had been accomplished. Many astronauts had to suffer with "demons" of hitting their career highs, being thrust into the spotlight, and dealing with wives who did not understand their new lives. Unfortunately, marriages broke up. Some sought refuge in religion, like Joe Erwin (Apollo 15), who tried to find the location of Noah's Ark. He had narrowed it down to Mount Ararat, Turkey, but he died in 1991 before finding it. Ed Mitchell (Apollo 14) started the Institute of Noetic Sciences, studying extrasensory perception. Buzz Aldrin (Apollo 11) set his sights on how to get to Mars. John Young (Apollo 10 & 16), became the Chief of the Astronaut Office and flew the first Space Shuttle mission.

Daddy started hunting in Africa. NASA would send astronauts on publicity tours, and when they asked where my father would like to go, he chose Africa every time. He took Mama on some trips along with fellow astronauts and their wives, including Charlie and Dotty Duke and Jim and Marilyn Lovell. NASA finally said, "Stu, we've got to have you go on other trips," but he refused. Daddy was working out his mental demons through the challenges of hunting big game. The game became bigger and bigger, and he went on hunts for elephant, the trophy animal of Africa. These hunts were extremely hard, as elephants cover a lot of ground, and it takes stamina to keep up. Daddy was becoming more distant from the family and my mother. At one point, Mama asked if they should get a divorce. He came back quickly with his answer: he loved her and wanted to stay married to her. They never discussed it again.

• • •

As for me, not much was going on in the years after the Apollo program. I progressed through Ed White Elementary to Seabrook Intermediate School and started the sixth grade. The school we were attending was a rough environment. A lot of the kids were prone to fight. The school was laid out like a rectangle, with an open square cement area in the center. Rather than walking a big horseshoe inside, you could cut across the center space outside. There were no trees, no benches, no playground toys, just cement.

The rough kids would stand smack-dab in the center, and if they so chose, would bully the kids walking across the courtyard. There were a lot of fights, and I think my brothers were involved in several of them. I wasn't close with my brothers growing up. My brothers never wanted me around, for they said I would "squeal" to Mama about them. Maybe I would have, maybe not, but anyhow, I did not interact much with them at school or afterwards.

For the Thanksgiving holiday, Daddy took the family hunting. We ventured out to West Texas to go deer hunting. I am not sure where we were in Texas, but it was in the middle of nowhere. Just perfect for hunting. My mother generally hunted on her own or stayed at the camp and fixed meals for the family. My father always hunted with me. I was twelve years old, and was borrowing my mother's .243 rifle. My first deer was a doe at the age of eleven that I shot at dusk with my father's .30-06 rifle. It was close to the heart, but not a clean kill, and it hit the lung. We followed the trail of blood until it got too dark. We never found the deer. This year I was determined to make a clean kill if at all possible.

I felt a bit of déjà vu as evening approached, and the deer started to stir. It was the last feeding prior to settling down for the night. My father and I were in the blind together, just sitting in the silence as our eyes scanned a field. We saw some doe venture out, and a few more on the periphery of the field. My father whispered to wait, knowing that the large male bucks would make sure the females didn't spook, and once assured, they too would venture out for easy grazing in the field. Then there he was — a nice buck with a decent rack, about eight points. My father motioned for me to raise the gun slowly and to get it tucked nicely in my shoulder. Looking at the deer in the scope allowed for more light to come through, and I could easily follow the buck as he made his way to the center of the field. Some young hunters experience "buck fever" which is a nervousness that kicks in at the sight of game. Not me. Some adrenaline was going, but it was not overwhelming. Then my father whispered that when I felt ready, to shoot. He had instructed me to slowly take in a breath, let half of it out, hold it, then slowly squeeze the trigger like a handshake. I was cool, calm, and steady. I was focused on making that one shot, one kill.

BANG! The gun went off with a huge noise, and I could see the fire expel from the barrel of the rifle. A moment that seemed to last an eternity passed. Then my father yelled, "You got it!" I was almost emotionless but could feel the jubilation inside. We quickly got out of the blind and ran to the buck. My father taught me that the way you know if you have killed a deer is to poke the barrel of the gun gently in the eye. If it blinks, then it is not dead, and you must quickly shoot it again to put it out of its misery. It did not blink. I had killed my first nice buck.

That night at the camp we cut the horns off, and Daddy skinned the deer. We prepared the body for the meat packaging company. We would eat what we shot, and every Thanksgiving our meal consisted of things that we had killed or caught during the year. We had red snapper, trout, venison, duck, quail, and all the trimmings. It was normal to find shotgun pellets in our meat as we ate, and it became a game to see who had the most BBs by their plate after dinner. Mama would cook the rest of the venison during the year, for we were on a tight military budget. It was a misnomer that astronauts got paid more, for they received their military rank pay, with some hazard duty. Feeding a family of six was tough, and the hunting helped.

Back at school, my teacher asked me if my father would be willing to give a speech to the sixth-grade class. My father loved to speak to school kids and hoped to inspire them to have a meaningful life. When my father came to my class, I remember telling him that this big kid, who was also the class bully, was bragging about shooting a deer. I told the boy that I had just shot a deer too, but he did not believe me. I mentioned this to my father, and he tucked this little piece of information away. Daddy did the usual grade-school talk about lift-off in the rocket, floating in space, and landing down in the Pacific Ocean... and then he talked about recently going hunting with me and how important it is to have adventures.

The big kid questioned him and said, "You mean to tell me your daughter just shot a buck on her own? No help?"

Daddy said, "Indeed, she did it all on her own."

The kid suspiciously asked, referring to the recoil of the gun when shot, "And who picked her up?"

My father firmly answered, "No one!"

That bully never did bother me that school year.

. . .

As the year went on, home life was steady, and my father was into his usual in-and-out routine. Skylab was flying, and my father was doing what he could on these missions. Another mission was also in the works, a joint space flight between the Soviet Union and the United States. It was named Apollo-Soyuz, for an Apollo command service module was used since there was a surplus from the terminated Apollo program. Soyuz was the name of the Soviet spacecraft. As a symbol of détente between the two superpowers, a joint flight was planned to ceremoniously mark the ending of the space race that had begun with Sputnik in 1957. The launch date was set for July 1975. The commander of the Soviet team was Alexei Leonov, the first Russian to complete a spacewalk. NASA asked if my father would fly on this mission. My father refused. He could not, would not, work with the Russians. The whole purpose of Apollo was to beat the Soviets to the moon and plant the United States flag.

My father thought it was a mistake to name the mission Apollo-Soyuz, for it implied the Russians were of equal footing, and some could infer that the Russians had stepped foot on the moon, too. But the spirit of cooperation was in the air, and NASA was working on not only a new spacecraft called the Shuttle, but also the concept of an International Space Station. The family attended the launch of Apollo-Soyuz that summer in 1975, but since the mission was in earth orbit only, the Saturn IB was used. A metal structure was built where the first stage had been on the Saturn V rockets, and it looked odd to me not seeing the stage that once propelled the astronauts into deep space. The "half rocket" quickly popped off the pad. It foreshadowed the winds of change at NASA.

The Shuttle was a new type of vehicle that would transport astronauts into space then return them home by landing on the ground, like an airliner. I was used to water splashdowns, as were many of the astronauts, so this new form of space travel was intriguing. The goal was to build a permanent space laboratory and use the Shuttle to transport crews to and from the earth. The Shuttle program was much different from Apollo, for the Shuttle design was totally different from the Saturn V rocket, and it was to remain in earth orbit, at a range of 115 to 400 statute miles above the earth. Deep space operations were now on the back burner. It was a whole new dynamic shift at NASA, and those left from the Apollo era were feeling the change. By now all of the Mercury men had moved into different fields. John Glenn became a U.S. Senator, Alan Shepard went into business, and others became consultants or retired. Same with the Gemini crews, and by the mid-seventies, with the ending of moon travel, many Apollo astronauts were leaving, too. Daddy would have been guaranteed to fly and command a Shuttle mission, but my mother later told me that he was grumbling about how NASA seemed to be moving backwards and not forwards. She said he would come in from the day saying, "Joan, the scientists seem to have taken over, and we are discussing things that we discussed ten years ago as we were developing Apollo. They are talking about taking spiders and bugs into space, and not the big picture of continuing the journey into outer space." Daddy became frustrated and disappointed that we were not being more aggressive. The new NASA personnel and astronauts were more geared for engineering and science programs, and the last of the hot-jock fighter pilots were moving on. NASA was undergoing a fundamental cultural change, and the learn-as-we-go, and fly-by-the-seat-of-your-pants attitude was changing.

• • •

Most every astronaut loved to drink beer; it was just part of the astronaut good-ol'-boy way of relaxing. Alan Shepard had started a Coors distributorship in Houston, Texas. Charlie Duke from Apollo 16 also partnered with someone to start a Coors distributorship in San Antonio, Texas. My father and a hunting partner, Kenneth Campbell, started looking into a distributorship, too. They applied but were turned down. My father told the Coors executives to let him know if they ever thought of expanding into Mississippi.

Our summer came and went, and we continued to go to The Place, visit family, and ride bikes. I started the seventh grade in the fall and began the routine. We usually started out the school year having tornado drills and nuclear bomb drills. They were generally both the same: huddle into the corner and hope for the best. My parents were traveling a lot, and I was never really sure where they were going, but we generally had a sitter who stayed out of the way. Sometimes the maid would stay with us, or most of the time we had a sweet old lady named Mrs. Irons. She lived in a small, modestly decorated home, and I would ride with Daddy to pick her up or drop her off. Her house looked like a perfectly square white cube. I don't know where Mama found her, but Mrs. Irons said she would sit only for us, and to not give her name to other families. My brothers just ignored her and did their own thing. I kept to myself and continued with my studies.

As the school year progressed, my parents returned from a trip to tell us life-changing news. My father announced that he was retiring from NASA and the Air Force. The family was going to move to Athens, Greece, and my father was taking a job with an international conglomerate called U.S. Industries that was helping develop the Middle East. My father retired in 1976 after 10 years with NASA and from the Air Force as a full bird colonel. The family went out to the flight line for his final ride in his T-38. Daddy took a low pass over the runway before going straight up with the afterburner. Then he circled back and landed. It was at sunset. Fitting, since it was the setting of his military and astronaut career. Giving up that jet was tough, but it was back to following the trail of Richard Halliburton and having new adventures.

T-38 NASA jet

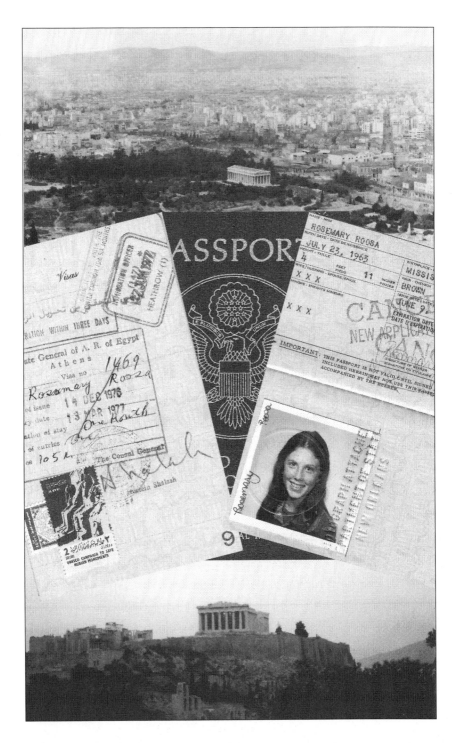

CHAPTER 4

Greece

Who are we? Where are we going? Where do we come from? These are philosophical questions that have plagued humankind for years and were pondered by great thinkers like Socrates and Plato. Soon I would be considering the questions in the same places that piqued the curiosity of philosophers. Our family was about to see firsthand the ancient ruins of Greece and step foot at the base of the Parthenon. The opportunity came about via a chance meeting through a hunting buddy of Daddy's — Sam Pancotto, from the Chicago area. He was not college educated, but he was quick with numbers and could make an accurate proposal for real estate developers on the spot. It helped him get ahead, and he made millions in a day when millionaires were scarce. Sam and my father hunted on safaris in Africa, being introduced by a big-game professional hunter. Sam invited Mama and Daddy to a wedding in Chicago in early 1976, where my father met a man named Gordon Walker, a soft-spoken, handsome and distinguished gentleman who ran a conglomerate called U.S. Industries.

The wedding in Chicago seemed like a scene from *The Godfather*. There were rumors that Sam was mafia connected, but Sam refuted being a "made man." Yet this wedding seemed like a mafia-merger, and all the big names and corporations in the area were invited to attend. Gordon and my father started chatting at the lavish reception, and Gordon seemed very impressed with my father's intelligence and work ethic. He felt that Stu Roosa needed to be in the corporate world earning some real money. Gordon Walker took

Daddy underneath his wing and offered him a salary of $75,000 a year and the first-class, corporate life. Since the Middle East was emerging in the oil industry, that would be my father's territory to sell U.S. Industries' products. Gordon offered the family a choice to live in London, Cairo, or Athens. My mother chose Athens.

We prepared for a summer move to Greece. It was the year of our American Bicentennial, 1976, and before the big family move, we traveled to Philadelphia, Pennsylvania, to plant a "Moon Tree" at the Liberty Bell. The term Moon Tree affectionately came about after my father took seeds on board the Apollo 14 flight. In honor of the Forest Service and my father's days of smoke jumping, Daddy took along approximately 500 seeds of five different tree varieties – the Loblolly pine, Douglas fir, sycamore, redwood, and sweetgum. It represented trees that grew across the United States. The Forest Service germinated the seeds and started planting them during the patriotic "red, white, and blue" time of the bicentennial.

At school I went to the library and checked out a few books on Greece, for I knew nothing about it except for what I had studied in history class. It looked beautiful. Most of the books showed whitewashed homes with the deep blue Aegean Sea in the background. I flipped through pictures of the Parthenon and Greek monuments and statues. It was going to be an interesting time. The plan was to live there for three years. There was debate about whether to sell the house in El Lago or rent it. I pushed to rent it, thinking the home would be an historical marker one day, having been the home of an Apollo astronaut. I finished my seventh-grade year and prepared for a life-changing journey.

We readied for an early July departure, planning to spend about a month touring Europe and then winding up in Greece prior to the new school year. My parents headed to Greece by themselves in June to search for a temporary place for us to live and to start laying the groundwork for an office. They came back from that trip very excited and talked about how, when they were in a little fishing village called Piraeus, they feasted on the biggest lobster they had ever seen. We were going to love it! They also found us a nice duplex that overlooked the entire city of Athens. They had researched schools and visited the U.S. Embassy.

Mama and Daddy rented our house in Texas to an elderly couple, who allowed us to leave some NASA photos and household items in the attic. The rest was packed for storage or Greece. In the few days before we departed for New York, I closed my bank account. I had received small amounts over the years for Christmas, birthdays, etc., and had accumulated about $500. A lot for a little girl almost thirteen years old. I put the money in a square, hard purse lined in flowered fabric and put it behind my bed, where it was when the movers came the day before departure. That night before leaving, I went through my purse, and $200 was missing. I had been robbed by the movers. I felt a sinking pit in my stomach, for there was nothing I could do. Who would steal from a little girl? My parents were upset, but my father said that the movers were smart to take only some and not all, or I might have discovered it missing while they were there. On the airplane to New York, I thought about the Ten Commandments and for the first time pondered forgiveness.

In New York, we stayed at the Waldorf Astoria. I had been getting used to nice hotels since Daddy's mission, but this was special. New York was exciting, and we were about to have a real summer adventure. Our first evening we had dinner at Tavern on the Green in Central Park. It had beautiful, sparkling crystal chandeliers and an "elite" feel. We spent the next few days seeing the sights, and Gordon Walker had arranged for us to have classes about Greece. No telling what it cost, but U.S. Industries hired the best and the brightest scholars, professors, and experts to indoctrinate us into the Greek culture. One instructor was Ernestine Friedl, an elderly woman whom my mother adored. She knew Greek history like no other. We also learned that Greeks like to play a game of sorts…they would short-change a person to see if he or she caught it. Important information to know. Over the next few days we experienced Greek food and one evening had a typical Middle Eastern dinner. We learned to say "al-salaam alikam" in Arabic, which was "peace be unto you." We sat on carpets, and servers brought out a cooked baby lamb. The tradition was that the guest of honor would eat the eyeball, and Daddy said he suspected that honor would go to him. He said if he got it, he was not going to chew, but just try to swallow it whole. I could tell he was dreading the evening. But when time came, they presented the eye to Gordon Walker's lovely wife, a former Miss Taiwan pageant winner. She gasped and refused. Daddy was relieved. The night before we left to fly overseas, we had dinner at the Bull & Bear Steakhouse at the Waldorf Astoria. It felt like Wall Street money with its rich, dark wood and large, comfortable chairs. We toasted to our last night in the United States.

The next day we flew on Air France first class to Paris. We boarded, and the beautifully dressed flight attendants handed out champagne in crystal flutes. I asked if I could have one, and my mother said "yes." I was fascinated with the bubbles, and the taste was exquisite. My father said that we were supposed to be on TWA but that when he called for six first-class tickets for the Roosa family, the clerk said, "Is this a joke? My father said, "no," and hung up. As I was slowly sipping on the champagne at 35,000 feet above the Atlantic, Daddy told me that while the family was in the Air France first-class lounge waiting to board, he went over to the TWA counter and showed them the tickets. He wanted to show Trans World Airlines that they had missed out. My father did not like his integrity questioned.

We arrived in Paris and stayed at a modest hotel, the Cecil, near the Champs-Elysees. We could have stayed at the deluxe Hotel De Crillon, but my father had met the Cecil hotel manager at a function and promised that he would stay at his hotel when in Paris. We rented a car the next day and soon learned that when going through round-a-bouts, cars had to give way to the right. We entered the circle at the Champs-Elysees at the Arc de Triumph and kept yelling for Daddy to move in, move in — they had to give way! And they did. We laughed… until Daddy tried to get back out of the circle to exit. This was much harder, and thus, we circled a few times while Daddy moved his way back out in break-neck speeding traffic. It was like circling the moon a few times before escaping its orbit.

From Paris we flew to Germany, where we had a big, beautiful metallic gray Mercedes-Benz waiting for us. It was a 450 SEL, the largest Mercedes built at the time. The plan was to drive from Germany to Italy, then board a ferry to Yugoslavia (now Croatia). Even though the car was large, we were a large family with a lot of luggage. Houston, we had a problem. Mercedes suggested a luggage rack for the top, but Daddy thought the look might cheapen this sophisticated vehicle. So, for about an hour my father tried all kinds of ways to squeeze the luggage into the trunk. Then voila, it fit. NASA problem-solving in tight spaces paid off. It was a tight squeeze for us kids too, but generally, I sat between my parents, and the boys sat in the back.

My father's new employer, U.S. Industries, paid for the best hotels along the way. Daddy planned a flexible itinerary. The trip would take about three weeks. As we drove through the quaint German towns, everything looked like a postcard. There were wooden window flower boxes and rolling green hills. In Europe, it is customary to view hotel rooms prior to accepting, so I would generally accompany my father to see if the rooms were acceptable. Not that my opinion much mattered, but he made me feel important by giving me a say in it. And if I didn't immediately get out of the car when he did, he would look back at me with a "Well, come on, let's go check it out" look. One little hotel had an indoor pool with a mural of the countryside painted on the wall. I came back to the car yelling, "It's got a pool!" My brothers looked at me skeptically, like I was trying to play a trick on them, so after checking in, I put on my swimsuit, and they followed me, wearing their street clothes and saying not a word … and then their eyes lit up with excitement when they saw it was true. Little sister would not take a hit on this one.

The autostradas and autovitas were the coolest. No speed limits. We'd encourage Daddy to drive fast as if he were in one of his supersonic jets. We zipped through Europe, and soon we were in Italy. Since my father liked guns, a man named Zoli made my father a special rifle engraved with Apollo 14 images and my father's signature. We joked that the guy would make a great forger, for my father's signature was unique. He signed his name as "Stu A. Roosa," but he would cross the "t" in Stu with the end of the "u" in a loop, and then the "A" looked like an "O" with a tail. We visited with Zoli and stayed as guests in a castle near Lake Garda. Turns out the place was haunted. Since I generally stayed with my parents, they slept on a double bed, and I stayed in a twin bed near the bedroom wall. In the middle of the night, I woke to hear the sound of someone running up and down the stairs. My first thought was that it was one of the boys. "Please tell them to go to bed, Mama," I said in a sleepy tone. She calmly answered back, "Just go back to sleep, Sugar. All is okay…" are the last words I heard as I drifted back into a slumber. The next morning the owners of the castle came out for breakfast and hesitantly asked, "How did you sleep?" My mother answered, "We slept fine." Later in life she talked about how she didn't sleep a wink, that she heard all the classic haunted sounds like clapping thunder, heavy rain, running horses, and chains dragging in the night. Daddy had a pillow over his head and didn't hear a thing.

Next stop was Venice, the romantic city on the water. We arrived in Venice the day before my birthday, which was July 23. A friendly gentleman greeted us at the boats, which took us from the mainland to Venice. He was our personal escort, and he and Daddy exchanged cards. I thought, "How do people know we are here?!" Since my father had led a rather secretive life being in the space program and Air Force, people suspected our move to Greece was a CIA cover. Daddy always denied it, but many would smile and wink as if to say, "Right… I won't blow your cover." I started to wonder. Sometimes I would ask Daddy how he knew people in Europe but would not get a straight answer. Perhaps my father was in the CIA, but I had no way of knowing. All I knew is we were staying at the Hotel Danieli on the Grand Canal and were arriving by a beautiful wooden boat. Gondolas were drifting by with men in black striped shirts and wearing red bandanas around their necks and waists. The lobby of the hotel was exquisite with Italian marble and a beautiful staircase leading up to the floors. Green plants in large pots sat in a cozy sitting area. It was an elegant place to leisurely watch the tourists. The rooms were outfitted with carved wooden beds and tasteful artwork. The large antique keys to the room were on red tasseled plastic that would float if dropped into the water.

The next day my father asked me what I would like to have for my birthday dinner, and the answer was obvious to me – pizza! My mother knew there was a famous place in Venice that Ernest Hemingway frequently visited and Richard Halliburton had mentioned in his tales, but she could not remember the name. She said it had a simple name, like "Sam's Place." So my father asked the concierge. The well-dressed man answered him, "I believe you are referring to Harry's Bar." "Nooo, that's not it," my father replied… now convinced the name was Sam's Place. The concierge politely tried to convince him otherwise, and a "bar" did not hit me as the kind of place to have a birthday dinner for a 13 year old, but we headed out to try and find it anyway. Soon thereafter we found a typical pizza place off the pigeon-laden San Marcos square, so we stopped.

Italian pizza is not like American pizza. It is thin crusted, and the portions are generally made for one person. Pepperoni and mushroom pizza is my favorite, but it was not on the menu. Daddy asked the English-speaking waiter if the restaurant could make a "special pizza" for my birthday with only these toppings. The waiter in the white shirt and black bow-tie said the chef could. As the pizzas arrived, mine came with all kinds of toppings. This is not the birthday pizza Daddy ordered for me. Soon we could hear the waiter and the chef arguing in Italian with their hands waving at each other and pointing at me. Even though we could not speak Italian, we could figure that the chef heard "special" and started fixing that pizza right away. It was clear someone was going to pay for the mistake. But my "special" pizza finally arrived after everyone had long finished theirs. By then the birthday evening was not turning out to be so special after all, but on the way back, my mother led us into a jewelry store. She wanted to purchase a nice gift to commemorate my turning 13 years old. After discussion, the distinguished sales clerk brought out a variety of Venetian cut-glass necklaces. Mama had a way of choosing items quickly and zeroed in on a short, clear necklace about a half-inch wide with rich, deep ruby-colored glass along the bottom row that circled just below the neck. I felt like a princess. My parents purchased it, and the night was unforgettable.

The following morning, the same man who had met us at the boat dock arrived at the hotel to show us some sights. He managed to get us around the long lines, and I still wondered who he was. Then the mysterious man turned to me along the way and said he heard it was my birthday and that he was going to throw a party. "What?! For me?" I thought, undeserving of such attention. Later that day we traveled to a large home with long tables shaped in a squared U-like fashion. "Who are all these people?" I wondered as the festivities began. The wine was flowing, but I was too young to imbibe. After we feasted for hours, the cake arrived, and the man said to me, "Speech, speech!" I was horrified at the prospect of standing up and talking. "No, grazie, no, no, no," I answered, nervous that the spotlight was on me now. He was insistent and finally seemed irritated that I had declined to speak. Later I felt guilty for not doing it, but impromptu speaking - or any public speaking at all - was not my forte. My father gave a toast to thank them for a great time and the drinking continued. He had my back.

Rome, the Eternal City, was next on the itinerary. Rome made for difficult driving. One-way streets abounded. Or the street signs were not always visible. As we went through European cities, my parents quickly learned to hire taxi drivers to lead us to our locations, and at first, the drivers would look confused because no one was getting into the taxi, but they would figure it out and lead us along. If they got too fast and we could not keep up, then my father would say, "There goes his fare." When we could not find the Hassler Hotel, we stopped and asked a cab driver to lead us. With Italian flair, he gestured, pondered, waved his hands, scratched his head, and finally said, "It is impossible. There is no way to get there from here." "What?!" we exclaimed. We were in Rome, and the hotel was in Rome, but after my father showed him some money, he said he would try. Sure enough, suddenly we were driving the wrong way on one-way streets, in back allies, and practically on sidewalks. The cab driver was right; it was nearly impossible to get there!

The Hassler Hotel is just above the famous Spanish Steps. Another five-star luxury hotel, it is known for providing unforgettable memories and breathtaking views of Rome. That evening while dining at the top restaurant in all its elegance, my father proposed a champagne toast. He gave us children a half glass and declared, "Here's to the Roosa Dynasty." Ahhh, those bubbles. We clicked our glasses together. Our family was on its way to becoming long lasting – a dynasty. It was a magical evening. The next day we visited the Vatican, and being raised Catholic, I saw this as a special place. The sheer architecture of the Vatican is impressive, and my father timed it so that we would attend a Mass conducted by the Pope. The Pope entered St. Peter's Cathedral on a chair carried by men of the church. We were sitting in a pew at the front. As the music played, I watched in wonder at the person who could speak God's words, and then watched as the chair was lowered to the ground. Pope Paul VI started moving down the row to meet us! My mother leaned over to me and whispered, "Kiss his ring when he extends his hand." I did not know much about the ring, but did as told, and he handed me a keychain. It was an honor to be in his Holiness's presence. During Mass, he spoke in several different languages, and he acknowledged Daddy being in the audience as the astronaut from Apollo 14. I wondered again how the Pope knew we were there, but my father had arranged many things that surprised me.

As we wound up our trip to Rome, it was time to board the ferry to cross the Adriatic Sea to Dubrovnik. Somehow Daddy got lost around the port area. We started into some dark areas. Then we saw garages with men working with blow torches in the shadows. We had hit the "stolen car" area, where cars were being transformed and tags removed for the black market. It was spooky. As Daddy was trying to find the entrance to the ferry, a small car came out of nowhere and started flagging us down. Someone was trying to get us to pull over. Daddy sped up. We were now in a *Mission Impossible*-type get away. After a few hairy twists and turns, we finally found the entrance to the ferry area, and the car sped in front of us and stopped. Out jumped the polizia. "Why did you not stop?" The policeman demanded to know.

"Because I did not know who you were!" my father said with a firm voice.

"I was waving my baton!" he shouted back.

"Exactly why I did not stop… I had no idea what it was that you were waving at me!" my father answered, staring at him. He took out his flashlight and saw all us kids wide-eyed as he did a quick scan of the inside of the car.

"Do you know how many cars are stolen around here?" the policeman said in exasperation. Having just seen the stolen car area, we did. The policeman saw a big, beautiful new Mercedes-Benz in the wrong part of the docks and was trying to catch a car thief. He waved us on, and we boarded the ferry.

Once again, I stayed in the room with my parents. As we sailed away, Daddy and I looked at the lights of Rome through the ferry window and sang, "Arrivederci, Roma…" But we really didn't know the words, so we would hum a bit, then blurt out again, "Arrivederci, Roma…" We did this over and over until Mama told us to stop. We smiled and laughed after our tense day.

After having been introduced to a whirlwind of different countries on our trip to Greece, we finally arrived at our new destination, where we would be for the next three years. The first thing that I wanted to know was where was all the whitewash that I had seen in the books? Little did I know that was only on the Greek islands. We were now in a major metropolitan city, and settling into the duplex Mama and Daddy had rented earlier. The place had a magnificent view overlooking Athens. At night, Mama would sit on the back porch and watch the lights twinkling in the ancient city. She commented that it is always nice to have a good view, and I tucked that bit of information away for "life's lessons."

Being the only daughter, I was oftentimes lonely, so from the time I could remember, I had cats. I loved cats. As a child, instead of dolls, I would play with cats. As soon as it was allowed, our Labrador, Beau, and my Siamese cat, Siam, joined us at our new residence. Siam had a dark face and sky-blue eyes. In Greece, this color of blue eyes meant good luck. Our landlord made it clear that the general belief was that cats should remain outdoors. The housekeeper kept throwing my cat outside. I would have to go search for my precious cat, telling the housekeeper, "oxi, oxi" meaning "no, no." "SiiiiAAAammm," I would call with a shrill voice, panicking that I'd lost him. Fortunately, I would find him in the bushes, scared to death of this new land, fearfully looking at me with those blue eyes, seeming to ask, "Where am I?" The top duplex was rented by an English family whose grandfather owned a Bentley and puffed on a pipe. We used to call him "Puff, Puff, Bentley," as we never learned their names. One day while I was frantically calling for the cat, the young boy who lived upstairs walked out and asked, "Why do you wake my Mummy up?" I looked at him blankly. It was mid-day, and I figured most people were awake. I did not know that afternoon naps were part of the Greek culture.

Daddy set up shop in a big top-floor office between Athens and our home base, also with a view of the city. He soon learned that corporate life in Greece was not as easy as in America. Simple things like hooking up a telephone line were complex. But Daddy found a secretary who was part American and part Greek. She was a bombshell and looked like Barbara Eden. Blonde hair and big… well, two things I did not have at my age. Her name was Aphrodite, like the goddess of love. She was able to speak the language and helped set up a beautiful office with flokati rugs, big wooden desks, modern chairs, and marble ashtrays with matching cigarette boxes and lighters.

Aphrodite was so friendly to us kids, and I could not tell about Mama's reaction. Soon we were having guests come visit, and they would say, "Stu, you got a nice set up here!" implying something else. But I always saw Daddy stay professional. He was not a flirt. Mama used to say you cannot keep a man on a tight leash, that if a man wants to cheat, he will find a way, but she also used to say, "Beware of the firm flesh." And as an astronaut, Daddy had already had women throwing themselves at him. Once at a party in Houston, my mother happened to be standing in front of two curvaceous young women, and one slyly said to the other, "I've slept with every Apollo astronaut." My mother wheeled around and said, "Not all of them!"

We stayed in our temporary residence overlooking Athens while searching for a more permanent home. We found one in a new subdivision at 22 Proteus Avenue in Kifissia, north of Athens and closer to the mountains. The three-story home was owned by a local soap-opera actress and was meant as a duplex for two families, with the maid's quarters on the bottom level. We rented it as one house, and the boys went upstairs into quarters that had three bedrooms, a kitchen, game room, patio, and a circular back stairwell that descended to the ground level. My parents had a wing of the house, and the bedroom was painted deep, almost blood, red. It was not soothing, but this actress must have liked the dramatic effect. My bedroom was next door to theirs, with a sliding glass door leading to the front of the house. I decorated my room with Purina Cat Chow calendar pictures and set up my desk next to the glass door. That desk was about to get a lot of use from studying.

We enrolled in a British boarding school called Campion, which was near downtown Athens. The American school, where most of the embassy children attended, was "full of drugs" according to a source, so even though we were living at home, we attended the British school. It was right out of *Tom Brown's Schooldays*, complete with a headmaster and strict uniform policy. Since the women's lib movement was going on, the school, for the first year ever, was allowing girls to wear pants. The girls wore navy blue skirts, or now pants, with a white top and a red vest. The boys wore navy blue pants with a light-blue collared shirt and blue sweater. No blue jeans. The school was not located in one building, but in several large converted homes in a residential area called Psychiko.

I enjoyed my schoolmates and bonded with Lisa Ann, an American girl whose father worked for TWA airlines. She was from Hollywood, Florida. Lisa looked like the actress Alicia Silverstone, and was a good foot taller than I and well developed. We were like Mutt and Jeff; she was so bubbly and full of personality, and I was so shy and reserved, but we became fast friends. I also bonded with an English girl named Helen from the town of Bath, which she pronounced with more of an "ahh" sound with her British accent. Other girls were from South Africa, Italy, Jordan, Australia, and other far-off places. Some students were from Lebanon, and their parents had sent them there to escape the civil war. These students talked about how beautiful and prosperous their country was prior to being riddled with tanks and bullets. The curriculum was grueling. Since the children boarding at Campion had nowhere else to go in the evenings, we were to study at night. Since we lived about 30 minutes north, it was quicker and easier for

Front of home in Greece, with my bedroom bottom left,
with our dog Beau

Back of three-story home in Greece

Daddy and me at the
base of the Sphinx

Riding camels by the
Egyptian pyramids

Sunset on the Nile
while sailing in a
felucca

us to take taxis to and from school than to catch the school bus that went all over town. The taxi drivers drove like bats out of hell. Each day was a harrowing experience. The drivers veered outside the lanes, drove onto sidewalks, ran red lights... it was if each ride were an emergency.

There was a military Air Force base across town, near Glifadha, south of the port of Piraeus, home of the big lobsters. Mama would go to the commissary at the base, making her way through the wild drivers about once a week to stock up on provisions. Mama was exasperated after those days, and she did not like driving that big Mercedes through traffic. Near misses were frequent, and it wound up raising her blood pressure permanently. Everything in Greece was bargained for, including the vegetables at the street market. Mama got tired of haggling over the price of tomatoes, so she dared the drive, especially when we had company coming in from the States and needed additional food and supplies. Sam Pancotto, his wife (also named Rosemary), and his pretty nurse traveling with them came to visit shortly after we had settled into our new, large home. After dinner, Sam and Daddy strolled out onto the terrace to have an ouzo. Sam took out a cigar and lit it while looking up at the moon. It was almost full. Sam took a puff, then with cigar in hand, pointed at the moon and asked, "Stu, is that the same moon that I see when I am in the United States?" Daddy flatly said, "Sure is, Sam."

• • •

1976 was coming to a close, and Daddy planned a trip for us to spend Christmas and the New Year in Egypt. Already, I had learned so much being in Greece and Rome — the basis of democracy — now we were heading to an entirely different continent and culture, with a highly advanced civilization that went back more than 5,000 years. Farouk El-Baz, the lunar geologist from NASA, had family in Cairo. We started our trip with a beautiful dinner in Farouk's brother's home. His wife greeted us at the door and kissed me on both checks. I was stunned, for our family did not outwardly express emotion, particularly women kissing women, even if it was on the cheek. I had learned handshakes, but this was a new one. It was a lovely dinner with all kinds of exotic dishes. Just one snag. She forgot to pour any water or beverages, so by the end of the night our throats were dry. But it was a fun experience.

We stayed in the famous Shepheard Hotel. It was an old and grand hotel where the explorer Henry Stanley, of "Dr. Livingston, I presume?" fame, went in search of the source of the Nile. Although the original hotel burned in 1952, it was resurrected near the same location. There were more modern hotels, but Daddy felt it appropriate to start our adventure where the adventurers started theirs. Having been working in the Middle East, Daddy understood some of the culture, and soon after a little "baksheesh" or small tip (stopping short of calling it a bribe), we were soon on our way to crawling on the Sphinx and riding camels by the ancient pyramids. Every single mode of transportation was visible in Cairo, from a Mercedes to a donkey-led cart, all traveling the crowded streets with horns honking constantly. Animals on the roads were something that we did not see in Europe or Greece, and it was a mixture of the past meeting the present. All forms of clothing were also visible, from women with covered heads, to men in long white "gowns," to people in Western wear. My eyes were wide in wonderment of the hustle and bustle. My father must have seen that I was a bit overwhelmed. He began to repeat to me, "Wait until we get to Luxor; it will be a sleepy little town..." and then his eyes would reveal his calm but somewhat mischievous nature, and he would chuckle softly.

One evening we saw a Sound and Light show in English at the base of the Sphinx and Great Pyramids. It was like a Disney show on steroids. The loud, booming voice said, "Man fears time, but time fears the pyramids." Against the dark night with the spotlights flashing on and off in sequence to music and the deep storytelling voice, these monuments were impressive. The next day Daddy had some business to attend to, so he rented us a car and driver to take us to see the Suez Canal. It was hot, and there was not much to see on the drive but desert. The driver was old, with leathered dark skin and almost bald, and the road was long without a lot of traffic. The driver started to fall asleep and was drifting off the road when he suddenly jerked the car and honked the horn! There was not a car in sight. Reflex for Cairo drivers is to just lay on the horn. We finally neared the Suez Canal, which had been a war zone, and remnants of broken-down tanks and bullet-ridden vehicles lingered. The day was interesting, but it was not a typical sight-seeing adventure.

That night at the hotel we went to the supposed five-star restaurant on top, and then we were to see a belly dancer afterwards. Mama wanted us to see all that the culture had to offer. As we perused the menu, we saw the selections were mouthwatering. Mama, being the gourmet cook, was reading the menu like a good book. We were in for a treat after our long day. The waiter went around the table, and we started to order.

"We don't have that tonight," he said apologetically. As another one of us would order, he'd say, "We don't have that tonight; what else would you like?" Then we'd pick something else and get the same answer.

Finally, my mother said, "What *do* you have tonight?"

"We have roast duck and potatoes."

"Fine" she said, "We'll have six of them."

The waiter seemed satisfied, and we laughed about the "extensive" menu. The duck was barely edible. After the dinner the lights went low, and I was feeling like we were about to watch something that was too exotic for our ages. The room had filled with patrons by that time, and then out came this huge woman in veils. The tantric-type music started playing, and she shook her belly fat and pulled off veils. As the fat wobbled down her body, the men in the crowd cheered with excitement. One of my brothers said, "I didn't know hippos came out of the Nile." It was an awkward evening all around. Yet beauty is in the eye of the beholder, and large women are considered sexy in parts of the world. It shows a sign of abundance.

After a few days, we boarded the plane for Luxor. I had had enough of crowds. "Just wait for that sleepy little town," Daddy would tell me again with a grin and a chuckle. I started to think that he was trying to fool me, and that we were about to hit an even larger city.

We landed after dusk and started out to the Winter Palace Hotel. "The Old Winter Palace or the New Winter Palace?" the cab driver asked.

"Don't know," my father replied.

It seemed like a big deal. Maps were pulled out, addresses pondered; conversations with airport attendees occurred. After much debate, my father finally yelled, "Just take us to one!"

Turns out the hotels were right next door to each other. We were booked at the Old Winter Palace, which showcased the splendor of the colonial days. I fell asleep that night exhausted, not sure about this trip. I woke up the next morning to the "clip clop, clip clop" sound of a horse-drawn carriage. Sure enough, it was a sleepy little town on the banks of the Nile. Turns out Agatha Christie wrote *Death on the Nile* while staying at the Old Winter Palace.

Soon we were heading to one of the most amazing places in the world, the Valley of the Kings. It was the location of the pharaohs' tombs. Tutankhamun's tomb had been discovered in 1922 and was "new," so we toured it first. Tutankhamun, however, was a blip on the radar compared to other pharaohs, and King Tut's tomb was small. Its claim to fame was being discovered almost fully intact by Howard Carter. The tomb had not been ransacked, and the treasures were found mostly in place from approximately 1320 BC. However, we learned the ultimate ruler was Ramses II. Ramses' father was Seti I, and his tomb was simply amazing, with deep pits for trespassers to fall into and false chambers to lure looters. The hieroglyphics and artwork carved into the pillars and walls were incredible. My mind had a hard time grasping that all of this was accomplished thousands of years ago. I enjoyed the fascination with the after-life and the connections with the gods. In one mystical chamber of Seti I, the ceiling depicted traversing into the after-life on a large boat, with the background painted in a rich, deep blue/indigo color. The soul was crossing over to become on par with the gods.

Close by was the Valley of the Queens, where the pharaohs' wives were buried. In one area, there was an incredibly large structure with a huge ramp leading to a grand entrance. It belonged to a woman named Hatshepsut (the guide pronounced it like Hat – Ship – Suit). She apparently was much more than a wife – she was a pharaoh. Yet the male rulers seemed to dislike having a woman pharaoh in their past, and they took great pains to eliminate her name from carvings to essentially erase her from history. Somehow the truth of Hatshepsut persisted, for the truth seems to come out in the end.

In one area, we stumbled upon an unfinished obelisk. It was to be the largest and grandest of all obelisks erected. Yet after all the intricate carvings and shaping, it remained there on its side. The effort was abandoned. My father turned and said, "This is just like the Apollo program. We were achieving something great, but just quit." My father always had a hard time understanding why the United States quit going to the moon during our technological height. He felt a kindred spirit with the unfinished obelisk.

We took a long day trip to visit Abu-Simbel, the great Ramses temples which were erected so that twice a year a ray of sun would shine all the way down the corridors and light up the face of Ramses, and he would be one with the gods. This made him on par with the gods while he was still living and before the after-life. How did this civilization accomplish so many complex structures and know about the movement of the earth, stars, moon, and sun? I was now really enjoying discovering this country in Africa and learning how this ancient civilization utilized the skills of its people, from the artists, to the craftsmen, to the engineers, to the scientists and religious leaders.

On Christmas Day it was 90 degrees, and we were looking at palm trees and desert. It was not a traditional Christmas. We went to lunch, and the waiter informed us the special was "Turkish."

"Turkish what?" my father asked. We had no clue anymore about the food.

"Turkish" was all the waiter repeated.

"Turkish what?" my father asked again firmly.

"Turkish" he replied with a final head nod. That was it.

Mama mentioned it might be a curry dish, or something with lamb.

"Turkish *WHAT?*" my father sternly asked the waiter, losing his patience. Finally, the exasperated waiter flapped his arms like he was doing the chicken dance and said, "Turkish, Turkish! A big bird!"

We all said at once, "Oh, turkey!"

The waiter said exhaustingly, "Yes, Yes, turkish!"

We ordered it, and he went away like we were idiots. At least some part of the day would be a traditional Christmas.

We returned to Cairo for New Year's, but this time staying at the Marriott. When we ordered off the menu, surprisingly, the food was available, and more people spoke English. It was definitely an international hotel catering to the business traveler. In the center of the lobby was a large decorated Christmas tree — not quite as elaborate as the one at Rockefeller Center in New York, but it gave us a sense of the holidays, despite the heat. At one point my father gently tapped my shoulder and said, "Look." All I looked at was the tree. He said, "What is interesting about this image?" He told me to bring my eyes down, and there sitting in the lobby, with his back to us, was an Arab gentleman in traditional dress of a black robe with gold trim, a white head cover, and a gold and black headband. He, too, was looking at the glittering tree. My father said, "Look at the different cultures, all merging together – Muslim and Christian." It truly was an image that was juxtaposed, but peaceful and harmonious.

Egypt wound up being a fascinating trip for me, having visited some of the great archaeological monuments in the world. Now it was back to Greece and seeing the Acropolis and Parthenon every day when I was riding to school. Ancient history abounded. It was back to the same routine at Campion, wearing our uniforms and walking from building to building, carrying almost 16 pounds on my back every day and attending nine classes per day. We were getting a college education, except I was only in the eighth grade.

Daddy was traveling for weeks at a time in the Middle East. After NASA, the long time away from home was getting tiresome for him. On occasion when he was in town, he would visit the American Embassy, sometimes taking me along to get a good ol' American cheeseburger and a milkshake. His trips to Saudi Arabia were a bit mentally exhausting, for when Daddy thought he had a deal, the players would suddenly go back to the negotiating table. There was never a quick handshake and sign-on-the-bottom-line kind of deal. And the price for hotel rooms was astronomical.

In 1976/77, a hundred dollars for a hotel room was expensive. Yet it is what my father had to pay to sleep in a room not larger than a closet. Daddy mentioned that one time when he was heading to a meeting, he passed by men who had just been hung in "Chop-Chop Square." He said, "I looked up, and there were three dead bodies hanging in the middle of the square. Arrest was Monday; trial on Wednesday, and death on Friday. The Court of Appeals is probably not very busy in that country."

• • •

The Easter break was coming, and my father decided to take the family back through Europe to go skiing. Since living in Houston and going back and forth to the Cape — both places warm, humid, and near the water — we had never gone skiing as a family. It was time for a new adventure. We packed up the Mercedes and headed towards Switzerland. We did not have a specific place in mind but figured we'd follow the hood ornament and see where it led. As we were driving through Austria, we stopped for gas, and the car next to us had skis on top. Daddy asked where they were going, and they said they had just come back from skiing at a place not too far away. "How was the skiing?" my father asked.

"It's snowing every day, lots of fresh snow… you should try it!" the fellow traveler answered in English with a German-sounding accent.

Daddy pulled out the map, and they showed him the location. It was a tiny town with a ski resort that was so high up, we had to park at the base of the mountain and take a funicular up, as no roads could reach the place during the cold season.

We arrived at the top and unloaded. Unfortunately, there was a snowstorm and we could not see much, but snow was everywhere, indeed! The accommodations were not the most luxurious; in fact, the restrooms were down the hall (no private bathrooms in the room) and to take a hot shower, a person had to put a coin in the water heater and be quick. The hot water lasted only a few minutes. Daddy used to love to take long showers after his experience as a child in the cold tub in Oklahoma, so he learned fast to take several coins. Mama had gone skiing with Daddy one time in Colorado years before, and on her first day, she saw the ski patrol hauling a man off on a stretcher. The man was nearly blue. She said to Stuart, "Honey, I don't know how to ski, but I know how to drink. I will see you in the bar!" And she never put on skis again.

My father believed in having the right gear for the right occasion, but since we were not skiers, we did not have the appropriate gear. Daddy outfitted us in rented skis, and we did our best to keep warm. He also hired an instructor to teach us, but the kind, elderly gentleman did not speak much English, and the best I could understand was "snowplow" — which was a maneuver of turning the tips of the skis inward to slow down.

Daddy was a natural athlete and always felt the need for speed, but on this trip, he stayed with me by my side as I tried to get the hang of it. The boys caught on quickly and soon were nowhere to be seen. The snow was blowing so hard, we could barely see our hands outstretched in front of us. Daddy had a mustache, and soon it became frozen and looked like miniature icicles hanging around his mouth. After a couple of hours of skiing — and falling for me — it was lunch time. Ahhh, warmth. The cozy chalet had a dining area of wooden bench tables, and the first course was hot soup. As we trekked in, Mama was sitting there already in the dining room and seemed pleased to see us. She told Stuart that something was wrong with the space heater. The room was cold. But Daddy checked it, and it seemed fine. Mama was relieved and said she was going to settle in with a book and read. As soon as lunch was finished, it was back out into the snowstorm to try again. Again, Daddy stayed by my side patiently, but it was just so darn hard to see. And wherever I was, the snowplow machine seemed to always be heading for me. I could hear the engine but not see it... then suddenly I would see two dim headlights coming at me and have to struggle to side step out of its way. It was a bit grueling. Daddy kinda laughed and said that he didn't think the driver could see where he was going but just knew to ride up and down the slopes since the snow was piling up so fast. Who knows, but it was a trying day.

That evening Mama informed us that she figured out the innkeeper was turning off the electricity to save money. Right before and right after each meal, the heat would come on, then go off. Daddy made some arrangement with the innkeeper to keep the electricity on for Mama, but he did not seem happy. This was a serious ski resort, and that is what you did during the day — ski! The next day was somewhat clearer, but that morning while I was in the restroom down the hall, a small window was open. I looked out and saw a cliff. It was straight down as far as the eye could see. A feeling of both panic and thanks ran through me, for what if I had skied right off the mountain in the snowstorm? It was certainly an eye-opening introduction to skiing. After that as I went through life, I made sure that I had the correct ski outfits. Like Mama, my favorite part was après-skiing at the bar.

• • •

Back in Athens, Daddy was spending time with me in the evenings, and we would sometimes ride our bikes on nearby trails with our dog, Beau, running alongside. Or if it was dark, he would teach me the constellations. Since Daddy spent so much time traveling with NASA and for work, when there was a moment to talk and discover his daughter's thoughts, interests, and feelings, he took advantage of the time. His father, Dewey, had taken the time to talk to him as a child and encouraged him to dream big. Daddy used to talk about growing up and sitting on the back porch in Oklahoma, looking at the stars and envisioning far-away places. Daddy was laying the same groundwork with me to dream and be adventurous. On some weekends, the family would pile up in the car and "follow the hood ornament" to places such as Marathon, Delphi, or Olympus. We weren't just hearing about these places made famous from mythology or the history books, we were experiencing them first-hand.

The weather warmed up, and we had more visitors at our home. This time it was Bob Perkins and his wife, Alice, from Coos Bay, Oregon. I had known Bob since NASA days, and we kids called him "Uncle Bob." Bob was an affable older fellow who slicked back his gray hair and would chuckle as he told joke after joke. He had met Alice during Vaudeville days, and they wound up making their living going to state and world fairs with a mind-reading act. Uncle Bob also knew a lot of card tricks, and he would entertain us kids with his sleight-of-hand and magic tricks. He even taught me a simple "mind-reading" trick of correctly identifying an object that had been silently pointed to by someone while I was out of the room. Alice and Bob's routine was much more elaborate, and one time while they were entertaining a crowd at a NASA party, Daddy bought a new deck of cards, convinced the cards were marked. "It's just magic, Stu!" Bob would say with his chuckle.

Uncle Bob rented a 100-foot sailboat, complete with a six-person crew, to take the family on a Greek cruise through the Aegean Sea. Mama prepared the menus for each day and purchased the food from the base commissary. Off we went to the Greek islands. At last, I was finally able to see the whitewashed buildings that I had seen in the library books. Daddy and I hiked to the top of Hydra one day, and we loved exploring the little side streets and quaint villages. The water was an exquisite shade of deep aqua blue, nothing like I had ever seen. Although it was approaching summer, the inviting water was still cold and full of jelly-fish, so snorkeling was out. Most times the yacht would motor from island to island, but one morning Mama got up and asked the crew to put up all the sails. It was quite the sight and feel.

Our first school year was coming to a close at Campion, and Mama decided to take my oldest brother, who was about to finish high school, to Russia as a graduation gift. My father was heading back to the United States at the same time. I was 13 years old, and my parents were leaving me and my two other brothers, barely 15 and 16, by ourselves in Greece. We were to call the American Embassy if needed. Mama had found a housekeeper who was an American and a trained archaeologist. Since there were so many archaeologists in Athens, the pay was not great, so to pay the bills, she took on the job as a maid. Her name was Janus, and she was not the best cleaner. The glasses from the cupboard were often dirty with specs of food, so we began calling them "Janus-glasses." Forevermore when we pulled out a glass that was not clean, we referred to it as a Janus-glass. However she was reliable, and she stayed with us at night while Mama and Daddy were away for two weeks.

When my father returned from the United States, he informed us that he had had enough of traveling alone and wanted to be with family. The three-year commitment initially promised to Gordon was null and void, and without consulting Mama, a rare move for Daddy, he had accepted an offer to move back to the United States. My father also said he was leaving the corporate world and was going to work for his friend, Kenneth Campbell from Texas. My mother's heart sank. She did not have a good feeling about it. However, since Daddy had no way of calling Mama during her trip to Russia; he had to make the decision then and there. Kenneth had demanded it. No waiting – yes or no. My father said, "yes."

Thus, our summer was spent moving back from Greece. Before returning to the United States, we took several weeks to travel through Europe, just as we had done during the move over. Seeing the world at such a formative time of life had an impact. I now felt "international." The world was an interesting and intriguing place, and I had enjoyed a sophisticated lifestyle that was a privilege to experience. It was life changing, and adventure and traveling was now a permanent part of my spirit.

CHAPTER 5

Back to Texas, Beer, & Flyin'

After Greece, the family moved back to Texas, this time to Austin. It was now July 1977, and Daddy started working for a company that Kenneth Campbell had invested in that was developing the electric car. Kenneth was the same businessman whom Daddy had partnered with to try for the Coors distributorship before moving overseas. Oil prices were starting to sky-rocket, and alternative fuels and energy were a hot industry. While we looked for a permanent place to live, we lived in a summer cottage owned by Kenneth. A comfortable, rectangular cottage on stilts, it was on Lake Travis and was outfitted with wicker furniture. It was far from the sophistication of old-world Europe. I enjoyed watching the boaters and would sometimes stick a fishing pole in the lake, usually with no luck. The partner in Austin was Mr. Bales, and he was a character. He was jolly and a fast-talker with a quick tale and a hearty laugh. He had a large houseboat and would invite us out for day cruises on the weekends. One of the first times on his boat, we passed some sunbathers on Lake Austin. A couple of them were standing up on the rocks, and Mr. Bales told me to take a look through the binoculars. I didn't think much of it, until I was suddenly looking through these high-powered binoculars and seeing naked young college men, waving and looking back at me! Embarrassed, I quickly jerked the binoculars away, and he laughed from his belly. I was shocked and ashamed that he had "gotten me." I was suspicious of him from that day on.

We spent most days looking at homes, and we had several real estate agents searching. We searched high and low, but nothing seemed to hit any of us as "right." Mama was preparing for a long stay in Texas and wanted a unique and beautiful home that could accommodate the family. One day we were shown a home that had everything on Mama's wish list. It was in an area outside of Austin called Pflugerville. It had big, nice bedrooms, a sparkling new kitchen, and a view of the hill country. When Daddy came home from work that day, we all told him about the house. But in private, Mama told Daddy that she got a spooky feeling from the house... something that she could not explain... and did not want to purchase it. We were all tired of being hauled around in a car going from house to house, but Daddy declared that we had to keep looking. Behind closed doors, Daddy told Mama that if she did not have a good feeling about it, then it was off the list. End of discussion. He trusted her instincts. We later learned that a murder had taken place in the house, explaining why everything was new and shiny. Mama had sensed it.

Then we got a call from a real estate agent who had worked with us early on. He drove us deep within the hill country, on a small, winding country road that eventually had a street named simply "The High Road." We pulled into a courtyard and saw a Spanish-style house with terra cotta tiles on the roof and white stucco on the outside walls. There were dark brown shutters around the large, arched windows, and we all felt good vibes even before we walked through the big, wooden front doors. There was a white entry wall with Mexican tiles on the floor. The house opened up into a large living room with a fireplace and high ceilings. The family room was next to it, separated only by a large frame, giving it an open feel. Then our eyes moved to a green area... it was an indoor atrium with skylights. It was beautiful. Close to the front door was a small, circular staircase that ascended to an upstairs balcony room overlooking the living room. It served as the library. The house had two large, guest suite-type bedrooms at each end, each with its own bathroom, and a large master suite with a white brick fireplace and a bathroom attached with two closets, two sinks, and an oval, step-up Jacuzzi tub. The kitchen was designed with small, square colorful Mexican tiles and had a formal dining room with a full bar attached. Out back was a dark-bottom pool, which from neglect, looked more like a pond. Large stones were placed around its S curve shape which complemented the surrounding terrain. Behind the pool was a forest, which led down a steep embankment. Deer loved that area. Beside the pool was a round cabana with a thatched roof and a stone pathway. We had found the house. It was one of a kind and custom designed.

When we described it to Daddy, he kept asking, "How many bedrooms again?"

"Three!" we excitedly shouted back, "But Daddy, you should see it… it has a pool!"

Daddy kept shaking his head saying, "No, it's too small. We need more bedrooms."

Finally, Mama convinced Daddy to see it, and it was like a moment of discovery. "Ahh, I see now why you are all excited. It's great. We'll buy it."

I started my freshman year at Westlake High School. It was hard to make friends, as I had just come from the ancient world of Greece. When I told the other students where I had been living, they would say, "Grease! That's what you cook your chicken in – where the heck is Greece?!" I had moved from the sophisticated, international community to a school where all the kids had known each other since the first grade. I was shy, and people took that as being aloof. It was hard to make friends. Plus, I was not developing much and still had a little-girl look. The boys were not interested. I didn't understand the dating game and was not asked to either my junior nor senior prom. Even though the house on The High Road was a great place, it was isolated, and the route driving there was not easy, full of twists and turns. Most high schools have a "turf" or cruising area where the kids hang out, but not at Westlake. You either hung out at your friends' houses or went it alone.

I kept up my studies and would hike in the hill country. Daddy would often walk with me, and many times the dog, Beau, and the cat, Siam, would tag along, too. One weekend, Daddy and I explored deep into the hill country, and although Daddy would not say it, I think we got lost. He had a good sense of direction, which he called his "direction bump," and finally we found a dirt road. The dog and cat had followed us that day, and we were all tired. No telling where we were, but we had no other option than to keep going until we made it home. About three hours later the cat just sat down on the road, panting. We couldn't get the cat to walk anymore. Daddy picked up the cat and put it around his neck and shoulders like a trophy animal. He grabbed its four dangling legs with his hands and kept hiking. I had seen dead animals carried like this when hunting, but it was either that or leave the cat, and Siam was content to be carried home.

My freshman year turned into my sophomore year, and then my junior year. Each fall we hunted, and at the age of 16, I shot my first big buck. On this particular hunt, Daddy and I were not in a blind, but quietly hiking through the brush looking for herds. Daddy was taller than I, so I could not see as well. I followed in his footsteps, carrying a .243 rifle strapped over my shoulder. He stopped. I stopped. He motioned to quietly move forward... and then we stopped again. He slowly crouched down and whispered to me that there was a herd of doe ahead and that a nice buck was feeding toward the back of the trees. He whispered, "Rosemary, two people can make a lot of noise. I want you to ease up on your own to the edge of the field, and when you see the buck, take a shot." So, I started to belly-crawl to the edge of the field. Suddenly, I was among two does, and they spooked. A white-tail deer flashes its tail up in the air when spooked — as a warning to the other deer. Most will run, and then it's back to hunting. But I kept crawling and found a little clearing. I was quiet as a mouse, moving slowly and trying to not spook any more deer. I did not know where the buck was or if it had already run away, so I slowly stood up to take a look around. Then I saw it, the big buck, on the edge of the forest. Suddenly, another doe spooked, and I froze. The buck did not run. I, ever so gently and slowly, raised my gun and tucked it firmly in my shoulder. I looked through the scope and got it in my crosshairs. I thought, "Aim just around the shoulder, where the leg hits the body..." I forced a breath out, took a deep breath... then half a breath out... hold... then BOOM! Immediately, all the does started to run, and I watched the buck start to take off, too. There was rustling of brush everywhere as the herd ran, and suddenly I heard my father yell, "Take a rest, take a rest!" He was running up to my side, and I starting thinking, "Take a rest... now's not the time to rest; I need to shoot that buck!" What he meant was to rest the gun on a tree limb or rock to shoot it again, but the buck was gone. Had I lost another deer like I did with my first one? We started tracking it, and lo and behold, we came across it quickly. I had killed it with one shot. Daddy shook my hand in congratulations, and we both had huge smiles. He told me how he had watched the whole thing, and how very proud he was of me. The head of that buck is in my home to this day.

Back at school, it was time to start thinking about my future. Career day was coming to high school, and the counselor asked if I would like to meet with someone in a particular field. My mother raised me to believe I could do anything, and that this was the time for women to break the career molds. I mentioned that since Daddy was a pilot, that maybe I should think about something to do with flying. My mother immediately said, "You should be a commercial airline pilot, not a stewardess, but a pilot." She would say, "Just think, Rosemary, you are meticulous, very organized, love to travel, and you never have to bring your work home with you – your job is in the air!" I liked that idea, so I told the high school career counselor. When career day came, sure enough, there was a commercial airline pilot on hand. The pilot told me that I should learn how to fly, get as many hours as possible, and go to college. He said, "Even if you graduate in basket weaving, you need to have a college degree."

Since I was back in Texas and had been essentially raised in Texas, I started looking at Texas schools. Mama wanted me to look at other colleges. Mama had gone to an all-women college, Mississippi State College for Women, or MSCW. It had since gone co-ed and is now called Mississippi University for Women (MUW). But I grew up singing "MSCW... we sing our song to you..." and even had a license plate with MSCW. Mama thought women colleges gave a young lady the best education because a female student among all women could concentrate more on the books than trying to look pretty for class or "play dumb" for a boy. In the '70s, Mama got intrigued with the Women's Lib Movement and started calling herself a feminist. To her, the term simply meant equal rights and equal pay for women. She did not complicate it. Mama got so intrigued with the opportunities occurring with women that she ran for a seat in the Texas legislature after Daddy's mission. Not only was she the first woman to run, but the first Republican to run in that district. Her slogan was: Vote for Joan Roosa for all the right reasons. She lost by only a slim margin.

• • •

Daddy joined the aeroclub at Bergstrom Air Force Base in Austin. He missed flying and would occasionally check out an airplane and fly me around. We'd have a hamburger at a nearby airport and then fly back. Pilots affectionately called it the $100 burger, for by the time you factored in fuel and time – the cost of that burger would be around $100. Daddy used to say, "Flying cures whatever ails ya." We talked about my being a commercial airline pilot, so he started teaching me his own version of ground school. As we flew, he would talk about the instruments and aerodynamics. I learned about lift, and he reminded me of the stalls we used to do when flying the Citabria at The Place. He obtained an instructor's rating so that he could officially teach me how to fly.

Daddy had gone from supersonic jets to single-engine land aircraft, but he was flying, and about to teach me, too. One day early on with the FAA instructor, Daddy asked me if I wanted to tag along and sit in the back seat. On this particular day, the FAA (Federal Aviation Administration) instructor was in the left seat, showing Daddy some maneuvers and teaching him about the instruments. The left-seat pilot has the command. After about an hour, we headed back to Bergstrom to land. The sun was setting, and the sky was darkening. The control tower stated in a monotone voice, "Beware of vortices. C-130 departing." The FAA instructor brought the plane down on final and was almost on the runway when we felt a sudden jerk to the left. We were starting to flip due to the vortices. In a split second, I heard Daddy yell, "I got the stick," and kept us from crashing into the ground. His astronaut and flying instincts were right on. The FAA pilot seemed shaken and stunned, and half blurted out a thank you. Daddy soon got his license, and we were off to the races.

I was 16 and could barely drive a car but was learning how to fly. I purchased a log book, and my first entry was February 23, 1980. The plane was a Cessna 152, a small side-by-side two-seater. Daddy wrote in my log book, "Local from BSM" (Bergstrom) and under remarks and endorsements wrote, "Demo T/O (take-offs) – Level Flight – Turns – Climbs." He listed my hours as 1.1 and signed it. An hour in a logbook delineates a flying hour, not the time spent on the ground preparing. The next entry was cross-country in a Piper Lance, flying out West in March to Salt Lake City, Boise, Twin Falls, and Durango – the place my father was born in 1933.

We entered Durango at night, and by clicking the radio button in rapid succession, we turned on the runway lights. Daddy hit the button too many times, causing the lights to go extra bright, making the approach almost blinding. But I was able to squeak it on the numbers, and he was impressed. Daddy listed in my log book, "Night – Demo Landing" and logged my hours 3.7. Our next trip was in a Cessna 210 to Hot Springs with 3.3 hours. In July, Daddy rented a Grumman AA5-13, and we flew cross-country to Skiatook and Max Westhiemer for a total of 7.8 hours. When we took these trips, Daddy put me in the left seat, the place reserved for the pilot in command. He used to sit in the right seat with his arms crossed, just to let me know that he did not have the controls. It was all up to me to fly the plane. Every now and then on a long flight, without saying a word, he would tap the altitude instrument – it was supposed to be exactly on the designated altitude determined in pre-flight, plus or minus nothing.

Finally, it was back to the Cessna 152 and flying local every few days in the month of July. My entries would read, "Slow Flight. Stalls. Forced Landings. Short Field T/O. Turn about a Point. Go Arounds." I studied hard and was probably the only girl around who would have sectionals on her bed in the evening, slide rules for calculations, and books on aviation. I learned about restricted areas, controlled classes of airspace, and how to code for airports. My birthday came on July 23. I turned 17 years old.

My father started calling me "El Tigre" – The Tiger – for he instructed me that I could not be timid with the airplane. I had to grab it and take control of it, like taking a tiger by the tail. He told me to growl at the airplane as I kicked the tires and drained the sumps during pre-flight. My shyness was always near the surface, but my father was teaching me about confidence. The one area that troubled me was the radios. I did not like talking on them, and it required using a lingo that my brain could not easily grasp. The tower talk was quick, and the numbers and directions would get confusing. I was learning the airplane by feel and was doing a good job by sensing whether to add power or pull back on the throttle. Then one day in early August, as we were driving out to Bergstrom to go flying, Daddy was particularly adamant about my being "El Tigre." He kept telling me that soon I would be flying on my own, but in my mind, that day was a long way off. I had reached over 30 hours in my logbook. I did not know how many hours it took for most people to solo.

The date was August 5, 1980. As we were doing some touch and goes that day in the pattern, my father said for me to pull off the runway onto the tarmac. I didn't understand at first, but he was stern. I pulled over, and he jumped out and locked the door of the plane. He quickly said, "Now go! Go! *GO!*" I pushed in the throttle and lined up on the runway and watched the airspeed approach 60 mph. I barely pulled back on the control, and soon my wheels were off the ground. I was flying solo! I gained speed and entered the pattern again. I looked over, and there was an empty seat. No Daddy to save me if something went wrong. I suddenly heard noises that I had never heard before, and my adrenaline kicked it. Take-offs were easy; it's the getting down part that's difficult. I looked down on the ground as I was on the downwind and saw Daddy standing there with his arms crossed over his chest, on the side of the runway, looking straight up at me. I felt another adrenaline rush, but it was time to focus. I said to myself, "Okay, El Tigre, it's just you to get this down. Show him what you got."

I entered base and started to lose altitude. I let down the flaps 10 degrees and pulled back the throttle even more. I was concentrating, "Flaps down another 10 degrees as entering final… full throttle back… stay on the

numbers... flaps all the way down... keep the nose down, keep the nose down, watch the airspeed..." Then as the ground was rapidly approaching, I pulled the nose up slightly, heard the stall warning sign go off... and "squeak, squeak"... the back tires were on the ground. "Push the control down a little more..." Keeping my feet on the floor pedals for braking, the front wheel touched the runway too. "Whew" - on the ground - all three tires! I quickly applied the brakes and sat there for a moment. I had successfully soloed. I looked over on the tarmac, and Daddy motioned for me to go again – yelling once again "GO, GO!" I pushed in the throttle and was off again. A pilot did not linger on an active runway. I accomplished three take-offs and landings that day. Daddy was thrilled. Just like when killing my first buck, I was not outwardly emotional – but was really happy on the inside. Daddy once said in a speech that his scariest moment in flying was not when the Apollo mission had trouble, nor when a fighter jet was acting up in a test flight — it was when his one and only daughter took off on her own in a little airplane, and all he could do was watch, helpless.

We spent August taking more cross-country trips, this time to Virginia in a Piper, a PA-28, a low-wing aircraft. As the summer closed, my last solo flight was on August 23, 1980, in a Cessna 152. On my first take-off I was feeling confident. I did a few touch-and-goes but then started to have trouble. My radio went out. I raced through the procedures in my head. This was a military base with lots of aircraft in the area. I called out to the tower that I was entering downwind and that I could not receive radio transmission. Was it safe to land? I looked up and saw the tower flashing the green light. They could hear me, but I could not hear them. I taxied back to the aeroclub and parked the plane. This subconsciously put a fear in me. Those darn radios.

The school year began, and I was a senior. After intense studying of aviation books, I drove to San Antonio to take the FAA written test for a single-engine land airplane. I passed. The clock was ticking – I now had only two years to receive my flying license or I would have to take this extensive written test again. Daddy encouraged me to keep up the flying, and for Christmas that year, Santa Claus brought me a brown bomber jacket with a map of the world on the inside. However, those radios were intimidating, and I did not fly anymore for awhile. The year turned to 1981.

• • •

As I tried to figure out my future, Daddy had been struggling at the electric car company. After a couple of years in, he surmised that his boss, in his opinion, was nothing more than a high-class con artist. My mother was never happy in Austin, as she did not get immediately accepted into the right social circles. She was lonely, without friends in the area. She later said that perhaps Daddy's business associates had prevented them from getting to know the proper people. My parents hid a lot from me, but I could tell Daddy was not happy. Mama told Daddy that the one thing he had going for him was his good name and that he needed to maintain his integrity. Daddy drove to Houston and met with Kenneth to discuss how he felt and to express his opinion that his electric car partner may be ripping him off. Rather than being relieved, Kenneth seemed upset with Daddy and told him that if he needed to quit that job, that he would lessen his salary and Daddy could help him in the real estate business. So, Daddy started working on developing strip malls in shopping areas. He would meticulously track population data, review high traffic flow, and analyze the best ways in and out of an area. But times were tough. Daddy later told me that he would sit on the edge of the Jacuzzi tub in their bathroom at night, just holding his head in his hands and pondering what to do. We were financially struggling, but my parents did not show it. Daddy was stressed and worried. He had children in, and more about to enter, college – and the economy was struggling too. Jimmy Carter was the President, and interest rates were over 20 percent. No one was investing in real estate.

Even though we were struggling, Daddy felt we still needed to be a part of space history, and in April, my parents and I traveled to Florida to witness the first Shuttle launch. The spacecraft was different from the Saturn V. It looked more like a sleek airplane than a traditional rocket. It was pointing straight up on the launchpad, with an external tank and reusable solid rocket boosters on each side, providing the majority of thrust in the first two minutes of flight. Only two astronauts flew this mission, STS-1, of the Shuttle program – John Young and Robert "Bob" Crippen. John Young had flown in Gemini and Apollo, and we knew him well. We had not been to the Cape since the Apollo-Soyuz Test Project in 1975. It seemed like a world ago. It had been 10 years since I'd watched Daddy launch on Apollo 14 in 1971.

Since the Shuttle program was the prelude to the International Space Station, its mission was to remain in low-earth orbit, circling on average between 200 and 250 miles up. The Apollo missions had gone nearly 240,000 miles from earth. A big difference. And so was the launch. After a couple of days' delay, this new spacecraft launched on April 12, 1981. As the countdown went to zero, I saw the familiar white mist from the water jets cooling the launchpad… but then the Shuttle popped up in the air like a champagne cork, and poof, it was gone! Wait… what?! No sitting on the launch pad with the ground rumbling in anticipation? The quickness off the launchpad hit me the most. As it turns out, the launch was exactly 20 years from the day that Yuri Gagarin launched from the Baikonur Cosmodrome on April 12, 1961, sending us into the space race.

• • •

Daddy said it seemed that Kenneth wanted to punish him for quitting the electric car business, so eventually Daddy quit all together. Unbeknownst to me, Mama and Daddy were borrowing money from friends and family to meet the monthly bills. Then along came a large package in the mail. It was a Coors application. The Coors Brewing Company had decided to expand east of the Mississippi River and wanted to know if Daddy would be interested in applying for a distributorship in Mississippi. The packet had gone to the address in El Lago, then to the address in Greece, then eventually found its way to Austin. It was beaten up and torn, and Daddy saw that the application deadline was rapidly approaching. He had about a month to prepare. He told Mama that there was no way he could put it all together, but Mama said to do it. This would be the ticket. Daddy worked day and night and put together large maps like ones he had prepared for real estate analysis. Distributorships were competitive, and many people applied. Daddy eventually won the rights to a Mississippi distributorship. On the application, Daddy had to indicate whether he would accept another area in Mississippi if he were denied his preference – the Mississippi Gulf Coast. Mama and Daddy discussed this, and they decided he would not accept any other area. Mama wanted to live near the water, and thus, it was all or nothing. After an extensive process, Coors granted Daddy the lower six coastal counties for exclusive distribution, and so my parents began to sell everything we had in order to start a company. The family was now in the beer business, and Daddy would be drinking beer for a living.

During my years in high school, Daddy had a mustache, but right before the move, he shaved it off. He came into the kitchen as we were packing up the house in Austin and kept looking at me. I was chatting away about little things, and finally he said, "Do you notice anything different about me?"

I said, "You look more youthful. Is it because you are happy about starting this company?"

He started to get a little impatient and asked again, "Do you notice anything else…?"

I stopped what I was doing and looked intently at him. He was standing proudly and took his hand to his face and stroked his cheeks.

I said, "Noooo… did you get a haircut?"

He finally blurted out, "I shaved my mustache!"

"OOOOHH," I said, "Oh my gosh, I did not notice!" I felt embarrassed that I wouldn't even notice that a man no longer had a bushy caterpillar on his face! But I've always been slow to notice people's exteriors, for I generally pay attention to the personality of a person, and I've been chastised for not noticing when someone lost weight, or when they wore a new outfit or piece of jewelry.

I said, "Daddy, why did you do that?"

He answered, "Because I am starting a new career and a new job, and I want a fresh start." He never grew any hair back on his face after moving to Mississippi.

I had applied to college in Texas at SMU, Southern Methodist University, and was gung ho. My mother said that she still wanted me to consider a women's college, but she had heard rumblings that MUW was not the school that it used to be, so she asked me if I would consider a private prestigious women's college with Tulane University in New Orleans, called Sophie Newcomb. I applied there, too, to make her happy. I was accepted into both schools. As my parents were preparing to move to Mississippi, I drove up to the SMU campus in Dallas. I did not get a warm-fuzzy feeling from it, although I was there when the campus was on break. I wrote to Newcomb to say that I would be attending in the fall, sight unseen. It turned out to be a good choice, as it was only an hour and half from Mama and Daddy in Mississippi, and Newcomb was a small, welcoming campus with red brick buildings and large oak trees.

The beginning of the Shuttle program in 1981

CHAPTER 6

Becoming An Adult

At first, I was not looking forward to Mississippi. I felt that I was a Texas girl, having spent my formative years in The Lone Star State. However SMU was out, and I was looking forward to the cosmopolitan city of New Orleans and Newcomb/Tulane in the fall. When we crossed over the state line into Mississippi early that summer and started driving along the white sand beaches on Highway 90, I saw the sun glistening on the water and the shrimp boats with their high nets out in the Gulf. As we drove by the large, old Southern homes along the north side of the road… a feeling hit me. "I'm home," I thought. A wave of "this is where I ought to be" came across me, and I felt at peace. It was like a salmon swimming upstream to find its breeding ground again. There is just something about returning "home" – and since I was born in Mississippi, I was returning to my roots. Maybe because everything is bigger, bolder, and bodacious in Texas, perhaps subconsciously the state was a little overwhelming to me. The South has a subtle sophistication. The people are polite, courteous, genuine, and friendly. Everyone likes to eat, drink, tell a clever joke, and generally be happy.

I soon noticed that one of the first things people ask when a guest enters their home is "What would you like to drink?" Drinking is part of the culture. Most of the older generation drink J&B or Dewar's with a splash of water and lots of ice. Bourbon still is a favorite, but not as popular as scotch. The drinking age was 18 at the time, and it was only a technicality that I was turning 18 in July. It was not far off. The introduction to libations started. However, this summer was all about the beer.

Daddy moved to Gulfport, Mississippi, prior to my high school graduation and rented a little yellow house near the water on Pratt Avenue. It was only two bedrooms and one bath. It was a shotgun house with a long living/dining area and a kitchen towards the back. The house was a big change from the spacious and luxurious home in Austin, but Daddy assured Mama it was only temporary. He needed all funds to manage the cash flow of starting a multi-million-dollar company. As we adjusted to our new surroundings, Mama tried to put her touch on the little house and decorated one of the bedrooms for me in a silver wallpaper with cherry blossoms. I later heard folks called it the "microwave" room, but Mama had funky, modern tastes. I thought it looked cool. Mama was immediately accepted into the social circles with the support of her sister, Patti. Patti and her husband, Knox, made sure that applications to the yacht club were submitted and that Mama and Daddy went to all the right parties. Mama joined the bridge club and the garden club, and she was happy.

My sweet Aunt Patti had a luncheon party one weekend and introduced me to several girls around my same age from the old families of Gulfport. I appreciated meeting them and instantly bonded with one, Mandy McHugh. She was a cute, curvaceous blonde, only 5 feet tall, and was engaged to be married to her high school sweetheart. I was a shy girl with a ballet dancer's body and didn't know much about sex or boys. I was in awe. Mandy's best friend was Kelly Houston, who dated a local boy who was from an old and prestigious Gulfport family. Kelly was also at the party, and she was a little quiet, just like me, but the three of us sat next to each other at this beautiful outdoor luncheon that my aunt had prepared in Southern fashion. I told Mandy about my flying and wanting to be an airline pilot, and she said that the day that I received my private pilot's license she would prepare a champagne brunch to celebrate.

During the week, Daddy put me to work as the receptionist, answering the phones and doing general paperwork for him at the beer company. The summer was all about opening Gulf Coast Coors, Incorporated, the first distributorship east of the Mississippi River. Prior to 1981, most folks had to "smuggle" Coors across the state line. Doing this was so popular that a Hollywood movie, *Smokey and the Bandit,* glorified it. Most folks in Mississippi have a story about smuggling Coors in for an event. The Rocky Mountain spring water it was made with seemed to have a mystical effect.

The Mississippi Gulf Coast was buzzing about Coors hitting the market. It was the only brand my father had at the time, as Coors Light had not yet been developed. We were a one-brand operation. July Fourth was approaching, and all the money was going into business operations, payroll, trucks, and inventory, but no money was coming in. My father was starting to run out of cash, and then word came from the Coors Brewery that he could start selling earlier than planned if all was in place. Daddy pushed the "launch commit" button, and on the first day of selling at the end of June, it was all hands-on-deck. The route schedule was to cover the entire coast in a week's time. The phones were ringing off the hook, as everyone wanted their beer on the first day, which was impossible. At 8 p.m., the first truck rolled in. It was midnight before all trucks were in. My father had a hospitality room that had several round tables and chairs, a keg on tap, and was decorated with his African animals. We stayed there and drank beer until all the trucks were in. The cash intake that day was over $50,000. Daddy was in business.

Mama decided to throw Daddy a dinner for the tenth anniversary of the Apollo 14 mission since he had been busy in the winter preparing for Coors. The event was an intimate and elegant affair at Grass Lawn, an antebellum two-story home converted into a venue for weddings, parties, and special occasions. The view was over the Gulf of Mexico, with a large green lawn stretching out to the white sand beaches. That evening in the candlelit dining room, Mama stood up and toasted Daddy. "Wow," I thought, "what an amazing 10 years it has been, from NASA, to Greece, to Texas, to Mississippi." Soon I would be starting a new life on my own in New Orleans. I wondered what was going through my father's head as we sipped champagne in this new, genteel culture. Gone were the supersonic jet days, the fast and furious dogfights, and the tough competition among the best of the best.

I started school in the fall and during orientation learned that over half the students were not from the South. I laughed that I was a minority in my own part of the country. Freshmen were not allowed to live off campus, and I had chosen to live in one of the oldest dormitories, Josephine Louise. No one from my high school was there, for most had stayed in Texas. Prior to starting, I had filled out a compatibility form and had no clue who was going to be my roommate.

As it turned out it was a girl from Baltimore, Maryland. Her name was Jill Reamer, a stocky blonde with tanned skin. I soon found out she was Jewish and a liberal. She was a little messy and liked to jog. My dresser drawers were always closed, and I made my bed every day. She would leave her drawers half out and powder sprinkled around the room from when she would throw it on her body after running. She never pulled up the covers to her bed. I thought it wasn't going to work. But she turned out to be the perfect roommate. We were respectful to each other, and in the end, quite compatible. The form had worked. We used to talk at night about our families, life, and music. I used to laugh with her about my being a Southern, Catholic, Republican who got along well with this "Yankee," Jewish, Democrat. She would sometimes say she was not a "Yankee" as Baltimore is below the Mason-Dixon Line, but she knew I was only kidding. I did talk her into voting for Ronald Reagan that year. We are still friends to this day, and later in life, she wound up marrying a Catholic boy.

I joined a sorority, Chi Omega, which was the family tradition, and started to meet interesting people. Tulane was a national and international college, and the atmosphere was enjoyable. New Orleans was a party town, and I was naïve about its ways. The drinking age was 18, and there were many fraternity/sorority socials called mixers. There was also Bourbon Street – full of bars, restaurants, and the seedier side of "The Sin City." New Orleans was unique though, and I liked the French influence with the iron balconies and the street cars. Newcomb College was essentially a part of the Tulane campus, and right next door was Loyola University, a Catholic university with a large cathedral with stained glass windows and a long aisle to the altar. I wound up praying a lot in that church for my grades, and I thought I might get married there, too.

I met a girl in Chi-O, Michell (pronounced Michelle) Lausen. She was a striking, tall brunette with a model's body and deep brown eyes that looked almost Asian. Her family was from New Orleans, and her father was in the oil and gas industry. Her parents bought a beautiful, Italian-style 8,000-square-foot home not far from campus. Her father, Fritz, had been in the Navy, and they had an elegant 49-foot sailboat. Fritz loved to invite the pretty sorority girls aboard for weekend sails. Michell and I bonded and started going to mixers together. My grades plummeted as I tried to learn my limit on drinking. I weighed 100 pounds when I graduated from high school and entered college, and then gained "The Freshman 10," putting on 10 pounds that year. My first semester finally ended. I made mostly Cs and Bs but made an A in English. My mother was so pleased that we went to Godchaux's, an upscale department store on Canal Street in downtown New Orleans, and she bought me a fur coat — a dyed fox, waist-length coat that gradually turned from light brown at the top to darker brown at the bottom. She bought herself a dark mink coat with a dark brown fox collar. We went to Commander's Palace to celebrate. We had champagne in the Garden Room overlooking the green flora and beautiful oak trees.

My freshman year opened a new world. I didn't know that boys stayed in girls' rooms all night and that girls talked so crudely. I did start dating which was nice, for there were always parties and functions. I wasn't seeing anyone special, and I wasn't so sure about "The Rules." I had missed out in high school learning about the dating game, but it was all innocent enough, and my phone was ringing for dates. Mandy had started college at the University of Southern Mississippi, or USM, and we kept in touch. On weekends I would usually drive home to Mississippi and we'd hit the town. When I picked Mandy up from her house, we would visit with her father first, and he laughed that we were "combustible" together. Mandy and I were high energy, and we felt on top of the world.

When home, sometimes I would walk down to the beach from the little yellow house on Pratt Avenue and ponder life. It was a time of figuring out who Rosemary Roosa was — I'd ponder religion, philosophy, beliefs, and what I would and would not stand for as I moved forward as an adult. During my freshman year, just as soon as the cash flow had built up in the beer company, Daddy bought an airplane, a Cessna 172 with the tail letters 4640 J (J is called Juliet in aviation language). My father wanted me to keep flying. My ground school test I had taken was expiring in two years. To inspire me, Daddy had some business cards made with the Coors logo and business address. He listed my name, and underneath my name, he put the title of Corporate Pilot.

I spent the summer after my freshman year flying. College books were closed. Flight books were opened. I took out my logbook and resumed flying on July 2, 1982. That day had three separate entries. The first was for 1.2 hours, and Daddy listed in the Remarks and Endorsement section: "T.O. – Stalls – Slow Flight – LNDS." Later that day he listed the flight route from GPT (Gulfport) to LCL (local) and STENNIS, an airstrip near the Mississippi NASA facility which tested all the engines for rocket flights, including Apollo. Stennis was a long and well-maintained runway with no control tower. Time in logbook, .9 hours. Remarks were T.O. (take-offs), Forced LNDS (landings), and EMER. PROC (emergency procedures). When we arrived at Stennis, Daddy got out of the airplane and told me to solo. I did. He just listed "SOLO" in my logbook and marked .5 hours. He had thrown me in the deep end. Now it was about gaining those solo hours and getting my license. Daddy instructed me to fly every day, several times a day if possible, to keep the momentum going.

From that day forward and on most mornings in July 1982 I got up early, went to our local airport, kicked the tires, drained the sumps, and practiced maneuvers in our new Cessna 172. I would fly along the beach, out to the islands, up to Hattiesburg and Meridian, and sometimes to New Orleans. Daddy had every instrument possible installed in the cockpit, except for radar. He said if the weather was that bad, we would want to land anyway rather than fly around it. On July 10, I had four entries in my logbook. On July 13 and 14, we practiced, and I performed my required 3 night-landings. Daddy said I was ready. I called and scheduled a time

ROSEMARY D. ROOSA
Corporate Pilot

GULF COAST COORS, INC.
603 Industrial Seaway Blvd. — P.O. Box 2007
Gulfport, MS 39503
(601) 896-8100

with an FAA certified pilot to take the oral exam and flying test. On my birthday, July 23, I turned 19 years old, and Daddy and I flew together. We flew to Stennis, and he listed, "VOR PROCEDURES (radio navigation) – STALLS – SOFT (soft field landings and take offs) and 1.2 hours. I had accumulated over 23 hours' solo time.

The next day, July 24, I flew to Stennis on my own. It was crisp clear day, and "El Tigre" was ready. I had studied all the restricted airspaces, had practiced what I would say on the radio, and knew the radio frequencies by heart. I took off from Gulfport, and even though a pilot did not chatter on the radio, I told the tower that I was about to take my check-ride and to wish me luck. They knew my voice from flying every day, but I'd never met anyone from the control tower in person. Gulfport was a commercial and military field, and oftentimes the C-130s and I would fly the pattern for touch and goes, and we got to know each other's voices. I took off and headed west to Stennis airfield, the huge runway near the NASA facility in Mississippi. Remembering that this was the same place that Daddy used to fly in with his T-38 jets to watch the Apollo engines being tested, I felt like I was coming full circle from Daddy's NASA flying days to mine.

It was a short, 15- to 20-minute flight, and I landed near the small FBO (Fixed Base Operation) facility. These operation facilities smelled of aviation fuel and leather, with a feel of nervous energy. Inside was a pilot's lounge with tables and chairs, leather seats in case a pilot was delayed and needed sleep, telephones with direct lines to the weather briefs, and aviation charts on the wall. I walked in and shook hands with the FAA pilot. We sat at the table and he started to quiz me about what paperwork was required in an airplane at all times...."Hummm..." I answered. I was prepared to talk about what the colored lines and purple squares were on the map. I don't think Daddy talked about what was required in the airplane on his talks to Bergstrom AFB.

I said, "a checklist... your sectionals... your airport flight codes..."

"No," he answered, "It's the basics." I looked bumfuzzled, and my heart started to sink as I thought I was going to flunk before I even had a chance to fly.

"It's called ARROW," he said.

"Let's see, arrow…" I hesitantly murmured.

He gave me a hint: "One of them is on the side of the airplane, by the left leg of the pilot."

Ah, ha! It came to me – "the airworthiness certificate."

"Right!" he said, "Now the others…" With a few more hints I struggled through and came up with radio station license, registration, operating manual, and weight and balance. These were supposed to be the easiest questions, but I finally muddled through them. Then he started with the harder questions, and these were a piece of cake.

Finally, he said, "Plan your cross-country, and let's go fly."

My calculations and math were right on, and I got the latest weather brief. He was satisfied. We walked out to 4640 Juliet, and I thoroughly went through the pre-flight check, starting with the wing on the left side of the airplane, checking for nicks and dings, then to the front prop, looking for the same. I checked the engine for oil level and leaks, kicked the front tire to make sure it wasn't low on air, rubbed my hand down the right front wing, checked the pitot tube to make sure it was clear of debris (this reads the airspeed during flight), and drained the fuel tank to check for water and appropriate AvGas. The color should be light blue. Red is for jets like Daddy used to fly. I loved the smell of aviation fuel. It smelled cleaner than regular gasoline. I took in a deep breath, then I checked the flaps for no obstructions, then went to the back of the airplane, moving the rudder side to side to check for obstructions. I returned to the left wing and the cabin door. I crawled inside and buckled up. The FAA pilot did the same from the right side. I picked up the checklist.

A good pilot follows the checklist to a T. This was one reason my mother wanted me to be a commercial pilot. She always said that I would not overlook anything on the checklist. I had a lot of Daddy's traits, and being thorough and meticulous were some of them. After completing the list, I yelled, "Clear prop!" out the window and cranked the engine. Stennis airport did not have a tower, so I did not have to worry too much about the radio transmissions. I taxied to the end of the runway and did my run-up.

I held the brakes and pushed in full throttle. The airplane shook and tried to jerk forward, but I held the brakes firm. I weighed no more than 110 pounds, but "The Tiger" was in control. I wasn't sure how all the mechanics worked in an airplane, but I knew that when checking the magnetos, the RPMs should drop. They did, and all tested well. Time to take the runway. I rolled the plane to the center line and stopped. I pushed in the throttle and let the plane start rolling down the runway, watching the airspeed increase. At 60 mph, I lifted the nose, and we were off. We proceeded to the practice area, and the one thing that I dreaded doing on my own were stalls. I loved them when I was a little girl in the Citabria, but I trusted Daddy's skills. Now it was only me at the stick, and a plane could easily go into a spin from a stall. The FAA pilot wanted me to do stall after stall after stall. Upward stalls, turning stalls… I thought it would never end. Then he suddenly pulled the throttle back and said, "Lost engine. Emergency landing." I immediately started to prepare and started looking around for a road, a clear field, or some other smooth surface where I could land. I called out a small country road and started to descend. He tapped me on the arm and said, "How about that landing spot?" It was the long and wide Stennis runway.

"Ah, okay," I said, a bit embarrassed. With no power I lined it up on the numbers and made a smooth landing. I taxied back to the FBO and shut down the airplane, again following the checklist. We climbed out of the airplane. I waited, almost holding my breath.

"You passed!" said the FAA pilot, and I said, "Thank you," once again not showing a lot of emotion, but elated on the inside. My father would be proud. He would often tell me that I would meet people who soloed but never finished getting their license. I would not be such a statistic. That day on July 24, barely 19 years old, I received my single-engine land, private pilot's license. I flew back to Gulfport and called to the tower as I started to enter the pattern. They cleared me to land.

Then I heard a call, "How did you do?"

"I got my license," I answered back, trying to keep that cool, calm voice of a professional pilot.

Flying in our Cessna 172

Getting ready to take off in 4640 J with Mama in the back seat

"Congratulations," the voice said over the radio.

Sure enough, Mandy had me over for champagne. I drank the first sip straight from the bottle.

After I earned my license, Mandy and I convinced our parents to let us drive to New York for a vacation. We were the original *Thelma & Louise*, minus throwing ourselves off a cliff – and the crime spree. The two of us had a ball driving up, listening to Ozzy Osbourne, AC/DC, and drinking beer. When we finished a can, we would toss it in the back seat, yelling, "Used!" We were driving a deep green Cutlass Supreme, and we both agreed that if one of us got a ticket, we would split the cost. The speedometer was a needle that went from 0 to 80 miles per hour, and our slogan became, "Bury the needle!" meaning to go faster than 80 miles per hour, so fast the needle would go below the dashboard, and we would have no clue how fast we were going. Mandy got the ticket. We ate blueberries along the way, and every two hours, we switched drivers. In Virginia, we stumbled upon the oldest continuously run inn, The Wayside Inn, dating back to 1797. The staff wore colonial costumes and made us ham sandwiches with homemade bread. It seemed like an episode from the *Twilight Zone*. The next day we drove all the way to the military academy of West Point, staying at the history-laden Thayer Hotel in the hills of New York. We flirted with the cadets before heading to New York City and back home. It was the end of the summer of 1982, and the freedom of two young women, pre-cell phone era, made it our summer of emancipation from our younger to older selves.

For the Christmas holidays my sophomore year in college, Daddy planned a trip to the Bahamas, with the first leg being to North Carolina to go skiing. My parents had purchased some land outside of Asheville in a place called Wolf Laurel. My father rented another Cessna 172, and we had our own 172 – 4640 Juliet. Mama would sit in the back of one plane, and Daddy the other, so that our parents were separated in case of an emergency. After the ski trip, we headed to West Palm Beach and stayed the night in a nice but nondescript hotel. Two of my brothers were on the trip, both pilots, so we rotated left seat to right seat in the two airplanes. The night before the overwater trip to Nassau, the boys invited guests to their room and

Mandy and me in college

Mandy (former Colleen) and me (as the current Colleen)
later in life for St. Patrick's Day celebration

ordered champagne. The next morning when Daddy went to check out, he disputed the champagne purchase, and the boys had to fess up. Daddy was mad. He said, "Rosemary, you pilot one plane, and I will pilot the other." I made the first landing in the Bahamas, at Treasure Cay Airport. Daddy was proud of me for doing that and mentioned it many times over the years that followed. We traveled to Marsh Harbor, San Salvador, Georgetown, and North Eleuthera, finally circling back to Freeport, and St. Lucie in Florida. In 10 days, from December 23, 1982, to January 3, 1983, I had added another 20 hours to my flight time. As a memento, Daddy plotted out on a sectional flying map the course of our island hopping and gave it to me along with pictures of the trip.

The flying was on hold as Mardi Gras approached in February 1983. Mardi Gras is a festive time that celebrates the time between Epiphany to Ash Wednesday, with the few days leading up to "Fat Tuesday" (the day before Lent begins) as a time to party-hearty. On the Mississippi Gulf Coast, one of the largest Mardi Gras organizations is the Gulf Coast Carnival Association. The group has a King and Queen along with a Royal Court. I was chosen to be a part of the court and was instructed to not tell a soul. The official announcements were to be a closely guarded secret until right before the big ball on the night before Mardi Gras. The theme that year was Mississippi's Legendry Lovers, and I was decked out in costume as a young Indian woman who sang a tale of forbidden love with a young Indian man from another tribe. Since their marriage was forbidden, the two lovers went into the local river and drowned together. Local folklore claims the river "sings" with a mystical humming sound. I thought it was funny that I was chosen as the Indian with my reddish hair, fair skin, and blue eyes. For the Mardi Gras festivities, we checked into a local hotel, and Daddy got a suite and put a Coors keg in it for all to enjoy. The night of the Royal Court Ball on February 14, Daddy escorted me out to meet with my Duke in the court. As the spotlight shined on me, I got nervous and started walking fast. Daddy said softly to me as he held my arm, "Slow down. Enjoy the moment." It was like my "coming out" party and formal introduction to society. I think he enjoyed it more than I. He was "Proud Papa" of his "El Tigre."

Sectional flying map of our Bahamas island hopping

Mardi Gras Ball with my grandfather Dewey Roosa (left), grandmother
Lorine Roosa (middle by me), and "Proud Papa" (right)

I decided for my junior year that going abroad to France would be fun. I called it my "rebellious year," although I really did not have much to rebel against. It was my way of becoming an adult. It would be a time away from family, friends, and the known — to "discover myself" — and go back to the international life. I applied to the American College in Paris, ACP. Now the name has changed to the American University in Paris, AUP. It was a very small school and partnered with the Parsons School of Design in New York City. My parents said they would take me to France. Uncle Bob, who taught me the mind reading act as a child, came along with us, as his wife had recently passed away. We visited the wine country and many of the chateaus in the region of the Loire Valley, including Chenonceau (which spanned a river), Cheverny (inhabited by the same family for over six centuries), and Chambord (the largest chateau in the area). Mama introduced me to Kir (white wine with crème de cassis, a currant flavor), and my favorite, Kir Royal, which is champagne with crème de cassis and a sugar cube. While sipping on one at a restaurant, Mama jokingly said that if I should meet anyone with the last name of Cheverny, to pay attention. We spent the night in a chateau towards the end our trip, and I stayed in a turret. That night I heard all kinds of sounds and thought the place was haunted, now knowing the story from Lake Garda. I was spooked. The next morning while having a café, after not sleeping well, I looked up and saw that the turret had a weather vane on top. The wind had blown it all night long. No ghosts, but my nerves had been rattled.

Next was Paris. As we looked for a place for me to live, I was starting to get nervous about my decision to trek halfway around the world not knowing anyone. I did not have a good feeling about it but did not say a word to my parents. When they dropped me off on the final day, I purposely did not turn around. I knew if I did, I would not want to stay. I had hit the "launch commit" button. I walked away with tears in my eyes but looking straight ahead. Mama told me later that as Daddy was driving away, he kept looking in the rear-view mirror. If I had turned to look back, Mama said he would have stopped the car, gotten me, and taken me home. He had sensed my tentativeness.

The college was so small that it did not have dormitories; it placed the students in homes. Before my parents had left, we found a place for me to live in the 16th arrondissement, near Trocadero, because my mother insisted that I live in a good place. It was a beautiful apartment on Rue de Longchamp. However, the paperwork to move in with the family, the Morals, was going to take a few days, so the school put some of the students in a hotel while the details were sorted out. On my first night alone in Paris, I met Leigh Ann Preston from Kentucky, a pleasant and easy-going soul with short brown hair. During our conversation, I learned that she, too, was a pilot. She said her family had a Cessna Citation, which is a corporate jet, sleek and fast. I said we had a Cessna, too, (just conveniently leaving off the 172 part). As we talked, she asked if I had ever had an accident.

"No," I said, "have you?"

She admitted that she had run off the runway and gotten stuck once while taxiing. Those types of accidents were preventable, and Daddy drilled into my head to be extra careful on the taxiways. But I had found a friend in the City of Lights with Leigh Ann.

Before entering my junior year, I had declared my major to be political science, as I was intrigued with government and cultural ideologies. The Cold War was still going strong. In Paris, I continued my political science studies and was living in a time when the United States was deploying intermediate-range nuclear missiles in Europe, and some Europeans did not like it. I looked American and would sometimes be hassled on the bus and metro. Paris was a beautiful big city, but I soon started feeling like beach-front Gulfport, Mississippi, was not such a bad place to live, and that I was a just a "small-town country girl" at heart. My sweet friend Mandy wrote me often, and I enjoyed the letters from home. Although it was nice to be in the sophistication of Paris, I was lonely. Leigh Ann lived across the city, and visiting each other was not easy nor often. We did travel together to Venice for Thanksgiving and to Germany towards Christmas. I also went on school-sponsored trips to the south of France and around Paris – but after a few months, I was ready to come home. I realized that traveling without someone to share it with was not all that fun. When I left Paris, I threw everything in the trash. It was not worth keeping the lonely memories. I went back to Newcomb for the spring semester.

· · ·

Before I started my final year of college in the fall, Daddy said we were heading to the Cape again in August to see his good friend, Hank Hartsfield, take off as the Commander of a Shuttle mission. Hank and my father first met at Edwards Air Force Base as part of the class of 64-C. Hank had been accepted into the military space project called MOL – Manned Orbiting Laboratory. This knocked him out of NASA and thus some competitive slots for the moon. But Daddy thought he was an excellent pilot and personally appealed to the NASA decision-makers to transfer Hank to NASA after MOL was canceled. Daddy never told Hank he had helped him into the program, but Hank joined the NASA team in 1969. He was support crew on Apollo 16 and Skylab and became an integral part of the Shuttle program. Hank's wife, Fran, and Mama were good friends, and the Hartsfields had purchased a home in El Lago, where my parents loved to talk politics and flying with them. Hank and Daddy were on the same page politically, and Fran and Mama enjoyed friendly debates while smoking cigarettes and drinking beer. They had often times come to The Place, along with their two daughters, Judy and Keely.

Hank's launch had been delayed by two months and originally was scheduled for lift off in June. The crew was only four seconds from taking off when a faulty main engine forced the program's first-ever abort, followed by a hydrogen fire on the launchpad. Daddy heard about it and decided we needed to be there to support his mission. Fran was happy that Mama was there, too, for support, as a fellow astronaut's wife. On August 30, 1984, we watched Hank Hartsfield command the maiden voyage of Discovery, STS-41D. It was exciting to be back at the Cape and see Daddy's buddies flying into space. Also on the flight was Charlie Walker, a payload specialist, who decided to take some tree seeds into space after being inspired by Daddy. These trees were later dubbed Space Trees.

· · ·

As my senior year resumed, my flying time dwindled. Those darn radios. My shyness about speaking did not seem to lessen in college. In fact, all through my four years, if on the first day of class the syllabus required a speech, I dropped it the next day and enrolled in another class. Senior year was different because of certain classes that were required for my degree. If I absolutely had to give a speech, I would write it out, sentence by sentence. I went carefully by my notes. The hours in my log book started to taper off, but every now and then I would take up the Cessna 172 for a spin. If I was going to fly for a living, I needed to start concentrating on an instrument and commercial rating. I bought the books, and Daddy and I practiced sometimes "under the hood," meaning I would wear a special head piece, like side blinders on a horse, to eliminate outside sight so I could focus on the instrument panel. When I would from habit take a quick look at the ground for reference, Daddy would laugh and say, "Just one peek is worth a thousand cross-checks."

Of my four years in college, my senior year was the best. I had started dating a "younger man" – a junior by the name of Martin – and we both had a passion for politics. He was the president of the Republican Club, and conservative views on a liberal campus were not always in favor with the professors, but we had fun discussing the world's fate and debating political systems. In January 1985, a small group of us attended the inauguration of Ronald Reagan in Washington, D.C. Little did I know that I would soon be living in our nation's capital, but that winter of the inauguration was cold. We did not get to see much, as the snow caused the parade to be canceled. We toured some monuments anyway and visited the Smithsonian museums.

I had accepted an invitation to live off campus with Michell my senior year. We had a cute shotgun duplex. In the other apartment were a married couple in graduate school. Our house had a screened-in front porch with a swing for two. It had two bedrooms, one bath, a long living room and dining room combined, and a small kitchen with a cement back porch.

We used to love to grill, and Michell was the "pyromaniac." We would spray lighter fluid on the charcoal and make the flames "whoosh" as high as possible. I found out that I liked to break glass and used to laugh that it was in my blood since my mother threw that champagne glass in the fireplace all those years ago. Michell would save up the burned-out light bulbs for me to break, and when we had a few, we'd throw them into the outside garbage can with a "pop."

The shotgun house was decorated with nice furniture, antiques, and pieces of art. It was not the typical off-campus home with school posters on the wall and a mattress and box spring on the floor. Martin started to pal with some fraternity brothers from Central America, and I was back into running in some international circles. We had parties like ones Mama and her girlfriends threw and would hit downtown New Orleans from time to time. I specifically remember being at the Hilton hotel bar at the end of Poydras Avenue one night, and we were all dancing. Latins loved to dance, and there was a certain way to move the knees, feet, and waist that was different and fun. The song, "Born in the U.S.A." by Bruce Springsteen started to play, and one of the guys from El Salvador grabbed the U.S. flag and started waving it while dancing around on the floor. Michell and I looked at each other and smiled because I think only a handful of us had been born in the United States. Even Michell had been born in Japan when her father was stationed there with the Navy.

One evening Martin and I had a spat, so Michell and I sneaked down to his house, and I threw a few light bulbs at the front door while Michell remained in the bushes. It was a harmless way of getting the point across that I was upset with him. Instead of Martin coming out of the door, the porch light went off. We got bored waiting for him to open the door and went home. The next day Martin told me someone attempted to shoot at the house, most likely due to his political leanings, and that his life was in danger. I never told him it was me, and Michell and I later laughed at his ego. My mother never seemed to like Martin, and she tried to discourage any thoughts of a serious relationship.

College graduation was a special day. It was in May 1985, and the spring air was full of promise. At Newcomb a tradition was the "daisy chain" in which the graduating women would wear a white dress under the black cap and gown and would carry a linked daisy "rope," which everyone held together as they entered the auditorium, one behind the other. The action showed unification and sisterhood and symbolized the links that the graduates would need to succeed in life.

To celebrate my graduation, my parents planned a weekend with family and friends to two plantation homes. The first night was at a show-home called Nottaway. It was the quintessential Southern plantation home and was one of the few spared in the Civil War. The house was large and had a grand white ballroom, as the owner had only daughters and he wanted to entertain well for future suitors. My mother did not want Martin to come along, so she didn't invite him or Michell to make it seem non-bias. It was so sad waving goodbye to them, but we had several cars of grandparents, family friends, brothers, and some of their friends, so off we went to White Castle, Louisiana. We had champagne with dinner in the grand ballroom, and guests staying in the house could roam at night freely. I ventured into the billiard room, where the men used to gather for brandy and cigars. The home had portraits of former owners, silver candelabras, antique chairs, wooden curio cabinets, and crystal chandeliers. The next day we toured more plantations and spent the night at a place called Tezcuco. I slept in a room that had a four-poster bed with a white canopy and was full of memorabilia. I wished that Martin and Michell could have been with us, and I could not understand why Mama did not like Martin. He came from a prominent well-to-do family in Ladue, Missouri, and I envisioned him being a corporate lawyer for some big company like AT&T. He was not a smooth-talking "charmer" but was not bad looking, either. He was starting to lose his hair, and he was… well, a bit nerdy. Daddy thought he was wimpy, but I thought we were a good intellectual match. Mama so frequently mentioned that she didn't like Martin that I began to think I might be missing something. After all, my mother knew me better than anyone else. Maybe we weren't right for each other. Still, I think both Martin and I thought we would get married after his graduation the following year, although we did not talk about it. It was a bit like Mama and Van had been.

After graduation, the world was my oyster. I thought the next few years would be career, marriage and kids. The young women of the '80s from the feminist moms of the '70s were ready to conquer the world and have it all.

Michell and me at a Chi Omega party shortly before graduation,
wearing the necklace from Venice

Holding a daisy after graduating from
Newcomb/Tulane with Daddy & Mama

CHAPTER 7

Washington, D.C.

I graduated with a Bachelor of Arts degree in political science and started wondering what to do. My flying was off and on, and I started to lose interest because of my insecurity on the radios. My desire to become a commercial airline pilot waned, and I wondered what to do with myself as I turned 22 in July. I started working again at Gulf Coast Coors, helping out where I could in the office. Then one winter day I received a phone call from Sherwood Bailey, a local entrepreneur and successful businessman. He mostly made his wealth through real estate and was active in charities and politics. He said, "Rosemary, you should be in Washington, D.C. with your degree. I have a son working up there for our local congressman. I'll set up an interview for you." I hung up the phone not even knowing who my local congressman was, but I would soon find out his name — Trent Lott — a big name in D.C. He was also the Minority Whip in the U.S. House of Representatives. I sent my resume and waited. Not too long after, I received a phone call:

"Rosemary?"

"Yes," I said.

"This is Leigh Ann Preston – your friend from Paris!"

"Wow, Leigh Anne – how did you find me?"

"It's an interesting story…"

She told me she stayed in Paris for her entire junior year abroad, and then came back and graduated from Stephens, a women's college in Columbia,

Missouri. She took a job with her local Kentucky congressman and moved to Washington, D.C. His congressional office was in the Rayburn building and just happened to be across from Trent Lott's office. She was walking down the hall during her lunch break and heard two gentlemen talking. One of them said, "We have someone named Rosemary Roosa coming up for an interview..."

Leigh Ann stopped. She turned around and said, "I did not mean to be eavesdropping, but what name did you say?" When they repeated it, she informed them that she knew me and asked for my phone number. The next thing you know she was inviting me to stay at her place with her roommates.

I then received a call for my interview with Trent Lott's office for early December 1985. Since Leigh Ann offered her place, I flew up a week early and interviewed around town so that I would be "skilled" when it came time to meet my congressman. I had in mind a salary of around $20,000 to $25,000 a year, but when I got to D.C., I was told that was too high. I interviewed with the Secretary of Transportation's office, Elizabeth Dole, and was offered a salary at $16,000 a year to be her receptionist. I interviewed in other offices and went shopping for a new suit. I found a Brooks Brothers navy blue suit with a white, high-collared shirt. It was expensive for the time, around $200 dollars, but it looked conservative and smart. By the end of the week, I was ready for my interview. I was feeling good, looking good. On Friday I went to Capitol Hill and was escorted to the Minority Whip's Office just off the House floor. It was a one-room office with a receptionist's desk near the door. The room was gilded and furnished in Colonial New England style. I was impressed. I felt confident and ready to help shape policy and change the world.

A gentleman entered, and I stood up. I had not met Trent Lott, so I did not know what he looked like. The gentleman was Trent Lott's floor assistant. We chatted, and he left. Another gentleman came in. I stood up again. It was Trent Lott's committee staffer. I sat back down and waited awhile. Finally, the doors pushed open forcefully, and in came Trent Lott with his administrative assistant. Congressman Lott was a good-looking man with glasses. He had perfectly cut light brown hair and quick, determined movements. His eyes caught everything as he smiled at me. He took my resume and some letters of recommendation that Daddy had thought to procure for me. One was from the president of a bank in Pascagoula, Trent Lott's home town. Another was from a businessman Daddy had met while starting his beer company, and one was from Mandy's father, Bob McHugh, editor of the *Sun Herald*, the local Mississippi Coast paper. Although Mr. McHugh was supposed to be neutral in his political leanings, he was thought to be a Democrat, and Trent Lott wanted to know why he would be writing a letter for me. I told him that his daughter and I were friends. Trent Lott's eyes were inquisitive and revealed a hint of suspicion about my running around with liberal thinkers.

He then looked at my resume, and I was prepared to talk about all that I had learned studying political science, working at Gulf Coast Coors, my capabilities, and cosmopolitan background. Instead he looked up and asked if I had boyfriend. I was shocked. I said I didn't. Then he proceeded to ask if I was pregnant. I was doubly shocked. I said, "Excuse me?" He quickly mentioned that he had once hired a young woman and that she was pregnant and left him a few months later. He did not want that to happen again. I assured him I was not pregnant and thought to myself that these questions might not be legal to ask, but I answered them anyway. I wanted the job. Then he asked my salary requirements. Because I was told earlier in the week that I had been expecting too much, I answered, "Between $15,000 to $20,000." I was offered the job at $19,500. I felt I could have gotten closer to $25,000 if I had stuck to my original thinking.

Congressman Lott was a good boss, though, and I never got the sense he was prejudiced or biased. He did not abuse his staff by making them work weekends or unreasonably long hours, like I saw with Leigh Ann's boss. Trent Lott was fair, except for paying the women less money than the men, but that was a practice that existed in all fields of the workforce. I was grateful for the job and excited to be moving to our nation's capital. I accepted the position as legislative assistant and would start after the holiday break and new year celebration. Martin and I were only occasionally talking on the phone now, and life was moving on for both of us. I let our relationship go since my mother did not care for him. I trusted her judgment. My parents and I drove up to Washington before the Christmas holidays and searched for places to live. Leigh Ann had roommates, but I did not know anyone, so I started looking for a one-bedroom apartment. I soon found out that D.C. is an expensive place to live. My mother wanted me in a nice place, just as she had insisted in Paris. After a lot of searching we came across some new apartment towers that were close to Capitol Hill in an area that used to be a red-light district. The area had undergone an urban renewal program, but there were still pockets of danger, and the apartments were not too far from where D.C. Mayor Marion Barry, born in Mississippi, had been busted in a scandal involving prostitutes and drugs.

My complex was called Waterside Towers. It had a gate, underground parking, and a key to unlock the elevator service. The apartment was on the sixth floor and had a balcony looking over the street and row houses below. The floors were parquet, and the place was roomy and had a nice feel, with a large bedroom and bath, a suitable kitchen, and a combined living and dining area. Its rent was $600 a month, almost half of my take-home pay, but my parents said they would supplement $100 a month for food and essentials. We ordered a custom-made couch from High Point, North Carolina, that had a pull-out bed for guests. This would be the farthest from my parents that I had ever been on a permanent basis; thus, I was a little anxious but excited. My parents helped me move, and I began work in a city where most everyone wore suits, had a college degree, and was Type A++. I felt a long career coming on. I was in a cosmopolitan and sophisticated city. I was on a good path.

I settled into my work answering constituents' questions and answering the phone when the receptionist was busy. I was in D.C. only a few weeks when I heard about the Space Shuttle Challenger disaster. It was January 28, 1986. I ran to a TV and gasped in horror as the white plumes of smoke trailed every which way through the sky. Even though my father was an astronaut, I had never seen another astronaut die in space. I was in total shock, but had to get back to work. Suddenly, Congressman Lott rushed through the door and asked me to come into his office. I thought he was going to ask me about the explosion, but to my dismay, he asked how I liked working for him and whether I happy in his office. He spoke quickly and firmly and looked at me with genuine interest.

I said, "Do you know that the Challenger just blew up?"

He said "yes," and then proceeded with his questioning. I appreciated his concern and input about my welfare, but I stumbled on my words because I was so shocked. I never could quite get on his wavelength. He was a fast-talker, speaking in a gallop-like tone, quick and short. He was a to-the-point kinda guy who could process information rapidly. Trent Lott could work a room quickly, and it was an admirable trait in the town of deal making. It was a new style for me, for Daddy was slow and methodical. The tortoise and the hare difference. Since my traits followed my father's, I was a tortoise, too.

• • •

At the time of the Challenger accident, NASA was in full swing with the Shuttle program. The culture had changed though. The goal was to build a space station, place satellites in space, and conduct science experiments. It was a worthy mission but different from the competitive moon missions. NASA updated its logo. Designs for the Saturn V were tossed aside. Computers replaced slide rulers. Mission specialists trained for only a few months before flying. Space flight was becoming routine – which is what my father expected would happen, but NASA depended on congressional funding. NASA needed some good publicity to keep its hefty budget going. The government agency decided to fly a school teacher, a civilian, Christa McAuliffe. She would conduct educational lessons from space to inspire a new generation of astronauts. NASA was once again in "Go-Fever" mode, but not for beating the Russians to the moon. The agency was trying to keep members of Congress from beating back the dollars. Flying a civilian seemed to make sense and cents.

In Washington, D.C., Congressional members have a mission too – to bring federal dollars to their districts and states. The Shuttle program created lots of opportunity for many areas of the country: testing of engines in Mississippi, making the external fuel tanks in Louisiana, making O-rings in Kentucky and Utah, and the list goes on. Then all the various components would be assembled and eventually launched at Kennedy Space Center in Cape Canaveral, Florida. On January 28, almost 15 years to the day after the Apollo 14 launch, the Challenger took off. It was in the air for 73 seconds when it disintegrated. As with the Apollo 1 crew, emergency procedures were implemented, but there was not enough of the Shuttle left to follow through on them. The entire seven-person crew perished. The nation was in shock. How could this happen?

Daddy called his fellow astronaut, Hank Hartsfield. "This was not supposed to happen, Hank. We called the shots. If the ride was compromised, we were able to call it off," my father reminded Hank.

During Apollo, the astronauts were a part of the engineering process and knew how the systems worked, and most importantly, knew the weaknesses. "It's different now, Stu," Hank said, having flown on three Shuttle missions, "most decisions come down from HQ."

Investigators determined that the cause of the explosion was a weakened O-ring on the solid rocket booster. The freezing temperatures the night before loosened the seal. There had been warnings. Unfortunately, the warnings were not heeded, for the cast of thousands were in place that day. "Go-Fever" outweighed concerns. Space flight, no matter how routine, is still a risky business.

• • •

As people from Lott's Congressional district would come to Washington, I'd greet them and ask them where they were from. Most would first say Mississippi. Then when pressed, they would name the county. When I told them that I was from Mississippi, too, they seemed surprised. "Another Mississippian way up here in D.C.!" Trent Lott had the walls painted blue to represent the Mississippi Gulf Coast, and I had a picture of Ingalls Shipbuilding behind me. We used only blue pens, and Trent Lott signed his letters with blue ink. The blue represented the water.

Leigh Anne was across the hall from me, but she rarely got time off for lunch and had to work long hours, so we did not see much of each other. Next to our office was Congressman Sonny Montgomery, a stately Democrat from the Meridian, Mississippi, area. I met a tall brunette in his office named Cindy. Her family had a lumber company in Gulfport and imported mahogany from Latin America. She and I hit it off, and we palled around some. I also met Sherwood Bailey's son, Jody, but he worked in the Whip Office in the Longworth Building and lived in an area that was not close to me. I met more Mississippians in D.C. than I had at home. About six months later I got a call from a lawyer named Gaines who said he wanted to invite me to a party with some "home-folk" from Mississippi. I accepted. He did not indicate it was a date but more of a gathering with friends to help me meet more people. We entered the party, and I noticed a young man wearing a flowered jacket. His name was Tom. I thought that this person must be really confident to wear a jacket like that in this dark-suit-wearing town, and we started chatting. He was only slightly taller than I and had large blue eyes and blond hair. He had a dry, off-beat sense of humor that I liked. He was from Arkansas, but at the party with a Mississippi friend.

Tom worked as a receptionist on the Senate side of Capitol Hill for a Democrat. Tom's pay was $16,000 a year. He called me for a date, and I went. Soon he was calling several times a day, and we began seeing more and more of each other. We did not have a lot of money to spend, but he would take me to expensive bars just off the Hill, and we would nurse our drinks. We often went to parks. One of our favorite places was the botanical gardens. Since I had not dated much in my formative years, I did not realize that his showmanship stemmed from insecurity. He started belittling me and cutting me down in subtle ways. But since he was giving me so much attention, I brushed it off. He soon isolated me from any male friendships, then my women friendships. He wanted to be the "it and all."

Spring came, and my parents came for a visit to see the cherry blossoms. They met Tom, and he put on a good show. At first he charmed them, and wined and dined them at an expensive restaurant. But then Tom quickly seemed to find things for only him and me to do while my parents were visiting for the week. My parents said while they were packing up that they wished they had visited with me more, but that was about it. I was a grown woman working on my own, and I had to make my own decisions about life and love. Tom's affection was getting more and more possessive, and on one occasion he raised his hand to me but smashed something on the floor instead. In-between arguments, he would shower me with apologies and tell me how perfect we were together. I was confused and wished I had a "flight checklist" on love so that I would know whether this relationship was right or wrong.

• • •

At work, I was enjoying being a part of the legislative process. I realized that what I had learned in college was not the way our American government worked. In the U.S. House of Representatives, it was party-line all the way. If the Republicans introduced legislation that made sense, immediately the Democrats were opposed, and vice-versa. It was not a matter of what was best for the country, but who could outmaneuver whom and get the credit and headlines. Being in the minority party was frustrating, but to no one more than Trent Lott, who I believe had his eye on 1600 Pennsylvania Avenue. I was greatly interested in foreign affairs, and part of my job was to attend hearings and receptions after work. On occasion, I would be invited to an Embassy function or events at the White House. I attended the President's Dinner with Ronald Reagan, and still have the engraved champagne glass and commemorative champagne bottle. In October 1987, Soviet Foreign Minister Shevardnadze spoke at the Rose Garden along with the President, and Capitol Hill staffers were invited to attend. It was fascinating being near the heart of the two superpowers from the space race. When leaving, I walked past the limousine of the "Evil Empire," which was being guarded

In Congressman Lott's office with fellow staffers
and Walter Payton with me on far right

by a muscled Russian guard. I peered in. It was right out of a James Bond movie with leopard print inside.

I also attended Department of State and national security briefings. In one briefing I learned about Russian Spetsnaz in the United States. These were undercover agents posing as Americans and who were ready to do the will of the Communist Party when called upon by their country. The U.S. advisor warned that these special agents were "everywhere" and that we as Americans needed to be vigilant. I had never heard of them but was fired up after the briefing. I asked my father about them, but he was not familiar either. I started laughing, saying, "Beware, the Spetsnaz are everywhere!" This began a running joke between my father and me.

Since I did not care much for the beer hangouts for staffers and was on a limited budget, on occasion I would save up my money and have a drink at one of the finer hotels, usually at the Ritz piano bar called the Jockey Club or the Willard Hotel's Round Robin bar, which had recently been renovated and reopened. There were always interesting movers and shakers in them. Not too far from the Willard was the Old Ebbitt Grill, where Col. Oliver North negotiated selling used arms to Iran to fund the Contras in Central America. D.C. was a secret deal-making town. One of my favorite places to go was on top of the Hotel Washington, which had an open-air restaurant/bar overlooking the Washington Monument, the White House, and other federal buildings. The game was to see how many U.S. flags one could count from this point of view. I think my maximum was 28.

I involved myself in military issues and took a couple of fact-finding congressional trips. About 30 of us from the Hill went to Fort Knox with the Army and practiced maneuvers in a tank simulator, then on to Fort Campbell, Kentucky, where we fired rifles and participated in "confidence builders." Tom happened to be on this trip, and one military exercise had us lined up in a row of four. We linked arms at the elbows. We were then strapped with helmets and ropes, which led to a helicopter hovering above us. The helicopter lifted us off the ground to about 500 feet, and we flew around with the wind beating the heck out of us. Tom decided it would be cute to "push off," creating a motion like that of the toy that has four silver balls hanging on strings — when one ball swings, it hits the two center balls and knocks the last one out. Tom pushed off the group as we were clinging for dear life and came swinging back in and knocked into the three of us like a Mack truck. No one went swinging out like the toy, so he pushed off again. He came back, aiming at me. This time he hit me squarely and knocked my helmet off. I watched as my helmet fell to the earth below, and I thought, "What if that had been me?" It was like watching a slow-motion movie as I lost sight of the helmet and hoped that no one got conked on the head with it. That should have told me something about him.

Another military trip was with the Navy, and we staffers went on a week-long tour to Hawaii, where we saw the U.S.S. Arizona from World War II. I was struck with how many Japanese visitors there were on the island. We also went to the Navy's elite gunnery school in San Diego, and I sat in the same seat as Tom Cruise did in the movie *Top Gun,* when he described his "friendly relations" with a Russian MiG. We ended the trip in San Francisco at a Navy shipyard. The military was doing well under the Reagan years.

Time progressed. Tom and I had been going out for more than a year, but it was not a healthy relationship. He managed to bring out the worst in me, and we would quarrel over the simplest of things, like whether modern or antique furniture was better. The arguments never really had a point, but if I took one position, he would take the other. He was whittling away at my self-confidence and making me question my beliefs and thinking. I remember calling home one time and asking my mother if I was even a good person, for he had made me feel guilty about something insignificant. She was subtly disapproving of Tom but liked him better than Martin.

Then one day without warning, Tom asked me to meet him at the botanic garden during our lunch hour. We walked through the gardens not saying much, and while crossing a bridge, he took my hand. He put a two-carat diamond on my finger. His parents were in the jewelry business in Hope, Arkansas (the hometown of Bill Clinton). I was stunned. Tom did not ask me to marry him, rather just looked at me with his big, blue eyes and half-smiled. I did not say yes, but time was ticking on my lunch hour, and

I had to get back to the work. I walked in the door and showed the girls in the office. One woman who monitored my work was Martha Fortenberry. She was approaching 30 years old and was attractive with shoulder-length black hair and red lipstick.

She said, "Let me see! Can I put it on?"

"Sure" I said and took off the ring. I let her wear it most of the afternoon. In my heart, it did not mean much. Tom called my parents that night to say we had gotten engaged, and my father was almost speechless. My mother managed a few words. I felt like the cartoon Pepe Le Pew, where the little black cat couldn't seem to run away from the adoring clutches of the striped skunk.

The arguments continued with Tom and me, and I just did not know what to do. After each one he was again apologetic and promised to improve. I was now 24 years old, stably employed, and it was time to get married. However, I kept thinking of my parents' marriage and thought that a relationship should bring out the best in a person, not the worst. Had I not had that comparison, I would have been totally lost about how a relationship should be. Time clicked on, and once after an intense nonsensical argument, Tom asked for the ring back. I called home, and my parents said they would come the next day. My mother flew in that morning while my father drove the car. My father gave me the best advice in the world. He said, "Don't take the ring back unless you are ready to walk down the aisle." Tom waited for them to leave and then came over, sheepishly apologized, and tried to put the ring back on my finger. I refused; however, we kept seeing each other off and on. He had managed to isolate me from my friends, and I did not have a strong support system to lean on for advice and guidance.

At work, a woman had left the Whip Office, and I asked for her position. Since Congressional expenses are public record, I looked up her salary. She was earning about $27,000 a year. I thought that I would get a nice pay raise. Trent Lott's new administrative assistant called me into his office and said that I got the job, and that I would have a raise of $500 a year. That amounted to about $25 more a month after taxes and insurance premiums. I was disappointed but happy to now be working in the inner depths of politics. The Whip Office was not made up of all Mississippians, and I shared an office with a smart, older woman from New Mexico named Mary Martinek. She had been divorced and recently remarried. She gave me words of wisdom about relationships.

Then my friend, Michell, called and invited me to spend the Labor Day weekend with her. I did not have the money on my limited salary. Michell offered to purchase the ticket, so I went to Houston, where she was now living after graduating from Tulane. Having gotten her degree in geology, Michell was making better money working in the oil and gas industry. She knew me from sorority and college days, and during the weekend, she turned to me and said, "I don't know what exactly is going on with you, Rosemary, but this is not the person I knew from college." My belief in myself was eroding.

Trent Lott decided to run for the U.S. Senate, but I was removed from the race in Mississippi. I had no doubt he would win, and I presumed that I'd go with him to the Senate side. Working in the Whip Office gave me some great insight into the political world of Washington D.C. and deal-making. Part of our job was to keep track of how Republican members were going to vote on major pieces of legislation. If a member was not going to vote party-line, it was the job of Trent Lott and others, including Newt Gingrich and Jack Kemp, to "whip" them into voting the right way. I'd sit in meetings with the party leadership and listen to their strategies and thoughts on how best to capitalize with the media. Since members of Congress are busy with various meetings, press functions, committees, hearings, greeting "home folk" and many other duties, our office was responsible for knowing what legislation was coming to the House Floor and providing a synopsis of the bill. In the House of Representatives, once a vote is called upon, there are only 15 minutes to get to the floor and cast a vote. It is impossible for a member to know all that is happening, so it was our job to keep them informed. I was fascinated being in the pulse of power, and I enjoyed it.

I had some vacation time, and it was now the spring of 1988. My parents were heading to a Shikar-Safari Club meeting in Pebble Beach. Shikar-

Safari was a big-game hunting club with the who's who of the hunting world. Since Daddy had hunted frequently in Africa after his mission to the moon, he was invited to be a member. Shikar-Safari Club International required prospective members to go through a sponsorship program, like joining a sorority or fraternity, and be nominated by a member. It is a small group of elite big-game hunters from around the world. The group was formed initially by those who had the means to hunt but also had the vulnerability of being ripped off by fly-by-night outfitters. In Africa, they say, "This is Africa," meaning anything can happen. The term shikar comes from hunting tigers, which are now forbidden by the U.S. to hunt. The term safari generally means a hunt for one of the Big Five: elephant, rhinoceros, leopard, lion, and Cape buffalo. The founders wanted to have a club whose members would meet each year, visit, exchange experiences, and show pictures of their hunts. A requirement when hunting big game is to take a picture of you and your animal in the field. This ensures that you actually "collected" the animal, and no one shot it in your place. Shikar-Safari was proud of its founding ideals and ethics, realizing that hunting is an honorable sport to be engaged in for pleasure and personal recreation, and not for commercial purposes or personal aggrandizement. As a fellow hunter, I instantly fell in love with the mission, its purpose, and the people.

Daddy contacted Alan Shepard, who had a home in Pebble Beach, and we stayed on the Shepards' property. One night, my father and I stayed up late drinking… he liked to stay up late, and I did too. Not only did I have my father's traits of being meticulous, analytical, thoughtful… but of being a night-owl, too. Mama went to bed at 10 p.m., no matter what time zone she was in. If the clock said 10 p.m., boom, she was in bed. She even had the reputation of leaving her own dinner parties and going to bed at ten, leaving Daddy to entertain the guests. It had been an exciting time at Pebble Beach, hearing people's hunting stories and attending wonderful parties. On our last night there was a formal ball, and the excitement of it left both Daddy and me tired but awake. Mama went to bed. Daddy was drinking beer, and I was sipping on one. It was late, and then the room got quiet.

"Rosemary," my father started in a slow but serious tone, "Would you be willing to come back to Mississippi and run the distribution company?"

My mind kicked into gear, trying to comprehend the magnitude of the question. I figured one of the boys would do it eventually. The thought had never entered my mind.

"Do you think I can do it?" I asked, stunned.

He replied, "I wouldn't be asking you if I didn't think you could do it."

My immediate response was, "Anything for family."

I had a new, clear purpose: to help my father and the family beer business. Whatever was going on in my personal life had to wait – the career, marriage, and kids. I flew back to D.C. from California and gave my notice to Trent Lott.

Daddy at Southern Circle home drinking beer and eating blue crabs

CHAPTER 8

Back to Mississippi

My father was a man of challenge, and he enjoyed setting up the business on what he called "A quarter in his pocket and on a wing and a prayer." He was proud of his accomplishments, but soon he started to get tired of the day-to-day operations. He had worked hard since 1981 to get things rolling and had purchased other brands along the way. He was now conducting business with over five major suppliers and had moved the company from selling off the truck to a pre-sell system where the accounts would order one day, and their beer was delivered the next. My father was the only beer distributorship at the time to have such a system, and it was the best way, considering all the brands that he was now carrying.

With his faith and confidence in me, I moved into my bedroom in the house on Southern Circle in Gulfport, the home my parents purchased during my later years in college. It was early July 1985, and my birthday was approaching. On July 23rd, I would turn 25 years old. My father gave me the title of executive vice president, and he let everyone know that I was the heir-apparent. My oldest brother had worked in the company a year before, but Daddy mentioned he spent much of his time going to military training schools to further his career and was not focused on the beer business. Daddy said the employees were grumbling that they didn't get as much time off as my brother, and it had put Daddy in a precarious position. I told him I was there to work. I asked about salary, and my father said he would pay me a bit more than what I was earning in D.C. I'm not sure he even knew what that was, but we agreed to $25,000 a year. I had returned home not for the money, but to help Daddy in the business. I felt the family obligation, and the company needed to prosper.

My brother advised me to start subtly and not make waves. My instincts told me differently. A new sheriff was in town, and although polite and courteous, I was firm and pushed for answers about how the company operated. Soon I learned the company was in bad shape. We had an office manager whom I believe was stealing from the business. No wonder Daddy could never figure out the checkbook. When I would ask for some petty cash to go buy something, the manager would pull the money out of his pocket. When I told him that was not proper, he would say, "oh, my money, the company's money – it's all the same. I'll figure it out later." Daddy had set up checks and balances, but the office manager was in control of a lot of cash and inventory, and I knew that Daddy was not paying close enough attention. I next went to the sales manager to learn how the marketing side of the company operated, how the salesmen would pre-sell, and how the delivery system worked. The sales manager was a short, paranoid man, but I was patient and slow with my questioning. I needed their help in understanding such a complex operation. I was only trying to learn, but within a month of my starting, both managers quit. I was now thrown in head-first in the deep end. It was sink or swim, and I persuaded Daddy to teach me as much as he could. Since he liked drinking beer, we would generally sit in the hospitality room in the afternoons, and he would sip on a beer as we went through the operations. He taught me a great deal, and I took notes and listened intently. He gave me the checkbook and said I was now in charge of the money, for he liked to say he lived by "The Golden Rule" - "He Who Has the Gold, Rules!" It was Daddy's way of giving me new authority and transferring power.

Shortly thereafter, we were in need of three new cars for the sales supervisors. Daddy sent me to a dealership. I wasn't sure how to buy cars, but I was determined to come back with three new cars and to make him proud. I arrived at the dealership and asked for the gentleman my father had called, whom I presumed was the fleet manager. He sent me to another salesman, and I proceeded to ask him about cars. He kept smiling at me, mentioning my looks, and asked if I had a boyfriend. I was polite and professional and could not seem to keep him on track. I was too shy to be rude, so I finally gave up and went back to my office.

I was disappointed that I had bought nothing. When I walked into Daddy's office, he looked hopeful. "Well, what type of cars did you buy?"

I said, "I think the guy was interested in me and not too interested in selling cars."

My father, without saying a word, swung his chair around to the phone and dialed the car dealership. He spoke with the fleet manager. Daddy said in a controlled, but angry tone, "I sent my daughter out there to buy three cars, not get a date!"

Daddy wheeled his chair around and told me in a softer tone to go back and speak only to the fleet manager. Before I left his office, he said, "Rosemary, you are small and petite and nice looking. The business world is going to be tough on you and may not take you seriously, but you keep persevering. I know you can do it."

I drove back and negotiated for three new cars. They were delivered the next day.

Daddy hired a new sales manager from Pepsi named Keith. Keith seemed to think he answered only to Daddy. I tried to have one-on-one meetings with him explaining that although Daddy was the president, I was handling the day-to-day operations and we needed to find a way to work together. Since Keith came from the soft drink industry, he did not know that beer could not be sold on consignment. Next thing we knew, we were turned in by another distributorship to the Bureau of Alcohol, Tobacco and Firearms for selling on consignment. A-several-months-long investigation ensued, and we were fined a few thousand dollars. Daddy had also given Keith a company vehicle, and one day out of the blue I received a phone call. The caller said, "If your sales manager would quit delivering pizzas, then maybe he could take care of selling me some beer!" The caller immediately hung up. I told Keith about it, and he confessed that he was delivering pizzas for Pizza Hut. He said that he did not earn enough money with us, so he needed to supplement his income. I asked him if he was using the company car and gas. He said he was, and I was surprised by his frankness. He was fired.

Together Daddy and I interviewed our three sales supervisors, and we chose one to be the new sales manager. Kerry Breland was energetic, young, and a non-stop talker. He was a salesman at heart, and it's just what the company needed. I learned a great deal about personalities and found out that salesmen were a whole 'nother breed. They don't stop talking until they have the sale; they can take rejection but keep on going and not take it personally, and when they're telling a story, it's best to just interrupt or the story will go on and on. Kerry and I worked well together, and our sales began to improve. I decided we would hold off on hiring an office manager until I could get a handle on the flow of operations. I wrote off in the checkbook over $8,000, just so I could have a clean start in calculating the numbers.

Daddy and I also hired a new computer operator, for the one we had had quit shortly after the office manager left. We hired a tall, no-makeup-wearing, chain-smoking natural brunette with a quick tongue. We had two other women in the office, an older woman who was the bookkeeper, and a young office assistant, who was also the receptionist. Her name was Lori Begley, and she impressed me a lot. She was a go getter who was organized, prompt, pleasant – and when she had nothing else to do, she would create a job, like dust the plants or reorganize the supply cabinet. We communicated primarily by notes, for if I was in the middle of a report or concentrating on a project, I did not want to be disturbed. Every now and then I would do what I called a "walk-about" – and go into the warehouse to physically see the inventory and chat with the warehouse manager, Fred Hart. He was an older, rugged, and handsome man with a mustache. He was affable, easy to get along with, and a hard worker. He was respectful to me and taught me how they loaded the trucks at night, how they would check-in the drivers, and how he kept track of the pallets and various brands.

The Coors Brewing Company required that their brands be kept cool, at 36 to 38 degrees, for the beer was cold-filtered, and Coors believed the best-tasting beer was right out of the tap and staying cool would preserve the flavor. We had a 5,000-square-foot cooler that could handle cars, forklifts, and dollies. Fred told me that when he started, my father, The Colonel, as the employees called him, showed him how to manually escape from the cooler if the electricity went out or the door failed to open. Fred said Daddy sliced his thumb while searching for the manual lever, and blood started to spew all over the floor. Fred said, "The Colonel never stopped talking and calmly and slowly showed me the entire procedure. I couldn't concentrate on a word he was saying, looking at all that blood! But he acted like nothing was wrong and just kept going." That was The Colonel, never show a weakness.

As I settled into running the business, my ex-fiancé would call on occasion, but that path had been run. I was slowly regaining my confidence, thanks to Daddy's trust and training, and I learned what I didn't want in a husband or relationship. I was living at home and saving money to get my own place to live. I had moved back from Washington D.C. with $28 to my name, so I was starting from scratch. I got involved in the social circles, and time moved on. I celebrated the 1990 New Year at the Gulfport Yacht Club with my cousin, Gloria, a beautiful brunette with big blue eyes, a striking body, and the quickest wit. Laughter was a guarantee around Gloria, and we enjoyed being each other's "dates" for New Year's Eve. The last 10 years had not been the decade that I had imagined, but I had a good job and was helping my parents. My father kept quoting to me, "Experience breeds knowledge, which breeds confidence." I was becoming myself again and running a multi-million-dollar company.

As with most things in life, when the pendulum swings hard one way, it generally swings just as far back before settling into a small, steady tick. In July, at a *Chamber of Commerce After Hours* social I saw a guy drinking a Coors Light. I looked at him approvingly, and he lifted his beer in a toast-like fashion. He didn't know that I was looking at what beer he was drinking and not necessarily him, but he looked like Tom Cruise with short dark hair and muscles. He came over and spoke. He was young, about to turn 21, and had just returned from the Gulf War. His name was Johnnie. Johnnie talked about living in fox holes, with all kinds of creepy crawly creatures, and having to suddenly put on gas masks when the warning sound alerted that an incoming missile was approaching. He had enlisted in the Marines after high school and wanted to prove that he was a tough son-of-a-gun. I liked to hear his military stories. I was 26, about to turn 27, but he asked me out. I thought, "What the heck, why not?" At least Daddy could not call him a wimp. I felt that if men could date younger women, women could date younger men. I didn't think it would last long, but soon we had been going out a year, then two. He was 180 degrees from Tom and easy-going. He had started college, and we would see each other on the weekends and during breaks. All the while, I was traveling with my parents, sometimes in the United States to brewery conventions, sometimes abroad with Shikar-Safari, or to visit family stationed in Europe.

• • •

In 1991, my parents were invited to Yuri Gagarin's 30th anniversary in Russia, and my father got me an invitation, too. I wanted to see who these people were who had fought so hard to beat us to the moon. Little did we know that we were visiting at a time when the Soviet Union was collapsing. Mikhail Gorbachev was head of the government and had implemented a policy of reform called glasnost, or "openness." Perestroika was taking place, which was a political movement for the reformation within the communist party of the Soviet Union. When we arrived into the country, our group stayed outside of Moscow due to "skirmishes." They were riots. We stayed at a sprawling government retreat, and the accommodations were nice enough. It was probably their Camp David. One translator said in passing, "In Russia, we are all equal. However, some are more equal than others!"

We visited Star City and saw the scuba tank and training facilities, which were fashioned like ours at Johnson Space Center. We walked around their new mission control, built by Japan, for the Russians had just flown a Japanese cosmonaut. The group toured the gardens, and we saw Laika memorialized in the form of a statue and plaque. Laika had been a stray

St. Basil's Cathedral in
Moscow, Russia

The Kremlin on the left

Standing near the center of
Red Square

dog from the streets of Moscow and was selected to be the occupant of the Soviet spacecraft, Sputnik 2, that launched into outer space and circled the earth in November 1957. In the early days of rocket science, since no one really knew the effects of weightlessness, animals were sent into space first. The United States sent chimpanzees. The French later sent a cat, but here in the Soviet Union, the Russians sent Laika, dubbed Muttnik by some American reporters. Laika was a young mixed-breed dog, mostly Siberian husky. Soviet scientists assumed that a stray dog would have already learned to endure the harsh conditions of hunger and cold temperatures from living on the streets. Unfortunately, Laika's trip was one-way. The re-entry strategy could not be worked out. It was unclear how long Laika lived in orbit before the life-support system gave out. But years later a Russian scientist revealed that due to stress and heat, Laika did not last as long as previously claimed by the Soviets.

Star City was originally a secret Air Force facility. We walked along corridors lined with pictures of pilots and viewed the worn-out classrooms. This was the home of "the enemy." Not on any map, it was the shining example of the communist way of life. We heard that the cosmonauts lived in "luxury," and to showcase that, the Russians invited us into a small home decorated in typical Russian style with white lace, blue and white Catherine the Great teacups and china ornaments, painted wooden trinkets, and Russian dolls. Later, when the United States started flying astronauts with cosmonauts to the Mir Space Station, an American wife told me that when she'd get tired of the heat not working in her Russian accommodations, she would pick up the phone and blurt it out, knowing the Russians were listening. About an hour or two later, a repairman would show up.

Under Soviet communism, everyone gave to "Mother Russia" and personal comforts were not considered a priority. During our visit, we toured a restricted area where the government was building a large rocket. We put on booties and scrub hats and entered a spotless area. We were up close and personal with this huge rocket, and I was impressed. After the tour, I needed to use the restroom. I politely asked, "Toilette? WC?" and was escorted outside the facility to a small bathroom with only a hole in the floor, a leaking rusty faucet, and a light that barely worked. The dichotomy was astounding.

The cosmonaut leading our trip was Alexei Leonov, the first human to complete an EVA (extravehicular activity), or "spacewalk." He was also selected to be the first Russian to walk on the moon had they beaten us. Alexei spoke English and had a sharp mind and wit. With him were other "Twice Heroes of the Soviet Union" who proudly wore their red cloth medals with a gold star. I wasn't sure what it meant to even be a "Once Hero," but it seemed like a big deal. One evening Alexei arranged for a bus to take us to Red Square. As we stepped out, there in front of us was the breathtaking St. Basil's Cathedral. Religion had been banned under communism, so the inside was bare, but the outside was spectacular. It had several onion-like domes in various sizes and colors, like multi-colored swirls of ice cream. Its complexity and design almost put me in a trance. Legend has it that Ivan the Terrible had an architect for each dome and asked them to produce their best work, then blinded them all so that they could not re-create the masterpiece elsewhere.

Red Square is a long open-area rectangle made up of grayish stones. On one side is the red brick Kremlin Wall and Lenin's tomb. At the base is St. Basil's and opposite the cathedral is a large government building. Next to it (opposite Lenin's Tomb) is, of all things, a shopping mall called GUM, the former government department stores. Alexei was proud to show the group the mall, so he started to lead most of us there. However, Mama was not a shopper and wanted to find a place to sit and have a glass of wine. Daddy and I found some others to accompany her at a small café where they could enjoy the night air. As Daddy and I started walking back to join the group, we found ourselves alone in Red Square. Daddy walked to the center and stood. He crossed his arms in determination like he would when we were flying, and started nodding his head in a pensive way. He looked around and I could tell he was in deep thought. He quietly said, "I sure would have hated to blow this up." I thought, "What?" and just looked at him. I remember Daddy used to talk about how he had an assignment early in his jet fighting career at a strategic target, but never identified the location. As all pilots do, he used his hands to demonstrate to me how he would have come in low, below the radar at "tree-top level," and then going straight up over the target (Red Square), released a bomb (it would have been nuclear). He then would've hit the throttle full speed and kinda reverse-split S over the top and fly inverted until he rolled out and cleared the area. The theory was the bomb would then arc up and back down, allowing the extra time for the pilot to get away. The Air Force called it the "Over-The-Shoulder" maneuver. Since the mission was assigned as a solo flight with no refueling planes in the area, at some point he'd have to eject and hike out behind enemy lines. In the way that Daddy nonchalantly described dramatic situations, he said, "It pretty much would have been a suicide mission." Now I was with him as he looked from the ground at what he would have certainly destroyed from the air if ordered.

Next we flew out to Baikonur "Cosmodrome" in Kazakhstan, which has been the launch site for Soviet and Russian space missions since the launch of Sputnik. Since it was also the site of Yuri Gagarin's mission, it was appropriate that we visit the facility. Located around 1,300 miles from Moscow, the area is a remote, harsh desert. It had been the site of the massive explosion that dashed the Russians' hope to reach the moon. However, the Russians had persevered with Mir and sent cosmonauts on long-duration flights. On the launchpad was a rocket ready to go, and the Russians said, "For the mere price of a few million, you may take a flight!" They were selling rides into space.

At the airstrip in Kazakhstan, the Russian pilots put on an air show to end all air shows. They flew every new and old military jet in their arsenal, and I wondered what it would have been like for Daddy to have gone head to head with one in a dog-fight. Daddy's motto was not to give way when heading straight on, and he would have been a formidable contender to the Soviets. After the impressive airshow, we went to the tarmac and walked among the planes. There sat a MiG-21, the ultimate enemy airplane that most of the astronauts trained to fight against in their military careers. One of the cosmonauts grabbed a ladder and told them to climb in. The astronauts were like kids in a candy store trying to jump on the ladder all at once. But the MiG is a tight fit, so it was one at a time. Standing next to me was cosmonaut Valentina Tereshkova, an attractive brunette with a commanding personality. In June 1963 she became the first woman to fly in space, completing 48 orbits around the earth. I told her I was a pilot, and suddenly she barked some orders in Russian and cleared the MiG's cockpit for me to climb in, moving all the astronauts out of the way. I was reluctant to make the men wait, but she told me to go ahead. I secretly snapped some pictures of the cockpit and felt like a spy taking reconnaissance in the Cold War.

Since there were three of us on the trip - Mama, Daddy and me - we stayed in the room where the cosmonauts stay prior to their launch. It was plain, no-frills, Soviet-style crew quarters, with minimal decorations and practical furniture. There was nothing ornate or expensive, but it was the largest quarters in the building. I heard that because of lack of space, Jim Lovell and Buzz Aldrin stayed in what was essentially converted broom closets. The Roosas were lucky to have the "spacious" two-bedroom suite of the cosmonauts. There was one unique item of interest in the place, and that was the back of the door that led away from the quarters. It had the signatures of all the cosmonauts. The tradition was that each would sign the back of the door before departing to the launch pad. It was a weird feeling staying in the same place as the men who competed against my father, and I felt like I was on Soviet sacred ground looking at those names.

We had translators who were probably KGB, but they were pleasant, respectful, and fun to be around. One woman was about my age, and she, too, had been a political science major at the university. She had also worked on the SALT II treaty and knew a great deal about our nuclear capabilities. We debated politics, life, and love. She was divorced with a young child, and life was difficult under communism. She explained to me that food was scarce and rationed by the government, and that if a line formed after work, she would just queue up and see what was at the end of it. Whatever it was is what she would have for dinner that evening. She explained that a person was assigned an apartment and that it did not matter where you worked, so there was a large black market "trading" of apartments to accommodate

Astronauts and Cosmonauts at Association of Explorers (ASE) meeting
(Valentina Tereshkova is bottom row, center)

Alexei Leonov, first man/Russian to conduct an EVA,
and me at an ASE meeting

one's work. Private ownership was not allowed for the majority of people. She spoke freely and openly, and I was a surprised by her candidness. I told her that in America, as long as you did not do anything illegal, that a person could speak out against their political leaders, including the President of the United States. She looked at me and said flatly, "I don't believe you." It was the one thing that I could not convince her of. She believed I was feeding her propaganda.

One evening while in Kazakhstan, our interpreter was tired. She said translating was mentally exhausting and that she just had to go to bed. Deke Slayton's son had brought some tequila with him, so a small group of us kept partying. We went to the sitting area in the crew quarters where Mama, Daddy, and I were staying. It had a small couch, a couple of chairs, and a table. After about 15 minutes, someone knocked on the door. I thought it was because the tequila was kicking in and we were being too loud. It was the woman translator around my age. She said "they" told her to come back. I presumed "they" were the KGB listeners. I later heard that Bruce McCandless, an astronaut who was part of the "Original 19" and the first to fly untethered from a spacecraft, helped sponsor the translator's move to the United States to become a teacher at a university. I wondered if she learned for herself that as long as she did nothing illegal, she would not be thrown in jail for speaking out politically.

• • •

After the official trip was over, Daddy planned for us to see St. Petersburg, formerly known as Leningrad. Traveling in Russia on one's own proved difficult. We had reservations at a hotel, but we needed internal visas to travel from Moscow to St. Petersburg. It was not like in the U.S. where one can travel from state line to state line without checkpoints. From the first day we arrived in Russia, we started the process of obtaining these visas. Throughout the trip, Daddy would ask the Russia coordinators if the visas were ready, and they would say they were "in progress." We started to wonder if we would get them. It was confusing and complex, and Daddy and I started to say to each other, "No way could they pull off a first strike," referring to the Cold War doctrine of complete annihilation in a nuclear war. The balance of power between the superpowers was kept in check by knowing that whoever launched a nuclear missile first would be hit with total devastation in return. The country with the first strike would have the advantage. As Americans, we were convinced the Russians could launch its nuclear arsenal at the drop of a hat. Now that we had been in Russia on this visit, it was clear that most of the time, the left hand did not know what the right hand was doing. Information was disseminated on a need-to-know basis, and we surmised that if most people had a complete understanding of the inner workings, then perhaps another revolution could arise.

On the last day of our trip, almost hours before the flight to St. Petersburg, the visas arrived. Daddy was pleased but frustrated it took so long; nevertheless, we were on our way to the city where the Tsars had their last stand. It was a European-looking city, founded by Peter the Great in the early 1700s to show that Russia could keep up with its Western neighbors. The hotel was luxurious by Russian standards but needed some work. As we looked at the menu that night, it read well. The waiter approached, a tall skinny man in his early 40s whose worn look made him appear much older, and he took out his black pad and pencil.

"What would you like?" he asked with a thick Russian accent but in perfect English. My father had a habit of asking waiters around the world what they recommended from the chef.

"What is the best thing on the menu?" my father asked him with curiosity.

In a slow and monotone voice, the waiter replied, "We are not allowed to eat the food, so I cannot tell you what is good," the waiter said with no emotion, and then stood there with pencil in hand. The food was not bad, but it was sad that this man had to serve it but never could taste it.

We needed some rubles for taxi cabs and little things, but smack-dab during our visit, the currency had been moved to float with world currencies and was no longer propped up by the government. One U.S. dollar was no longer equal to one Russian ruble. It was great for the U.S. dollar, but hotels hosting foreigners did not want to exchange money during this huge devaluation of the ruble. We put what we could on credit cards and started seeing the well-known sights, including the magnificent Winter Palace and Hermitage Museum, which had original artwork from the great European masters. I had a feeling this extensive collection might have been seized during WWII as "war booty," but there was no way to prove it. As we left the museum to find a nice lunch place, a man came out of the shadows, selling exquisitely painted Russian boxes. The artwork was so fine that he said human hair was used to paint some of the fanciful, thin gold design. There was a box depicting a prince and fair maiden on a horse. I had a U.S. 20-dollar bill. "I'll take it," I said, and he shoved it in my hand and disappeared. Another man approached my father and asked if he wanted to exchange some money. He gave us an excellent black-market exchange rate and started counting out the rubles, holding them up with his hand. I am not sure what American bills my father pulled out of his pocket, but Daddy asked him to count the rubles again, placing them in my hand. Then suddenly the Russian looked panicked and said, "Politsiya are coming! Quickly, exchange now." He shoved the rubles in my father's hand and took the U.S. dollars and ran off. We looked around and did not see anyone. Daddy looked at the rubles, and it was not the same amount as he held up initially. We had gotten ripped off. We both looked at each other and sighed in disappointment.

We were determined to brush it off, but the feeling of dealing with the underworld left us in a somber mood. On the bright side, we stumbled upon a small restaurant with red velvet interior and black leather seats, obviously an expensive place.

"Do you take credit cards?' my father asked, since we still barely had any rubles.

"Yes, we do," said the maître de, and escorted us to a corner table. He said they had a prix fixe menu, and asked if we would like caviar with our meal.

"How much for each, with and without the caviar?" my father asked, not wanting to get ripped off again.

The gentleman gave us the prices in rubles. We quickly figured it in dollars. With the new exchange rate, it was $15 without, and $30 with the caviar, along with a five-course meal. Both Daddy and I passed on the caviar, but Mama chose to have it. It was a true luxury to her. After we settled in, the waiter brought a huge bowl of deep black beluga caviar. My mother's eyes lit up as if she had died and gone to heaven. Caviar is rich, and it is hard to sit and devour an entire bowl at one sitting. As the different courses came, the waiter was reluctant to take away the caviar. When we hit dessert, there was still plenty in the bowl. Finally, Daddy said, "I now know what it feels like to be the richest man in the world. I gave Joan more caviar than she could possibly eat!"

• • •

In 1993, I purchased a home near my parents in a cute one-way in, one-way out neighborhood called the Enclave. It had taken me five years of living at home to save up enough for the down payment. The home was not large, about 1,700 square feet, but nice with three bedrooms, two and a half baths, a two-car garage, and a front and back yard. I viewed it as my starter home and figured one day I would get married, move to the beach, and raise children. I had fallen in love with Johnnie, and finally felt those feelings I had not experienced in other relationships. We had an easy-going relationship, but perhaps too easy-going. Johnnie was young and still needed time to figure out his future. He was attending college at Ole Miss in Oxford, but after his stint in the Marines, he had no clear direction. I mentioned to him that if he ever had thoughts of getting married, to not spring a ring on me, but for us to discuss it first. On New Year's Eve after ringing in the year on the Mariner III, a classic 122-foot yacht, he pulled a ring out of his tuxedo pocket as he was pulling the car into his parents' driveway. I was speechless as the family rushed out to congratulate us on our engagement. The ring was his grandmother's, and it did not fit. No wedding date was set. The words my father had said about not putting a ring on my finger unless I was sure I wanted to walk down aisle still resonated, and

My new home in 1993

My new cat to go in my new home

the ring sat on my dresser to be sized later. However, I was engaged for the second time.

By 1994, I was running the show at Gulf Coast Coors. Daddy rarely came to the office, and I could tell he was no longer interested in the business. I was making sure that he received his monthly salary of $6,250, or $75,000 a year, no matter if something else had to give. He had worked hard at building this company, and it was time that he enjoyed his retirement years. He loved to say with pride, "My daughter signs all the paychecks, including mine!" Daddy had entertained the idea of selling the business, as he was looking for total financial security. We had a few people look, but no real serious buyers. We hired a beer consultant, Chuck Parisher, who would keep us abreast of industry changes, advise us about our company operations, and let us know if someone was looking for a beer distributorship. Daddy said he wanted to be a millionaire – even though Coors was a multi-million dollar sales operation – but he wanted a million dollars in the bank, even if it was for a day.

One evening we were talking about how much we could sell Gulf Coast Coors for, and Daddy seemed convinced it was worth only a few hundred thousand dollars. I tried to convince him it was worth much more – so he said that whatever I could get over a million dollars was mine. I wished I had put that in writing. But as we explored the value, Daddy assured me that I would get a nice part of a sale for doing so much for him at the company. It would be my "golden parachute." The term came from a book about compensation called *What Color Is Your Parachute?* Although my salary had gone up since starting, it was certainly not comparable to the average business executive VP, and not even close to his salary. He was completely aware that I had turned this company around and was pleased with how things were going. I would be rewarded in the end and was patient.

He and Mama were traveling a lot, and I felt good that they were able to spend so much time together after spending many of their married years apart. They even took me on a few trips. We all traveled well together, with no stressful arguments or competing for different agendas. Daddy liked having a daughter he could talk to as a friend and adult, and we would stay up late and philosophize about life and discuss politics and current events. In May 1994, Daddy was asked to give a speech in San Antonio, Texas. The three of us, Mama, Daddy and me, drove over in our navy blue high-roof van that we used to travel to brewery conventions. My father gave an outstanding speech that brought the house down. He seemed to have a knack at reading and relating to crowds. It was one of the best speeches of his lifetime and was one of the few times he talked emotionally about the space flight and what the journey meant to him, seeing our world from approximately a quarter of a million miles away.

Our friends, Bert and Brigitte Klineburger, lived in San Antonio, along with hunting buddies who had ranches there. Bert spontaneously organized a turkey hunt at the ranch of Stan Studer, a Shikar-Safari member. The base camp was typical, with a few rustic cabins with bunk beds or twin beds in the rooms, a central kitchen/dining area, and in this particular camp, the Studers had added a cantina-type building, complete with designer-placed cobwebs to make it look like a scene from a South-of-the-border-style movie set. There was a full saloon bar and an authentic jukebox in the corner. We made up words to songs sung in Spanish. One of our favorites was to sing, "Pancho… Pancho Lopez… King of the Wild Frontier!" instead of Davy Crockett. Bert drank Cuba Libres (rum and coke with a lime) and I drank them right along with him. Bert had made my first Cuba Libre back in the day, and it was nostalgic that night drinking them again and telling huntin' stories.

The next morning, Daddy got up before anyone else to turn on the heat. The cabins were cold, and my bed was warm, and it was tough to leave those cozy confines. Since we were not prepared to go hunting, our clothes were definitely not all camouflage, but we managed with layers of sweaters and tops. As we stretched and prepared for the hunt, one in the morning and one in the evening, the muscles loosened up, and the brain engaged. Hunting turkeys is not easy. Turkeys have great hearing and eyesight. Brigitte lent me her old-fashioned bolt shotgun, which meant the turkey needed to be fairly close before attempting to shoot at it. Daddy always hunted with me, so Mama was placed in a blind by herself. After the morning hunt, Mama was now the proud recipient of a nice-sized turkey. She stayed in for the evening hunt and suggested we use her spot, as she had seen a lot of game, including deer and other wild animals.

Bert dropped us off around 4 p.m., and Daddy and I hiked into the blind. It was not large, so Daddy sat on the floor, and I sat on the stool. He had brought along two beers to sip on. After he drank a beer, he fell asleep. Staying still and quiet was the name of the game. I kept a sharp eye out, and right before dusk, I saw two large male turkeys coming down a dirt road toward the blind. I turned and tapped on Daddy's shoulder. He perked up and whispered to me to get my gun ready. That good ol' huntin' adrenaline kicked in. Since he was on the floor and could not see through the slits in the blind, he said to let him know when I was about to pull the trigger so that he could cover his ears. I got the gun ready and looked down the road. The turkeys were gone. Dang it. They were far away but must have seen or heard something that made them go into the woods. I looked back at Daddy with disappointment. He said to keep looking. After about 20 minutes, as daylight was beginning to dwindle, I saw two large turkeys walking away from me on another road 90 degrees from the first road. The turkeys had cut into the woods and out onto the other road, with their backs to me. I had to move fast. Daddy knelt up and saw them too.

"Which one do I take?" I whispered.

He replied, "The one on the right looks slightly bigger, but they are both great turkeys. Aim and take your shot at either one."

I looked down the barrel and lined up on the body of the turkey on the right. Deep breath in… and out… deep breath in… and let half out… hold it. Bam! The turkey on the left instantly ran into the woods. Did I get it? Can I see it? Where is it? My mind swirled from the blast and recoil of the gun in my shoulder.

"You got it!" Daddy exclaimed as he started to crawl out of the blind. I looked down the road, and there it was on the ground. As we ran up to it, we saw that it was huge! It was over 18 pounds and had an almost 12-inch "beard." The beard is the long string of coarse, dark hair that hangs from the turkey's neck. Anything over eight inches is highly respectable. Anything

Daddy, Bert Klineburger, and my big ol' turkey

over 10 inches is getting into trophy size. Daddy shook my hand, as hunters do when they are successful. He pulled out the remaining beer and gave me the first sip in congratulations.

"We will freeze the turkey for the holidays," he commented. However, since the shot was taken from the back of the body to the front, the breast plate was full of shotgun pellets. No wild game per the Roosa family tradition this year. Perhaps it was a sign that the upcoming holidays were about to be nothing like I expected. But that night at the camp, Daddy prepared the beautiful plume of the tail and beard for mounting, and we drank champagne to celebrate.

Daddy and me in San Antonio

CHAPTER 9

Final Flight

In August 1994, the Association of Space Explorers, ASE, was holding a meeting in Russia and were inviting astronauts to attend. A new policy dictated that an astronaut could bring only one companion. Since I had attended the 30th anniversary of Yuri Gagarin in 1991, Daddy was determined to get me back there with Mama. The American side held firm to its rule of only two people. He approached the Russians, who were intrigued by this man who was so determined to bring his daughter. I think Daddy just liked the challenge. I received an invitation. I had heard that the Russians like Eddie Bauer clothing, so as a thank you, I bought an Eddie Bauer down jacket for the Russian general who invited me.

My father had grown to enjoy the trips with the Association of Space Explorers, but it did not start out that way. His first trip was in the late '80s, and he traveled alone. While at a luncheon, he sat next to two cosmonauts who did not speak English. Daddy was polite, smiled, and said, "Have some mashed potatoes, you son-of-a-bitch," and passed the bowl. Then he would nicely offer them water while nodding, smiling, and saying, "Water, you bastard?" When Daddy told me the story, I was incredulous.

"You did not say that, did you?"

"I sure did!" he said proudly. My father had fought hard to beat the Soviet Union into space, and it is difficult to change a tiger's stripes.

However, my mother, being reasonable, said, "Stuart, if you don't participate in these meetings, then how can your voice be heard? The group should hear your conservative side." Then Daddy started to enjoy the encounters and the conversation, and soon he was taking Mama with him on trips. Now, once again, he wanted me along, too.

This time we stayed in Moscow, and it was just as fascinating the second time around. The Russians were treating us to the best of the best with parties at the Kremlin. Entering the gates into the Kremlin was like entering a monastery. It was serene, with gardens and cathedrals with the onion-like domes made of gold. Inside was a huge cannon and the largest bell in existence, the "Tsar Bell." On one building, the letters CCCP, for USSR, had been removed, but the outline was still visible. By now the astronauts and cosmonauts were "old friends," toasting with vodka and enjoying each other's company. It is hard to say who was with the Russian group, but I am sure the KGB were around and listening. Oftentimes there was a cameraman recording faces and events. As the camera would pass, I would smile and wave like I was on TV. The cameraman started calling me "cinema star" when he would zoom in on me.

On this trip, we were to see the sights in Moscow and then travel to Siberia to visit Lake Baikal, the largest freshwater lake in the world. Everyone was responsible for hauling his or her own luggage, a point we weren't aware of prior to packing. Since Daddy did not want Mama handling her own bags, he started carrying his and hers, while I dragged my own. When we arrived at the airport to fly to Siberia, Daddy instructed Mama to go ahead and secure three seats on the charter plane while we figured out where to put the luggage. Mama was smart and headed to the front, the first-class area close to the cockpit. The flight crew was excited to have such an elite group on their flight, and one of the stewards boasted that the plane was one of Aeroflot's newest airplanes. The crew were eager to show us as much hospitality as possible. The mood was festive, and the vodka flowed. After a bit, somehow the crew got word that I was a pilot, and the next thing you know I was in the cockpit, sitting on the pilot's lap in the left seat! They wanted me to fly it on my own, but I kept telling them that I was qualified for only single-engine land. They laughed with glee, and I wondered if they had been hitting the vodka, too. I wanted out of there, for I did not

Entering into the
Kremlin in Moscow

Russian church inside the Kremlin walls

Russian cannon to protect the Kremlin

want the possibility of flying a new Aeroflot jet with famous astronauts and Twice-Heroes of the Soviet Union into the ground. Finally, everyone settled down for the long flight to the Eastern Front.

The plane got quiet as we flew in the darkness to Siberia. In the middle of night, the plane needed to stop for refueling. After the plane landed, the cabin door opened, and a few people descended the portable steps. The steps were pulled away, leaving the door open with the ground 20 feet below. I got up to stretch my legs and peered out. The night was pitch black. No lights were shining from anywhere, so it seemed this was not a public airport with any towns nearby. I liked to follow my flying on maps, so I asked the crew to show me where we landed in relation to Moscow. I wanted to see where we were and where we were going. My asking this simple question caused a stir and quiet whispers from the Russians. I simply kept asking, "Where are we, and is it that difficult to answer?" The Russians do not like to lose face, so a flurry of activity ensued. I was wondering why it took so long to refuel, too, for our wait was going on 45 minutes to an hour, and we were the only plane on the tarmac.

Then out of nowhere a flight sectional was placed in front of me, and a Russian pointed, "You are here. We are in this part of our country."

I started to look over the map to get a perspective, and the Russian kept wanting to divert my eyes back to the spot he initially pointed. "You are here, here!" he said sternly but almost frantically.

"Ok, Ok, spasiba," (thank you) I said calmly, not having time to make heads or tails of the map before it was taken away.

Years later, I found out through Tom Stafford, who flew with the Russians in Apollo-Soyuz, that we were at a secret military base where many nuclear rockets were located, ready to hit the United States if launched in a first strike. Stafford also said the delay was due to the Russians pulling him off the plane to drink vodka with the top brass and military generals at the base. I realize now that the Russians did not want me to know where we were and deliberately misled me on the map. They could not figure out who I was, perhaps a spy working secretly with the U.S. government.

"You must be important," said the general to whom I gave the Eddie Bauer jacket, "for why did your father work so hard to have his daughter on this trip?"

Little did they know it was simply an experience that Daddy wanted to share with me.

The plane refueled, and after dinner and more vodka, we settled in again. Daddy was sitting next to me. Mama fell asleep, and the plane got quiet. Daddy started talking about religion and talked about destiny vs. choice. He asked me if I thought Judas had a choice or was just destined to be the one to turn in Christ, for Christ had prophesied that he would be betrayed.

"Do you think Judas went to Heaven or Hell?" he asked.

I did not know what to say, having not thought deeply about it. The afterworld was weighing heavily on his mind.

He talked about how things would be after his death, and I kept telling him, "Daddy, you are too young to die! You're only 60 years old and have spent your life being in shape!"

But he went on talking. He was in a serious, pondering mood, so I listened. He started to tell me about the Apollo 1 fire, and I could tell it was painful for him to discuss.

He was struggling with his feelings, and I finally said, "Daddy, you don't have to talk about this. Let's get some sleep." The fire and his initial thoughts were bothering his soul, but I shut him down. I wish now I had let him keep talking.

We got to Siberia in the morning and landed in a place called Irkutsk. We were back to hauling luggage. He struggled; I struggled, but we managed. We eventually boarded two speed boats on Lake Baikal and were told that we were going to have an afternoon lunch at a little village about two or three hours away. The vodka and beer flowed again, and everyone was jovial. Then three hours turned into four, then five, then six. Darkness descended on the lake, and we all wondered when we were going to get there. The boat kept speeding along, but our destination was elusive. Finally, around 10 p.m., we arrived at a tiny village. This was the biggest happening in the

Landing in Siberia after our long flight from Moscow

Drinking beer in speedboat on Lake Baikal

village in 100 years, and everyone greeted us, from the young to the old. They had prepared their finest, although it was humble food. Everyone got their second wind, and vodka toasts ensued. We ate, drank, and toasted, then without fanfare, the Russians stood up and said, "Let's go!" Everyone started to march out to awaiting buses, but Mama did the sweetest thing. She flagged down one of the translators and asked him to take her to the kitchen. I tagged along to see where she was going. Mama went to every person in the kitchen, shook his or her hand and thanked all of them for having such a lovely dinner. She told them that she knew how difficult it was to prepare for such a large group, and she wanted to personally thank the cooks and helpers. They were ecstatic.

The women wanted to use the ladies' room before boarding the buses to take us to the hotel. There was only one toilet, and the line started to back up. Everyone was ready to get to the hotel, so a young local woman motioned at me to come with her. I thought she was going to take us to her home to use the bathroom, so I grabbed Mama's arm and said, "Let's follow her." She had an Asian look and graceful gestures. She did not speak English. She led us down a well-worn path. I thought that we were going to bypass the long line at the toilet and be on the bus before you could say "sleep." We suddenly stopped. Which house were we to go in? I looked confused, and she gracefully raised her arms toward something. I was not sure where to go. She walked towards a large old tree and acted like she was squatting. She wanted us to go at the tree! We had no toilet paper or tissue, and I thought then that we should have waited patiently in line, but we went, and the young woman seemed pleased.

The bus ride was another eternity. We were deep in the mountains, but we could not see a thing. There were no lights and no moon. Our translators talked about how beautiful the woods and trees were, but we could not even see our hands outstretched in front of us. The heat was not working on the bus, and I had only a light jacket. It was cold. Really cold. If someone had been sitting by me, I would have cuddled up for heat and pardoned myself, but I was on my own. After about an hour or so into the bus ride, someone had to go to the bathroom, and the bus stopped. The translators warned those who got off to stay directly behind the bus, as we were in the steep mountains. There were no railings, and if someone fell off the edge, it could be fatal. I stayed on the bus and shivered. Finally around 3 a.m., we pulled into a town called Ulan-Ude and checked into a hotel. We were exhausted. By now we had been going over 40 hours almost non-stop with only catnaps in-between the various modes of transportation and drinking. I was given the key to a small room with one twin bed. As I was getting my toothbrush and a t-shirt out of my luggage, someone from the hotel staff knocked on my door. The staffer had brought me a small cup of tea. The warmth was soothing. It was nice being back in "civilization." Mama and Daddy were in a room down the hall, and Mama decided to take a bath. She got the only hot water in the hotel. The Russians proceed with schedules, no matter what, and a few hours later, someone knocked at the door to wake everyone up for the day's events. People tried to take showers, but the water was ice cold. I looked out my hotel window to see a large, bronze head of Lenin. It had to be at least three stories tall. It dwarfed the houses next to it.

The day was festive, and as the astronauts and cosmonauts proceeded to various official locations for speeches, their companions were about to be treated to a special event. We arrived at a building decorated with colored silk drapery and oriental carpets. The center of the room had a catwalk of sorts, with table and chairs at each side. We enjoyed course after course of flavorful dishes, and then, in Russian an announcement was made. Suddenly gorgeous women walked into the room, and one by one, they started walking down the catwalk like it was fashion week in London, Paris, or Rome. Each had an exquisite and detailed outfit. One tall and lean model with slightly Asian features walked out like she was a supermodel from New York. She was stunning and wore a sheer top with no bra. It was all avant-garde and haute-couture. I was shaking my head in wonder at this jaw-dropping event. "Was I really in Siberia? The land of banishment?" Later that evening, we were invited to a concert. Again, it was like being in a cosmopolitan city. The room had a ceiling painted like the Sistine Chapel and it was if the Boston symphony were performing. I looked at the Russian cosmonauts; many of them were asleep during the performance. I sensed that the Siberian people, although under the communist regime, had decided to build a fine culture for themselves out in no-where-ville.

We headed back to the hotel for a night of heavy hors d'oeuvre and vodka. Surprisingly, there was champagne — my favorite! As I was sipping on a decent-tasting glass of champagne, my thoughts were, "Here I am, just a small-town girl from Mississippi, and now I am in Siberia, a far-off and exotic land. Thank you, Daddy." It must have been similar to how Mama must have felt at the White House when Richard Nixon was holding her chair. About then two other astronauts' children (whose mothers stayed at home to give them a spot on the trip) walked up, and I spontaneously said, "Isn't this great? Just think, we are in *Siberia*! All because our fathers flew in space."

One of the children said, "Well, I don't know about you, but I think we are a little f#%!k'd up because of it." Whoa. My brain was not on that wavelength. The Program affected families in different ways, for it was not easy having pioneer fathers. The three of us thought about getting a bottle of champagne and talking about it, but as we looked around the room, we saw not only American kids, but also children of cosmonauts.

"Let's have a party tomorrow night, only us kids of parents who went into space," I suggested, adding: "No astronauts or cosmonauts allowed." Word spread quickly.

The next day was a "free day" with no official duties for the space travelers. We had a choice: 1) visit a folk festival similar to a county fair, or 2) visit a local healing and medical center. Mama and Daddy chose the first, but I was intrigued with Eastern medicine and practices and chose the latter. Our bus took us to the country to a building near a field of strange-looking plants. The tour was slow and thorough, like an exam. The guide explained that the doctors first take the time to understand the patient's lifestyle. Were there troubles at home? Was there a change in diet? What factors might play into a physical ailment? From there we toured an apothecary-type room that held homeopathic remedies. We sniffed and sampled the herbs and crushed plants and listened to an explanation of the healing powers that lie within their touch and taste. Massage rooms awaited to cleanse the chakra and bring harmony and balance to the inner workings. Then we saw the pharmacy, where pills were distributed. And finally, we visited the operating room, where if all else failed, minor surgery could be conducted. Major surgery had to be done in the city. It was fascinating, for at the time in the U.S., a person saw specialists. I had a specialist for my cat allergies, an ob-gyn, a dermatologist, a dentist, and whoever else I needed for a particular ailment. This was revolutionary to me, to treat a person as a whole.

We gathered at the hotel for dinner. Meals were strange at this hotel. We would have eggs for dinner and hot dogs for breakfast. We could tell when we had lunch, for soup was served. We knew when we were having dinner, for vodka was served. Time was irrelevant. There was a schedule, and nothing was being removed from it except sleep. By now the kids had gotten word of our planned gathering, and some of the astronauts were offended that a party was in the making, and they were not included. Around midnight, we gathered in a dimly lit room with a white tile dance floor. Someone had found a disco ball, another some music. There were about 12 or 15 or so of us younger ones from both the Russian and U.S. side. It was a jovial feeling, but my shyness surfaced when things began to take on the aura of a school dance. I sat down at a table. An interpreter's father sat next to me.

"What are you doing here? No parents!" I said, as he took a chair. His name was Leonid, and I was convinced he was more than an interpreter, but KGB. His daughter was on the trip as an interpreter, and she helped when the Russian and American wives wanted to communicate. Leonid said to me in almost aristocratic English, "I must keep an eye on my daughter."

The vodka was flowing by now. I was tired and wasn't sure how to break into the group, so we started chatting. "Tell me about how you became a space interpreter," I asked curiously, twirling my shot glass full of warm vodka.

I expected him to be tight lipped with the standard ops stuff, but he was genuinely open. His parents had both been educated, and he came from a well-off family. However, as communism took hold, he was placed in an orphanage. I gathered he never saw his family again and imagined they had been killed.

Leonid did not act superior or arrogant but was sophisticated. He was a rarity, for enlightenment and sophistication seemed squelched under the "we are all equal" doctrine of the USSR. During school, he had high marks and wanted to be a scientist. That led to his working on scientific experiments in space. As Leonid paused in conversation to eye his daughter, I took a swig of vodka, and thought I would be funny. I blurted, "Are you sure you're not Spetsnaz?"

"Well, Rosemary," Leonid looked back at me in all seriousness, "I was training to be one; however, I did not pass the physical tests." I gulped. They really did exist! Spetsnaz may sure enough be everywhere! Leonid's daughter was no longer in his line of sight, so he excused himself politely and left. I was stunned.

Morning came, and I could take a little time to get ready, for the astronauts and cosmonauts had a local event near the giant head of Lenin. I peered out my window and saw them on stage. I dressed and went down for breakfast: beef stroganoff. As I was sitting alone picking at the noodles, Daddy came and sat with me. I was surprised to see him away from the group.

"How was last night?" he asked. I told him about Leonid's shocking Spetsnaz comment.

"Ah," Daddy said, "that would explain it then."

"What?" I asked.

Daddy said when he came down for breakfast that Leonid came up to him and said, "I now understand your interests."

Shortly thereafter, Leonid introduced Daddy to a huge man in uniform.

"This man is Spetsnaz. He will protect you."

My father shook his hand and nodded, not showing any reaction. Daddy was good at going with the flow. At the Lenin head, as the speeches droned on in Russian, Daddy said he got bored and decided to come back to the hotel. He was trying to sneak away undetected, but the Spetsnaz man followed him, like a bodyguard. My father could not figure it out and tried to ditch him, but to no avail.

"He is in the lobby now," Daddy said.

We both laughed as I finished my stroganoff.

"I would like to meet him."

Daddy walked me to this man who looked like Jaws from the James Bond movies. All that was missing was the steel teeth. He had muscles upon muscles and was a giant in black military boots and a uniform. He shook my hand, probably not knowing why either, and Daddy pointed at a patch on his arm. Sure enough, I could make out "Spetsnaz" and something to the effect of "Special Forces" in Russian.

Next we visited a Tibetan temple, the only one remaining in Siberia, for during World War II, the locals here were instrumental in helping fight the war. We were not far from Mongolia, and the religion had made its way from Asia. Although religion in all forms had been banned under communism, it was now 1994, and religion was slowly resurfacing. My father said for many years to cover all bases — meaning to light incense or throw a lotus flower in the river — when visiting religious places. Although a Christian and Catholic, he said, "What if God is Buddha? Best to at least tip your hat in courtesy."

The Tibetan religion believes in reincarnation. This one was a little harder for Daddy to swallow. "What if you are a good slug?" Daddy turned to me and asked, half joking, half serious. Would you say, "I left a mighty good slime trail today!" He chuckled to himself.

But as with all religions, I try to tune in to the vibe… the spirit… the love. And this place, way out in the middle of nowhere, had a very peaceful feeling. The monks graciously took us on a tour of their brightly colored temple. They were quite hopeful the Dalai Lama would visit them one day soon, and they would be ready.

It was time to head back to Moscow. When we first arrived in Siberia, our passports had been collected. This made me nervous. The trip had been great, but after what we had heard of wayward Russians being sent to Siberia, the place of doom and gloom – I wanted to make sure we were not going to live out the rest of our days here either. We arrived at the airport and getting through security took a while. It was tense. I have learned throughout the years to not mess around when going through checkpoints and with border

Daddy, Mama, and me outside a Tibetan temple in Siberia

Inside the temple, adorned with colorful silks and fabrics,
hoping for a visit from the Dali Lama

patrol. They have the power, so do not give them any cause to delay or retain unnecessarily, particularly in a foreign land where freedoms and rights are not the same as in the United States. After a couple of hours, and after our entry papers were scrutinized, we boarded the chartered Aeroflot plane and headed back to the capital city.

Our final night in Moscow was August 16. It was Daddy's birthday, and he was turning 61. Since I was born July 23, 1963, he was almost exactly 30 years older. It was an easy way for me to remember his age. However, Daddy at times had a hard time remembering his own age. While giving a speech once, he was answering technical questions about how much thrust was generated at lift-off with the Saturn V rocket and how many pounds of fuel were used during the first stage, and so on, when out of the crowd, someone asked how old he was. "I am 47, next question." Daddy said quickly. After doing the math, I realized he was only 43 at the time. "I don't like those hard questions," he said later, shaking his head and laughing about it.

The Russians had a festive farewell, featuring circus acts, including a show with cats jumping on command from one birch to another. Having had cats, I thought getting them to act on command was a great feat. The vodka and champagne flowed again, and Daddy was given a gift of a bell, the symbol of this ASE's trip, as a birthday present. He looked tired as he accepted it under the spotlights. The trip had been grueling. He sat down at the table, and I decided to go say my farewells to the group. We had all bonded on this trip, and if you ask any astronaut today who had been on the trip, that person will remember it like yesterday. It was memorable in many ways, and each will have a story about it.

I returned to the table, and Daddy said in an excited tone, "Where were you? I was looking for you!"

"Oh no, I am sorry… I was off saying goodbye to everyone," I said.

He looked disappointed. "You missed him." Daddy said, and then continued, "He could have done it. He could have pulled it off." I was not sure what he was talking about. "He even gave me a watch for my birthday," Daddy said as he pulled out an inexpensive watch.

Daddy arm in arm with Leonid, while
Mama and I toast to our Russian hosts

Daddy receiving a gift of a bell for his birthday, August 16, 1994

"Who? Who did I miss?" I asked, feeling like I had missed meeting someone important.

"The man who had his finger on the button. The one who could have pulled off a first strike," Daddy said, still disappointed I did not get to meet him, "And he could have done it too," referring to the confidence and power the man must have exuded.

"Where is he?" I asked, searching around the room frantically.

"Gone now," Daddy said, and explained that Leonid had brought him by the table. After the Spetsnaz incident, Leonid must have figured Daddy needed to meet him, too. After all these years of Daddy and me saying the Russians could not have not done it, Daddy was now convinced they could have. No doubt in his mind. I regret not staying by Daddy's side that night.

• • •

We returned to Mississippi, and I returned to my home. I started thinking about how grateful I was about my life. In Russia, this house would have at least three families living in it. Life was going well for me, for I was running a multi-million-dollar company, had a home and a nice car, and a fiancé. Fall was approaching, and the holidays were coming up. In October, we prepared for our annual Halloween party. Halloween was my favorite holiday. Even as a little girl, I liked to have Halloween parties and once made a haunted house in the garage in El Lago, complete with a laboratory with grapes as eyeballs and spaghetti for brains. When I moved back home in 1988, I asked if we could have a Halloween party, and my parents got into it. They would invite their friends, and I would invite mine, so it was a nice mix of ages. Costumes were mandatory, not optional. All three of us would create a cute poem for the invitation, and Daddy and I would start decorating the house about a couple of weeks out.

Mama and Daddy had traveled to New England one year and saw that in the fall, storefronts would put out a "pumpkin-head" – a type of scarecrow that looked like a person with a painted pumpkin face. Mama would paint the face of the pumpkin, and Daddy and I would stuff the

Mama as Elvis for Halloween, with Daddy as Col. Parker
(Elvis' agent), and me as Pricilla Presley

Mr. Pumpkin Head by the pool drinking Coors Light on Halloween night

body. We used hunting boots for the feet, added corduroy pants and a plaid shirt for the body, and topped the pumpkin head off with a straw hat. We would stuff it with dry cleaning bags and attach garden gloves at the end of the shirt sleeves to look like hands. Daddy found it amusing to put a Coors Light beer can in one hand and a golf club in the other. It sat outside overlooking the pool with the golf course in the background, and it looked real. We hung bats, spider webs, witches and brooms, and put a Zorro mask on one of the animal heads in the house. Mama made chili and other Tex-Mex food and had Halloween candy for dessert. By this time, we had accumulated a bunch of decorations, and Daddy put out dry ice to give the entryway a spooky feel. For the party, he even decided that he would put a real beer by "Mr. Pumpkin Head" – and that he would periodically go out during the evening and dump some out, so that someone might think Pumpkin Man was really drinking it! The guests knew that no one without a costume was allowed entry, so people really got into it. Some of the older folks would have elaborate costumes like a "cereal" killer (a cereal box with a knife in it), a "card shark" (a shark with playing cards attached), and one couple dressed as a flower and bee. They laughed that their daughter had warned them when leaving the house, "Don't pollinate Mama in public!"

Some party goers would wear masks and make people wonder their identity until they got tired, wanted a drink, and removed the mask. I always dressed as a brunette and had been Elvira, Cleopatra, a black cat, and Scarlett O'Hara, but this year, Mama decided to go as Elvis. Daddy was Col. Parker, his agent, and I was Priscilla Presley with the '60s bouffant hair. My cousin, Gloria, loved to play on words, and she came dressed in a black leotard, a lamp shade on her head, and a "table" strapped around her with two champagne glasses and an ashtray with cigarette butts glued to it. She was a "one-night stand." Everyone had a blast, and the evening was filled with laughter and pranks. It was the fall party to attend, and our guest list was exclusive, not because we wanted to particularly exclude anyone, but because we had limited space and food. People would start asking around late summer if they were on the list, saying that they needed time to think of a costume.

In early November 1994, Corona was having its convention in Mexico. Each brewery had conventions and attendance was mandatory. It proved that the distributor was committed to its brands. I used to call them "pep rallies," as the breweries would show their latest commercials and marketing strategies, and in general, hype one up to get out there and sell their brands. At every Corona convention there was a chili cook-off. Mama had won it the first year but felt that now the blue ribbon went to the largest contributor to the local orphanage and was not really about having the best chili. We set up a chili booth anyway and decorated it with Corona paraphernalia. Mama decided to have fun with it and brought down her Elvis costume from Halloween. The booths were set up around the pool, and there was a DJ. Shortly before the judging, Mama went back to the room to get dressed in her white silk outfit, blue suede shoes, large gold belt and cape, and to slick back her dark brown hair. She asked me to help her to glue on the sideburns. I did, and then left to go speak to the DJ about playing an Elvis song, *"You Ain't Nothin' But a Hound Dog,"* as Mama strolled up to the pool. When the DJ saw her coming, he shouted above the noisy beer drinkin' crowd, "We have a special visitor here today at our chili contest! All the way from Mississippi… Elvis Presley!" And he started the music. Mama danced her way up to the pool area, jerking her knee on occasion, and curling her lip. Suddenly everyone ran up to her and started taking pictures! A couple that happened to be at the hotel with their baby shoved the child into her hands and said, "One day we want to show our daughter that she met Elvis!" People started asking Mama for her autograph, and she was taken aback. She had done it just as a joke, but she said people started treating her as if she were the real Elvis Presley!

Sure enough, Mama's chili was the first to run out, and everyone talked about how good it tasted, but she did not win the prize. The next day Mama and Daddy went deep sea fishing, but I opted to sleep in and piddle around the hotel. About mid-afternoon, Mama and Daddy came back. Daddy's face was red as a tomato, and he did not look good. I thought it was sunburn, but he was weak and shaky. He said he needed to rest, but that he had been successful and reeled in a big Marlin. It was a fighter and took him about two hours to bring it in, without help from the crew. Mama said she told him, "Stuart, it's not worth dying over." But knowing Daddy, he was going to get that fish one way or another. He was not a quitter.

Later that evening we went to dinner at an elegant restaurant called *Bogart's*. It was fashioned after the Casablanca movie, with large straw fans and palm trees. The lighting was dark with a purple hue, and the tables were mahogany. The maître d' placed us at a round booth with soft leather backing, and a waiter immediately came and placed a round cushion under the women's feet. I have not experienced that before, and it was a nice change of pace from the beer drinking and casual dining from the convention.

Daddy made it a habit to not compare us children to each other. He loved us each in our own way, and I was not made to feel inferior to the brothers. Daddy was not a *"Great Santini"* (as in Pat Conroy's memoir about his harsh military father) nor a male chauvinist. As Daddy's youngest child and only daughter, I learned right alongside the boys, and Daddy called us "The Troops." But saying that one child was better at something was generally not his style.

This night at *Bogart's*, Daddy was in a reflective mood, and he told me he wanted to tell me something. I looked at him solemnly, and he said, "Out of all the children, Rosemary, you are the best natural pilot. When flying you anticipate when to push in the throttle, when to pull back, and you have a great sense of feel about the airplane — better than the boys." I was stunned.

One of my brothers used to brag about his flying skills and how much Daddy thought he was the greatest pilot. I guess I believed him, but thought it was strange when my brother once asked if Daddy ever yelled at me in the airplane.

I said, "Nooooo…. has he with you?"

He laughingly said, "Yea, one time Daddy said, *'Get your head out of your ass, or your ass out of the cockpit!'*"

I told him Daddy had not once raised his voice to me in the airplane. My brother looked puzzled. Another brother had graduated from the Air Force Academy and had become an F-16 pilot. I just presumed he was the best pilot out of us kids. But Daddy wanted me to know his opinion about this, and coming from an astronaut and my father, it was high praise. These were the best words that he ever spoke to me. Later when I would hear my brothers brag again about their piloting skills, I would just smile and remember Daddy's words.

For Thanksgiving, we drove to Washington, D.C., to visit my oldest brother. He and I had essentially swapped places, and when I moved back to Mississippi in 1988, he moved to D.C. and got a job working on Capitol Hill. Daddy had not been feeling well on the drive up. My father hid physical ailments, not wanting to admit them – going back to his flying days. I could tell he was in pain, though. On the drive, we talked about the return trip. Daddy had made reservations at the famous Callaway Gardens in Georgia, for he wanted me to see the Christmas lights. Since I was "Daddy's little helper" each year with the big colored bulbs, he said this would be a treat for the eyes and would put us in the holiday spirit. Callaway Gardens was well-known for its Christmas extravaganza every year, and I was excited about driving through the decorations. It was a tradition of ours to drive through neighborhoods and look at the lights. Daddy would get a few beers; Mama would get some wine, and I would drink a little cheer, too. But when we arrived in Arlington, Virginia, Daddy was cringing in pain and grabbing at his stomach.

On our second night, I went and spent the night with Cristi, a pal from El Lago and the NASA days. After her father, Jim McQueen, left NASA where he analyzed lab work, he took a job with the CDC, Center for Disease Control, and was working on rare and strange diseases. Cristi's parents divorced a few years after the move, but the family remained in Maryland. Cristi's mother, Shirley, and Mama were also great friends, and Shirley was Mama's campaign manager when Mama ran for state legislator in Texas. It was a fun night reminiscing with Cristi, and she told me about her nursing career. The next day I returned to see Daddy in a lot of pain. "Why don't you at least go get a pain shot, so that you will feel better for Thanksgiving Day," I suggested, expecting "no" for an answer. He hesitated – and actually thought about it. This is when a pang ran though my stomach. Something must be terribly wrong. After not too much coaxing, the next morning he agreed to the shot. My oldest brother found a nearby medical center, and we took Daddy to the emergency room.

The doctors ran some tests and immediately admitted him to the hospital. He had a serious case of pancreatitis. They put needles in his arm and started pumping him with who knows what. "Wait," I thought, this was supposed to be an in-and-out trip. I wondered what was going on. On the first night, Daddy pulled out the needles and said he wanted to leave. The doctor threatened my mother, saying he could force him to stay, and the doc strapped my father down. The nurses gave him Ativan, and it made Daddy feel like he was on a cruise ship. He would say, "What deck am I on? I'm ready to go to my room now, please take me."

As soon as he would start to come off the drug, he would say, "Please do not give me that medicine. It makes me wacky."

So as the nurses came in, we would request that he not have that medicine, and they would reply, "Doctor's orders," and off on the cruise ship he would go.

My friend, Cristi, came to visit, and I asked her, "Is he going to die from this?"

She informed me that it was not likely, but he could, and that it was a very painful condition.

The doctors informed the family that Daddy would miss Thanksgiving dinner on November 24. Daddy told us to save some cornbread dressing for him. Since it was the holidays, doctors were coming and going, and there was not one point-person of whom to ask questions. Each doctor was prescribing different treatments, but after several days of touch and go, Daddy was feeling better and was sitting up in a chair. One doctor even asked if Daddy would come talk to his son's school about the Apollo mission when he got out of the hospital. I was relieved, for guilt was upon me for recommending that he get a pain shot in the first place.

Then another doctor prescribed Ensure to help get nutrients in Daddy's system. It was painful for Daddy to drink it, but we, the family, insisted. Each sip seemed to hurt his body, but we all said, "Drink it, Daddy! It is good for you!" Several hours later Daddy was in severe pain, and by now another doctor was on duty. The new doctor said adding fluids to an inflamed pancreas was the worst thing to do and ordered a tube down his throat to pull it back up. The doctor described his condition like a sunburn. It has to heal. Food and fluids make all the other organs work, too, to process the intake, thus causing the pain stemming from the pancreas excreting the juices to start the break-down process. Gall bladder issues ran in the family, but Daddy was a fighter pilot and an astronaut. All those years of training left him in good shape. He would pull out of this.

After the Thanksgiving weekend, it looked like it was going to be a slow recovery for Daddy. The beer company could not be ignored, and payroll was coming up soon. I booked a ticket home and planned to fly back up after about a week. It would give me time to square things away and then help with the drive home. The night before leaving, I decided to stay with Daddy for a few hours on my own to make sure he was comfortable. His throat hurt from the tube, and the nurse said he could have only chipped ice. Daddy wanted some ice cream. The nurse said, "We have frozen flavored water in a cup if he would like that instead." Perfect. I lowered the lights, and Daddy sat in a chair. I sat across the room with the hospital bed between us. He was weak, but he had an air of determination. We did not talk much, for it seemed to pain him to speak. I started to peruse a magazine when it dawned on me that Daddy was scraping and scraping at the frozen ice.

"Can I help you, Daddy?" I asked softly, looking up at him as he scraped the little wooden spoon over the ice.

"Here, I have this for you," he said proudly, and held up a semi-large pile of scraped ice toward the side of the cup.

"Daddy, you did that for me?" I asked, not sure why he would do that.

"Yes, I know you like ice cream," he said, looking at me lovingly, for he was a father who would do anything for his children.

"Oh Daddy, that is not for me, but is yours to eat!" I insisted. He seemed disappointed that I did not take it. He had worked so hard for me. It showed his soul.

I flew home and went back to work. My instinct was telling me that perhaps we should move Daddy to a bigger hospital. There were many top names in the D.C. area, including Walter Reed, Johns Hopkins, and others. I called every day and after several days started insisting that we move him.

"He is fine where he is," my brother would say, "And he is close by for us to check on him."

Daddy was still in the small hospital close to my brother's apartment, but his condition seemed to be getting worse, not better. After a busy week in Mississippi, I flew back. My other brothers flew in too. Daddy was now in an induced coma.

"When was this decision made?" I asked in surprise.

The doctor said it would help with the recovery if the patient was not conscious of the tubes and needles, and my mother had reluctantly agreed.

Seeing Daddy in this condition scared me. Tensions were building. The next day the doctor informed us there was nothing else he could do and to prepare for death. My head was spinning. It couldn't be. When I left Daddy he was in a chair... he wanted ice cream... he was supposed to give a speech at the doctor's son's school... he was going to recover... we had Christmas lights to see.... Suddenly my brother was on the phone to move him to a larger hospital.

We moved my father into the ICU of a larger hospital, but the situation was grim. His organs were shutting down, and his lungs were filling up with fluid. We started calling friends to let them know about the situation. One of the astronauts offered to call the other astronauts. Just in case, we started looking into funeral arrangements at Arlington National Cemetery. Daddy had filled out the paperwork there years before, which was helpful. It was now December and cold. After almost a week, Daddy was hanging on but still in a coma. Daddy loved gospel music, so I went to a Radio Shack and bought a portable CD player, then got a couple of CDs with a mix of old gospel tunes. I had heard that people in comas can hear and comprehend. On the evening of December 11 Mama was starting to consider taking Daddy off life support. Mama and Daddy had agreed long ago to not prolong a dire situation.

I decided to head to the hospital and check on Daddy's vitals and change out the gospel music. One of my brothers said he would go along. As we entered the ICU, the nurses were surprised. The hospital had visiting hours; however, we went in anyway. The TV in Daddy's area had been turned up and around to face the nurse's station, and one nurse was watching a late-night show that was blaring loudly. Irritated that they treated ICU patients this way, even if they were in a coma, I turned off the TV, closed the curtain, and quieted down the room. I stood by the side of the bed. I felt compelled to grab Daddy's hand. His eyes were closed. He looked pale. He was paralyzed by the induced coma and had a tube down his throat. As my brother left to talk to the nurses about Daddy's condition, my hand felt a momentary grip. Was that grip voluntary or involuntary? Had he mustered up enough will to let me know something? Leaning over the bed, I spontaneously said, "Daddy, it's your daughter. I want you to know that I love you very much."

Suddenly tears started welling up near the bridge of his nose. He heard me! I was so shocked that I immediately went to find my brother. "Look," I said, pointing at his eyes, which had small pools of water at the corner of each eyelid.

My brother started talking to him, telling him to hang on. He talked to him about the future. The water was receding. In my gut, I felt that he no longer wanted to hang on. He was ready to go. It was time. Daddy now felt distant. Looking at the headset, I put in a CD. One of the songs was about the Promised Land. It was not going to be long.

The boys stayed up most of the night, keeping vigil. I had crawled in bed with Mama. Right before daylight, the phone rang. No one was answering it. It kept ringing, so I got up and picked up the receiver. It was the hospital. "He is dying. Come now if you would like to see him," said the nurse.

"Wake up!" I yelled. Quickly getting Mama up, we dressed and grabbed the car keys. As we were about to turn the corner in the long hallway to the elevators, my oldest brother shouted down the hall for us to stop. "It is over, come back." Mama and I looked at each other in disbelief. We returned.

With no words, we all grabbed each other and hugged and sobbed. The dawn was breaking on the morning of December 12. Looking outside, we saw a streak in the sky going straight up. Daddy was number one on the runway. He was taking his final flight.

Stuart A. Roosa Funeral
Comments by Rosemary Roosa
December 1994 at Arlington Cemetery

When I think of my father – one word comes to mind – and that is love. Love for adventure, love of flying, love for his country, and most importantly, love for his family. He so deeply loved my mother, Joan, and gave us children everything he possible could. He lived such a unique life and was able to share with his family a unique bond. He also shared a special bond with many of you here today. And the fact that you are here shows the love he received in return.

My father taught me so many wonderful things, from hunting as a child, to flying as a teenager, to running a company as an adult. His trust and support in me was such a great feeling, and he always taught his family to strive for success, and to reach for the stars in our own way. Daddy was a generous, thoughtful, genuine human being who believed in living life full throttle. He never half-stepped anything he put his mind to – for he was an achiever, a true adventurer, and a great American.

Daddy taught us many things, but most of all he taught us that there was more to life than just wealth or fame, and that is true love. True love brings true happiness. And Daddy died a happy man, with lots of love around him, and with a sense of peace with himself, and with God.

He was a great man. Goodbye, Daddy. You will be greatly missed.

Chapter 10

Coors and Consolidation

The funeral at the Old Post Chapel and Arlington Cemetery was beyond moving. It was elegant, austere, honorable, and conducted with great military pageantry. Eighteen out of the twenty-four Apollo astronauts were in attendance, although three had already passed on, so almost all were there to honor Daddy. Alan Shepard conducted the eulogy. Charlie Duke did the Responsorial Psalms and the readings. My father used to say when he died, he had only a few requests that he would like honored. One was to play the songs he loved — *How Great Thou Art* and *Amazing Grace*. The other was to have a Missing Man formation fly-by. Other than that, we could bury him in a pine box. Mama picked a simple but elegant blue coffin, fitting for an Air Force career man, and we chose his full-dress military attire for burial. The music part was easy; the fly-by was more difficult. After we did some maneuvering and got in some high-level requests, F-15s were arranged to fly up from Langley, the base where Mama and Daddy had first met. It was fitting. The day was rainy and cloudy, and there was only a small window of opportunity to conduct a fly-by. Ronald Reagan National Airport had to halt flights for the F-15s to conduct the treetop fly over of the cemetery. The Air Force band strummed solemn music as the graveside ceremony took place. There was a 21-gun salute. The Under Secretary of the Air Force was in attendance along with several generals from the Pentagon. Friends and family had come from far and wide. I sat next to Mama, never far from her side. As she was handed the folded flag, suddenly there was a break in the weather. We could hear the jets soaring high above, waiting for the moment to zip in. Now was the time. The sound of the low roar became louder as the jets approached. The pilots came in fast, all four at once, then one went straight up. The other three zipped forward with the "missing man" now heading straight up for the heavens. Mama blurted out quietly, "Goodbye, Stuart." Tears burst from my eyes.

As my father's body lay in the casket, the family knew a secret. Before the casket was closed and sealed, the family had one last visitation. One of my brothers made sure Daddy's uniform was squared away and the medals were straight. Each of us kids had a private moment alone by the open casket. Then we pulled out a six-pack of Coors Light. We were giving Daddy one final toast. Then we came up with the idea that Daddy needed a beer, too, for his ride into the heavens. We put an unopened beer in the casket, next to his hand. As we drank our beers, we thought it might be funny to put an empty beer can by the other hand, so that if his body were ever exhumed, the examiners might think Daddy drank it!

Mama rented the Officers' Club for a post-burial reception, to thank all of those who had flown in from the corners of the world. The media was on hand at the graveside, and John Zarrella did a moving tribute on CNN. Some of the astronauts stayed for interviews, and Charlie Duke talked about losing his best friend. Our local television station interviewed some of the Gulf Coast Coors employees and aired a nice segment. *Time* magazine also ran a note about his passing. The White House sent a letter of condolence signed by President Bill Clinton. The word was out that our nation had lost a great hero of the Apollo program.

But some took this time to strike on the business. Daddy's sudden death caused a stir in the Gulf Coast beer market. I had been running the day-to-day business solidly for the last three years, thus did not understand the confusion, and almost panic, with our employees and the breweries/suppliers. My father's body was barely cold in the grave when one of our competitors started telling the market — and our employees — that the Roosa family was selling the company. The competitor told our customers to quit buying our products, saying we would not be able to service them properly. This rumor and strong-arm tactic directly affected our sales and income. My brothers came in for Christmas and New Year's and started to maneuver to have one become president of the company. They pressured Mama to make a decision to stabilize the market and the company by having a man in the family take charge. I was told Mama inherited everything of my father's, including his stock in the company – which gave her 90% control, with 10% divided among the four children. By this time no one in the family understood the company better than I, and I was surprised that the boys would even consider such – but my mother was actually debating the issue. The boys must have presented a strong case behind closed doors. I presented my case too, but thought to myself, "I came back for Daddy because he asked me. I have over six years' work experience as an executive vice president, and I'm only 31 years old... maybe it's time to move on to another job or career or even settle down." Mama announced to the family that she would think about it and told the boys to back off.

Soon after the new year, she assembled my brothers and me, and without telling me in advance announced formally that she had given it a great deal of thought and that I would be appointed president. One brother would become vice president of sales to send the message that the family was here to stay and that we meant business. Thus, I became President of Gulf Coast Coors, Inc., in January 1995. It had been almost 10 years since my graduating college. The youngest of the brothers chose to come back and would move from Florida to Gulfport as soon he could. He was engaged to be married in May, and his wife was active-duty Army, but they agreed to make it work. His job was to be a presence in the marketplace as I maintained the office and general operations. A plan and a strategy were put in place, and I continued as before at work. In preparation, I moved my office to Daddy's. It was a heady feeling knowing that over 50 families, plus Mama's financial security, was in my hands. A multi-million-dollar operation was going to fail or succeed based on my decisions. I kept my salary low. We were all in this together.

Personally, it was not an easy time, for the pressure was enormous. I was dealing with grieving and the passing of my father while stabilizing the company. I wanted to dye my hair black, but my hairdresser said that I should not show my employees a quick or radical change, for it might not elicit confidence in my ability to lead. It was good advice. My brother from Florida moved in with my mother, and I could tell she was reeling from the loss of her true love. Somewhere I had read or heard that when one spouse goes in a long marriage, that sometimes the other spouse goes within a year or two – or less. I asked Mama if she would promise me 10 years, and she did. I wanted her to have a goal through the darkest days. Later she said that if it weren't for that promise, that she might have wanted to quit on life. Not that she would have committed suicide, but depression and loss may have taken the best of her. My brother married, and his wife in the Army came in for a visit. One night she found Mama in her closet, slumped over and sobbing. My sister-in-law called me and said she was really scared, for Mama had never been that way before. It was a difficult time for all. My Uncle Knox, a meticulous contract lawyer, took care of the legal matters, kindly at no cost, but finally after a year had to threaten the doctors to quit sending bills or face legal consequences.

Emotionally after Daddy's death, I needed support too, and soon found that my fiancé, Johnnie, did not know how to help me mentally. His parents and grandparents were alive and well, and I'm sure it was hard for him to understand my feelings. One night when I really needed his support, he got a call from a friend who wanted to go out and hit the town. Johnnie did not particularly want to stick around his sullen future wife, and I was having doubts about whether he was the right person for the long haul. I had recently read *The Road Less Traveled*, by M. Scott Peck, and was pondering whether this was the right relationship for me. I had not put the engagement ring on my finger. It had been sitting on the dresser for a year. Our relationship, although not argumentative, was missing something deeper. We had been through some ups and downs, but when Johnnie wanted to go out that night, a switch went off in my head, and I told Johnnie that if he wanted to go out with his friends, then that was fine with me, but that the engagement would be off. I got the ring off the dresser and handed it to him. It was his decision, stay and help me through this emotionally, or leave. I am not sure if he thought I was serious, but he left. Although we saw each other after that night, I felt different. I was searching for the same type of relationship my parents had, and I did not see it with Johnnie. His looks got the attention of other girls, and he started seeing another girl shortly thereafter. It smarted, but I had a business to run.

The year progressed; the market stabilized, and I slowly started dating again. I was still grappling with the death of my father, so my relationships were on and off, and my emotions were all over the board. Time marched on, but the pressure to do well in the company was intense. After a while, my brother started acting on issues without my authority. I was little sister to him, not a boss. He was spending wildly, ordering merchandise and conducting big events. This was not the way to implement our plan. As I was trying to figure out what to do, a brochure came through the mail. It was from the Harvard Business School promoting a program called Owner/President Management Program, or OPM. The program required attendance for one month each year for three years – and the ending date of the first year was January 31, 1997. January 31 was the Apollo 14 launch date. This was a sign from Daddy.

Daddy had often said the last couple of years of his life that he thought that I should go to one of the Harvard Business School's executive education programs, for he had attended AMP, the Advanced Management Program, while he was with NASA. He would say, "But then that'd mean I'd have to go back to work while you are gone, and I'm not sure that I want to do that!" I have never received a brochure from Harvard before, so it's unclear how I got on their mailing list, but when I saw the date, something stirred in me to apply. It was an extensive and thorough application, but I was accepted into the class of OPM 27. I was one of six women out of a class of approximately 100, and one of two women in their 30s. Harvard Business School's way of teaching is intense. We were instructed to do all that we could to have our companies in order, for it would be almost impossible to run a company from afar and participate in three case-study classes a day. January in the beer industry is slow, so it was a perfect time. The course would meet every January for the next three years. The program was excellent. We covered a wide range of areas, from general management, to finance, to human relations, to marketing. Most of the professors were senior instructors from the two-year HBS graduate program.

The first day I arrived at the Harvard Business School, I could feel the history and intellect in the air. I was happy to be walking in the footsteps of my father and other great thinkers and doers. I remember my father talking about "the cans" – the dorm rooms for the participants. By the time I arrived, a new dorm had been built called Baker Hall, and each room had its own bathroom, but the accommodations were small. The room consisted of a twin bed on one side and a long desk and computer on the other side. We were each assigned a small group of about six to eight people, and we would meet each day to discuss the case studies prior to class. I made it a point to get to know as many people as possible, sitting with different people for lunch and dinner. Harvard B-School encouraged networking and would have cocktail parties and special events to help everyone get to know one another. We became a bonded and tight-knit group.

The typical day consisted of a group discussion from 7:45 to 8:55 a.m., with the first class beginning from 9 a.m. to 10:15 a.m. There was a 30-minute break, then another case study from 10:45 to 12:00 p.m. Lunch began at noon, and from 1 p.m. to 1:40 p.m., we would meet again with our small discussion group prior to the 1:45 to 3:00 p.m. class. Three cases a day for three weeks straight. It was like sipping water from a fire hose. We had to analyze each case thoroughly and be prepared to defend our decisions in the classroom. Best to make a financial mistake here, then with real money at home. On occasion, the actual president or CEO of a company we were studying was in the classroom, and after debate of whether to spend or not, the person would explain the decision and if it had been successful. The case study method fascinated me for there was no "one right answer." The cases forced us to hone our analytical decision-making capabilities.

In the late afternoons there were quick breaks, and some classmates would work out or play basketball. I would generally call home and talk to Mama, and then begin to read the next day's case studies. 6:30 p.m. was dinner, and then it was back to reading and studying. Sometimes a small group would gather and go out to restaurants, and I was kindly included. I remember one evening, a group of eight of us went out and I was the only woman. But that was not what distinguished me from the group, it was because I was one of two without a personal jet! These men started talking about their corporate planes and which ones were faster and better, and I could not contribute. The Latin Americans also included me in their clique, and they were fun to be around. I enjoyed their "joie de vivre" and sophisticated tastes. For the first time I tasted Cristal champagne within their midst, and it furthered my love of the bubbly. However most of all, I enjoyed the business analysis and challenging the brain to think in new terms. One of the professors taught about family owned and operated companies, and he specifically talked about its complexities. When I explained to him about my situation, he said I was in the most difficult of all family business situations. The professor explained how the pyramid was upside down, with the youngest leading older siblings, and it would be a hard road for me as the company moved forward. Also, an important lesson that HBS taught was just when you think you have it right, change it. Stagnant businesses would go belly-up either by competition, financial constraints, or technological changes. The market was ever changing, and a good business changes, too.

My business and market were changing, both internally and externally. After Daddy's death, I sought the advice of Chuck Parisher again, the beverage expert and consultant. Chuck had brought those few prospective buyers to the table when Daddy was looking at becoming a millionaire, but none had panned out. I started counting on Chuck's insight into the overall beer industry trends, and soon he called to tell me that consolidation was about to hit the beer market. Consolidation had swept the soft drink industry a couple of years earlier, and now the focus was on the independent beer distributor. I did not know it at the time, but the Coors Brewing Company was in negotiations with the Miller Brewing Company, which was owned by Philip Morris. Miller wanted to buy Coors out, so a strategy was put in place to first merge as many distributors as possible. All I knew was that the Coors Brewing Company started to put pressure on me to fulfill the smallest of obligations of the distributor agreement. Overall sales started to decline, and profit margins were squeezed. Chuck advised me that the family should consider either getting bigger or getting out of the business. I'm not sure Chuck knew at the time of the Coors talk, but he did see the consolidation trends starting to occur. He advised me that if the family wanted to get bigger that we should invest in a new warehouse and updated equipment. He said that if we wanted to get out, that we should start selling as many cases as possible, even at lower margins, and quit investing in people and projects. In both situations it would take about a year to groom the company for expansion or selling. In the interim, Chuck would start putting out feelers for buyers and said if we decided to sell, it was best to do it before the consolidation wave allowed for no options. At first, I started to look at expanding the company, for Daddy had put his blood, sweat, and tears into it. It was his legacy, and my first instinct was to preserve what he had started. Then as discussion grew with Mama, she started leaning towards selling. She said this was her financial security, and perhaps it was wiser to get out and take the money.

The second year of Harvard Business School rolled around, and I prepared to leave for the month of January 1998. The second year at HBS focused on obtaining operating effectiveness and efficiency, control, and implementation of strategies. It was intense and busy. While we were winding down the program, I got a call from Mama on the last day of classes. She had signed an agreement with Chuck Parisher to sell the business. I was half in shock. I knew she had been thinking about it, and Chuck and I had discussed the best potential buyers, but I thought Mama would have talked to me before signing anything. I remember going to the closing cocktail party, saying, "I've just been downsized – by my own Mama!" But in the end, it was the best choice, and it gave Mama the financial peace of mind that she was wanting, plus Coors was strong-arming us into selling. I wasn't sure if HBS would take me back for the third year but was told people often sold their companies while going through the program, and once you are in, you are in. I was relieved and went home to start the long and arduous negotiations.

The Coors Brewing Company wanted us to sell to the local Miller distributorship and was putting pressure on us to sell to them, although by law, Coors did not have a say. The family who owned the Miller distributorship along the Gulf Coast also owned the Coors distributorship in Jackson, Mississippi. I believe that the Coors Brewing Company was telling them behind closed doors that they were the only game in town; thus, the family kept low-balling on the offer. But Chuck, our advisor, was also courting another family-owned distributorship in town who sold Schlitz and Old Milwaukee. They were in the same boat that we were in and had been given the same advice – either get bigger or get out. That distributorship was owned by two families, the Fountains and Fallos, and was called F&F Distributing. They were more motivated to keep the two families employed and to pass down a legacy for their children. They were doing all they could to stay in the running. Chuck warned me that we might have to break up our brands and sell some to one and some to the other. I was determined to keep the company whole. The difficult part was trying to negotiate a sale in secret, for I did not want the employees to abandon ship and have the sales and cash flow go down the tubes. Our company now had nine different suppliers to agree to a sale, and it was tricky.

Another thing that the Harvard Business School does well is teach a business person how to negotiate. I came back with a high offer to both distributorships, and the Miller distributor balked. F&F mortgaged and borrowed all they could and bet the pot. F&F accepted my selling price. If I had put in writing that I could have kept anything over a million dollars as Daddy had once said, then I would have made myself a rich person overnight and provided for my own financial security. However, this was for Mama.

As we started the complex process of having each brewery/supplier approve the sale to F&F, my oldest brother called my mother and asked if she wanted to go to Asia with him. He was changing jobs himself and wanted to take several weeks off to travel. I was surprised that Mama accepted the trip during the make-or-break period of the sale, but she trusted me to do the job, and they left.

Chuck would call me every morning at 8:00 a.m., and we would strategize about the day's events. I needed to maintain a work-as-usual front while trying to talk to each supplier about selling to F&F. The Coors Brewing Company was not happy about the Miller distributor not getting the deal, and subtle sabotaging started to ensue. If F&F were not approved, then the Miller distributorship would be back in the running for negotiations. One by one, Chuck and I started with the smallest of our suppliers and started to secure approvals. One of the toughest to get on board was the Corona supplier. Corona was crucial to the deal, for one of the reasons F&F agreed to pay so much was because they needed this profitable brand. After one morning phone call, Chuck said he had a friend at the Corona supplier and that he would see where we were on getting the approval. The friend tracked down the contract and found it had been buried in a pile of papers. The friend pulled rank, and next thing we knew, Corona had approved the sale to F&F. Now everyone was in except for the Coors Brewing Company. After achieving the approval of the other eight suppliers, there would have been a lawsuit if Coors had refused. Legally, the brewery had to have a legitimate reason for saying that F&F was not fit to sell their brands, but with the others agreeing to the sale, they had no choice but to agree, too.

Mama came back from the trip, and I told her we had successfully kept the sale intact, and she looked at me like she expected no other outcome. We signed the papers to transfer the assets and funds on April 30, 1998. Professionally, it was the most stressful time of my life. After Daddy's death, things had been so hectic that there was no reading of his Will. I did not know that I had 26% of the stock, which would have yielded me $650,000 on the day of the signing. Daddy was trying to leave me a "golden parachute." This detail was not told to me after my father's death, and besides the 10% to the children, I was led to believe everything went to Mama, which now placed her in "The 1%" in terms of cash-on-hand.

My brother, the executor, found an investment broker and started maneuvering to handle the funds. My mother's friend, Mary Keegan, whom Mama had grown up with and had been the one to throw the dart that landed them in Virginia, had married a man in the wealth management business. Mama laughed that she married "fame" and that Mary married "fortune." Mary's husband was willing to help Mama, but my brother found someone at Bear Stearns in New York City. Mama sent some of the funds to Mary's husband as her "rainy day" money, but the bulk went to New York under my brother's control. I did not think much about it but started asking Mama about my golden parachute after the sale. My brother protested any large bonus to me, saying that I had been paid a salary over the years and that all was square. I persisted with Mama, telling her that Daddy had promised to take care of me. Finally, my brother called and offered me a severance of $65,000. I thought the amount was odd, for it did not correlate to any year's salary or familiar number. I wondered how he arrived at this number. I now know that a zero had been left off the amount due me, but at the time, I had no choice but to take it. I had nothing in writing from Daddy and was not aware of the stock inheritance.

· · ·

At least I had a little financial breathing room to look for the next chapter in my life. I took some time off to ponder my options. Since I was not in a solid relationship, the prospect of settling down and starting a family was dim. I was 35 years old, and in a way, it was an exciting time because I could do anything that I wanted. Mama and I started to take a few trips, including one on the Seabourn with the Harvard Business School. It was an all-class OPM reunion that started in Monte Carlo and ended in Barcelona. On board were business graduates from almost every OPM, including a gentleman from OPM 1. One of the first case studies our class read at the Harvard Business School was about a woman in Switzerland who worked in a family watch business. Her name was Pesca, and she was the only daughter among brothers. Her brothers were not all that interested in the family business until she got it going and running well. Then the brothers got interested, and one took over the company, eking her out. I could relate to her frustration and plights. When Mama and I arrived on the OPM Seabourn cruise in 1999, I just happened to run into her. I felt an instant kinship.

Mama and me sailing on the Seabourn for the
Harvard Business School OPM reunion

Toasting to our new adventures

With my days of being the "Beer Baroness" behind, it was time to find my passion. I thought, "I know the alcohol industry, and I like to drink fine champagne." I started researching champagne distribution companies and found most were located in New York City. Big Apple, here I come! I wrote to the best champagne companies and lined up interviews. One interview was with the company that distributed Veuve Clicquot. The history of Veuve Clicquot is fascinating, for the literal meaning is "Widow Clicquot." The Clicquot family started the champagne in France in 1772. In 1778, the founder's son, Francois Clicquot, married Barbe-Nicole Ponsardin. Francois was involved in trading, wool, and champagne production, but died in 1805, leaving the young widow in charge of the company. Under the direction of Madame Clicquot, the company started focusing on champagne and eventually made a name in royal courts in Europe during the time of the Napoleonic Wars. The champagne methodology was expanded during her reign, and she became known for her consistency with the brand. And most notably the "yellow" label. I once heard that Widow Clicquot instructed the print labelers to refer to the color of a chicken yolk for the brand's label color, which was more orange with free-range chickens. This is one of my favorite champagnes, so I liked the idea of working for a company that was pioneered by a forward-thinking woman, just like I had been in the beer industry.

A lunch interview was set up by the president of the U.S.A. Veuve Clicquot division, and I arrived at the office for our appointment. I felt more prepared for this interview than the one with Trent Lott and was excited about the prospect of working in the champagne industry. New York reminded me of Paris. I wasn't sure if I was prepared for the big city again, but I had studied how to negotiate salaries, sign-on bonuses, benefit agreements, moving expenses and all the formal business arrangements that Harvard Business School had taught. But once again, this interview threw me for a loop. As I came into the office, a young woman greeted me and said that she would escort me to *Le Cirque* restaurant, and it was there that I was to meet the madame-in-charge, a French woman who was the head of the U.S. Veuve Clicquot division. As we were walking there, this young woman told me that the Madame would probably offer me a salary, but that I could probably negotiate about $10,000 more. I thought this was strange talk from an employee but filed it in the back of my head. She also said that most people started with their company but then moved on to larger organizations after a year or two. I did not want to job-jump and was ready to get into a long-term position. Once again, I thought these were strange comments.

When I arrived, I was warmly greeted by a woman named Mireille Guiliano. I liked "Madame Boss Lady" right off the bat. She was sophisticated, elegant, and petite – just as I thought of myself. She said to call her Mireille, but even with my stint in France, I stumbled on pronouncing her name correctly. We started with informal chit-chat, and she ordered a bottle of Veuve Clicquot to start. I liked this already! We had a glass, and then she set the bottle aside. I had never started a bottle that was not finished, but I followed protocol, as this was a business interview. She had planned our lunch, and after the appetizers, she ordered a bottle of red wine. This was fun! She explained to me that the company had recently purchased the winery and wanted to know what I thought of the wine. It was excellent. I'm sure she was noticing my manners and demeanor, and the conversation flowed about marketing and the industry. The division handled the distribution of various brands, including the Krug champagne and other wines. She asked if I could write, which I thought was odd, but I told her I could. She explained that many of their press releases and ad campaigns were written in-house. I told her that I had the expertise and knowledge and could handle the job.

My only faux pas was when the espresso came at the end of lunch, I asked the waiter for a lemon peel, as most restaurants at the time served a curled lemon zest on the rim or saucer. I was curtly told by Madame Mireille that a lemon peel was from the olden days and that it originally served to wipe the rim to kill the germs. I had never heard that explanation before and was embarrassed. After the check was signed and paid, she said we'd go back to the office and talk. I figured the more formal interview was about to occur, but on the way back to the office, while walking along the streets of Manhattan, she started talking about places to live... and said that most people have roommates or live in a tiny studio apartment. I wasn't sure if I had been offered a job or why she was bringing this up. It seemed like an inappropriate time to be negotiating salary or living arrangements. I tried to explain to her that I currently lived in a beautiful three-bedroom home by myself, with a nice front and back yard, a two-car garage, and two cats. I know she had seen my resume showing 10 years' experience running a company and that I had been to the Harvard Business School. I had come a long way from days in Washington, D.C., and I wasn't ready to start again with roommates, a low salary, or have to look for another job in a couple of years.

Then out of the blue she said my starting salary would be $75,000 a year. I knew that I could immediately add the $10,000, according to what the young woman had said, but I was expecting about $100,000 or more. It was surreal to be discussing such a serious issue while zipping past yellow cabs and crowds of people. We arrived at the office, and I was introduced to the employees. There were around 40 people in the organization. I thought it was great, for it was run by a woman I liked, and it was a small unit, like Gulf Coast Coors had been. About the time I thought we would sit down one-on-one, she escorted me to the elevator and said, "I'll be in touch, and thank you very much for coming."

I was excited and disappointed. The next day I had an interview with the Dom Perignon distributor for the United States, but I met a mid-manager from the human resources department. The person did not understand my qualifications. I met with other companies too, but also could not get past mid-managers. I flew home and shortly thereafter received a letter from Veuve Clicquot. Ms. Mireille liked me so much that she created a new position that would be directly underneath her helm. My position would be to attend events and market for Veuve Clicquot, and personally handle the Krug champagne brand and the new winery. It was my dream job to drink champagne and wine for a living! I researched online to see how well my salary would support me in New York. New York was expensive, and in order to maintain my standard of living, I would need to almost double the amount offered to avoid living paycheck to paycheck. I countered with a high offer, thinking we could meet in the middle, but she said it was too much money and closed the door on negotiations. I think we were both disappointed. She later wrote a #1 *New York Times* best-selling book, *"French Women Don't Get Fat."*

I returned to Mississippi to keep searching. Then on September 11, 2001, the United States suffered the terrorist attack on the twin towers of the World Trade Center. As I watched in horror the collapse of the buildings and loss of innocent life, I thought that if I had taken that job with the champagne company, I would surely would have been working downtown. I couldn't help but think that God had a hand in my decision not to move.

As I regrouped on my career, Mama and I continued planning trips. She was lonely without Daddy, and the trips gave her something to look forward to. Although I, too, was enjoying the adventures, it was time that I looked seriously at finding a new job. My funds from the sale of the company were depleting. Moving to another location was on the radar. I started sending out my resumes, and decided to submit one to the Central Intelligence Agency. I was surprised but excited when I received a reply that I had made it through the initial screening. Next would be a phone interview. When the person from "The Company" called, I was asked if I could speak a foreign language. Although I had learned basic French while living in France, I had to answer "no." Not knowing a foreign language fluently kept me from progressing further with the CIA. My job hunting continued.

Then Mama approached me about running her day-to-day business affairs. She offered me a small salary to cover my bills. Mama was not liking the idea of my moving away. I agreed to stay. I had lost one parent so quickly. I was determined to spend as much time as I could with the other. They both had been so good to me all my life. It was time to live in the moment with my mother.

Traveling to the White House to meet President Bush
for an Apollo 11 anniversary event

CHAPTER 11

Travels

Joan Roosa loved the adventure of travel. She had an amazing life with Daddy and their travels, and once Mama received the financial security that she needed after the sale of Gulf Coast Coors, it was time to keep the traveling going. She said she married for love and that was it, so Mama had no real desire to date again. I became her closest companion, and we had a rare mother/daughter relationship. We respected each other and communicated without much dissent. Mama was a strong-willed person and independent in many ways. When she set her mind to something, there was no going back. But she was dependent in one way: she was a people-person and did not like to be alone. Daddy and I shared many of the same traits and we did not mind being loners. I could spend many hours, if not days, at a time by myself, but Mama needed people to talk to, to entertain and be entertained, and she had a wonderful sense of humor. She would practice jokes with me, and then the next time we were out and about, she would suddenly have a crowd around her and she'd be telling jokes like they had just come from the top of her head. She had her father Doc's bravado. People just liked being around her, and I never minded living in her shadow.

Mama was kind, generous, and steadfast. Daddy used to call her "The Rock." Daddy thought Mama could do anything. Sometimes I would hear Mama and Daddy banter about her being "The Rock."

Mama would say, "What if I don't want to be the rock?"

And Daddy would say, "Well, Joan, that's just the way it is. You are the rock."

And Mama would say, "Well I decree that I am no longer the rock! You can be the rock from now on, Stuart."

He'd come back with that consoling, loving tone, "I can't. You are it! That's just the way it's been and just the way it is." And then he would make some gesture with his hand, making a sign of an "S" and "R" – like the Pharaohs of Egypt would do – and say, "So it is written, so let it be done."

Mama would laugh, and then I would hear the same debate again a few months later. Daddy's pet word for her was also "Puddin'" — something that he called her for as long I could remember.

After Daddy's death, Mama and I used to talk about how we wondered whether Daddy almost willed an early death. For as strong a man as he was, he was dependent on Mama, and loved her completely.

She used to "prepare" him for when she was gone, and say "Stuart, you have my permission to remarry once I'm dead."

He would retort, "Joan, I cannot live without you." And he meant it.

She would counter, "But you are going to outlive me. I'm the one with the health problems. I have high blood pressure, tachycardia, and whatever else… so you must be prepared."

Daddy would quickly fire back, "Joan, I think that I would rather commit suicide than live without you."

Mama would then back off and approach the subject later. At some point Mama started wondering if he just might do it, so she quit talking about it unless she had another health scare.

After Daddy's sudden death at 61, Mama was only 60, and she'd say to me, "I'm too old to remarry, but too young to quit living." So we planned trips. Mama and I wound up flying out to California for Apollo 13's 25th anniversary. It was a black-tie formal event, and being from the South, when an invitation says formal, it meant long gowns. We dressed up in our sparkling clothes and headed to the event. A limousine picked us up. It turns out we were the only ladies in long dresses. But it was nice being around astronauts again. The movie *Apollo 13* with Tom Hanks had just

Greeting "the astronauts" at the party in L.A.

Apollo 13 movie director, Ron Howard, at 25th anniversary party

been released, and although Tom Hanks was not there, I had the pleasure of meeting Ron Howard. He was a red-head too, like Daddy, and was kind and quiet-spoken. He was used to the camera, for I asked someone to snap several pictures of us on my 35mm film Canon camera, and his smile never changed in the four or five pictures.

Several years later, we were invited back to California for a huge Hollywood shindig. In 2001, as I was going through Mama's mail, I came across an envelope that had already been opened but had a picture of a Playboy bunny on it. I thought that was a bit unusual, so I pulled out its contents. It was an invitation to attend a tribute to Arthur C. Clarke, the author of the book *2001: A Space Odyssey*, at the Playboy Mansion in Los Angeles.

"Mama, did you see this? We must go! It's at the Playboy Mansion!" I exclaimed.

"Yes, I saw it," as she sat on the couch in the media room, obviously not impressed. Mama and Daddy had met many celebrities and had attended some great events during their years together, but this one was at the Playboy Mansion! I wanted to go and meet the famous Hugh Hefner himself.

My mother said flatly, "I am a feminist, and I do not like the exploitation of women."

"Oh *noooo*, Mama, we are going to this one!" I insisted.

She grumbled, but I proceeded to RSVP and make the flight arrangements. For some reason, I made the flight to L.A. for only an overnight trip. Party in, party out. No reason to stay any longer.

As we checked into the hotel, we ran into several astronauts, and Mama started to relax about why we were there. It was fun to see astronauts ranging from Mercury, Gemini, Apollo, Skylab, and the Shuttle programs. The organizers said that since some of the Apollo astronauts were there alone, they would put a few of us in the limousines.

"Do you mind riding with Jim Lovell?" an organizer asked as she was marking through her white sheet with names.

Mama laughed and said, "No, I know Jim well."

Mama and Daddy had hunted with the Lovells in Africa on safari together in Mozambique. It was a safari full of adventures, including almost having a herd of elephant trample over them one night in a ravine near the water. A lead female elephant with a baby, and a large herd following, had come to drink from the river and caught the human scent. Daddy, Jim, and the professional hunters were all ready to shoot if the elephants started a stampede down the embankment.

Daddy leaned over to Mama and said, "I don't want to *scare* you, but if we have to shoot, keep your head down and don't move. I don't want you to get shot."

Mama, already frozen in fright with her hair on the back of her neck standing straight up, thought, "*Scare me*! I am already scared!"

The elephants did some loud trumpeting and stomped their feet in anger but moved on rather than attack. Mama came back from the trip learning how a female lion calls for "supper," and Mama would huff in this low growl at cocktail parties to entertain. Both the Lovells and my parents returned with some fascinating wood carvings, butterfly prints, and other exotic artwork — and several animals that had been "collected." On a safari, most times the hunters are placed in different areas so that they do not overlap, but one evening as Jim was driving back to camp, he went through my father's hunting area. There just happened to be a leopard feeding on some bait, so the professional hunter told Jim to shoot it. Daddy felt that this should have been "his leopard" but that is the unpredictability of Africa. Live in the moment and don't let opportunities go by.

As we were riding in the limousine to the mansion and sipping on cocktails, we reminded Jim of the leopard story. He said he was just doing what his professional hunter told him to do and laughed it off. We were all in an excited and festive mood, giggling with anticipation of the night ahead. As we pulled into the winding road leading up to the Playboy Mansion, there were cute street signs on the side of the drive saying: "Drive Slowly, Playmates at Play" and "Please don't feed the bunnies." We pulled around the famous fountain and got out to see a greeter whose hair was like Princess Leia's in *Star Wars*. There was a lighted tunnel leading to the pool

Mama and me with Jim Lovell (Apollo 13 Astronaut)
at Playboy Mansion

Inside the famous grotto at the Playboy Mansion while all was calm

area, and suddenly there were movie stars and people everywhere! There was a bar nearby that had drinks with lighted ice cubes in them, something I had never seen before. This was a true L.A. hip party! Jim wandered off to do interviews with *Entertainment Tonight* and other Hollywood media groups, so Mama and I mingled with the best of them, taking our pictures along way. I saw Morgan Freeman and knew he was from Mississippi.

I ran up to him and said, "Hi, I'm homefolk! I'm from Mississippi, too!"

He looked at me suspiciously, and then Mama said hello and greeted him.

He said, "I can tell by her accent that she is from there... but I don't know about you."

I never did pick up a Texas or Mississippi drawl in my years growing up, but I said to him, "No, really, I'm homefolk!" and we snapped a picture and moved on.

I told Mama we had to check out The Grotto, for I had heard much about it from Hollywood stories. We ambled through the star-studded crowd to a big rock with a waterfall. This must be it! As we were standing there, a gentleman walked up, seeming to be intrigued that we were intrigued. My mother said something about the grotto, and before we knew it, he was escorting us to the inside walkway, underneath the waterfall. My mother's jovial aura seemed to lure him in, for it turned out he was a manager at the Mansion and wanted to show it off for her.

"Tonight is a respectable night, with the astronauts here and all, so we have the jets turned off to discourage any wild play... but I will turn them on for you," he said to Mama with anticipated pleasure.

"Okay, sure," my mother said graciously.

SHOOSH went the water, and the lights in the pool came on. Wow, this was cool! The vibe in the air told me that some "thangs" had happened there.

"Thank you," my mother said, and started to walk back up the small stone sidewalk.

Mama and me with our fellow Mississippian, actor Morgan Freeman

With James Cameron, the speaker for the night celebrating *2001: A Space Odyssey* at the Playboy Mansion in Los Angeles

"I would like to meet Hugh Hefner," I gleefully commented. The manager said Mr. Hefner was flying back from Las Vegas and that it would be later when he arrived.

The dinner was under a big tent in the back yard, and the keynote speaker was James Cameron. The author of *2001: A Space Odyssey* was in Sri Lanka, where he lived, so he appeared via hologram to say a few words. There was even had a "Hal" (the errant computer from the film) set up with an actor inside. As the tribute went on, James Cameron was introduced. I had no idea he was so fascinated with space. Cameron began speaking, and his talk started to get long. But he was passionate with his speech.

Out of nowhere, the computer "Hal" told James Cameron to "wrap it up," but the directive was ignored. Cameron had a message to give, and he was going to give it. "Hal" tried several times again to end the speech.

"James… you don't want to do that, James… James… it is time to stop, James…," Hal announced, but to no avail. I wondered if that actor ever worked again in Hollywood.

Later that evening I met James Cameron and his lovely wife, along with some other actors from his films, and I found him to be most kind, despite his serious look. I could tell he was a "no-nonsense" man, and he gave me his business card. Unfortunately, I misplaced it. And Hugh Hefner was too tired from his trip to attend the party. But it was a fun evening, and the next morning as we woke up to fly home, I wondered why I did not extend our trip. Still, that was a wonderful 24 hours.

• • •

The United States Space Foundation invited Mama to Colorado Springs for a tribute to Apollo 14's 25th anniversary, and I went along. We stayed at the beautiful Broadmoor Hotel, with the mountains as the backdrop to the grand hotel and exquisite gardens. As we walked the grounds, we came along a dress shop. The boutique had a sale going on, and Mama bought me a two-piece black suit and two jeweled purses, which looked like Judith Leiber designs. Mama always loved to dress me, and she bought many of my clothes, sometimes choosing a style that was a bit more "sexy" than my shy, conservative side felt comfortable in, but the clothes were "spot on" haute-couture and fun to wear. It got me out of my shell sometimes. Her tastes were exquisite, and she liked having a daughter with whom she could discuss clothes, make-up, and fashion in general. Although Mama was not a shopper, she had a keen eye and "just knew" when something was right or cutting edge style. I used to call Mama "My Funky Mama" for the clothes were sometimes out there – but always cool, hip, and sophisticated. On the day of the tribute, Mama gave a touching speech of appreciation, and I said a few words after writing them down and reading them to the crowd. The U.S. Space Foundation gave us each an acrylic pyramid with the earth "floating" in the clear space. The earth was made up of gold continents and light blue seas. The world reminded me of the blue marble Daddy talked about from his childhood.

On the Apollo 14 flight, Daddy had carried some small silk flags in his PPK, Pilot Preference Kit. One flag was Spanish, in honor of Spanish explorers. Daddy was organizing a meeting with the King of Spain, who had been at the Apollo 14 launch in 1971, when the King was involved in a skiing accident and the preparations for the meeting were canceled. Then Daddy died. So later Mama decided to give the flag to the King anyway, and a meeting was organized via the embassy in Washington, D.C., to visit Madrid. Mama invited me along, and I decided to wear the suit from the Broadmoor. The acrylic tribute from Colorado gave us an idea, and we placed the flag in an acrylic frame. No doubt the flag was authentic, for the Franco symbol was on the flag, a symbol that was later banned. We also decided to gift the book, *A Man on the Moon, The Voyages of the Apollo Astronauts*, by Andrew Chaikin. While figuring out the best way to get there, we got a flier in the mail with an offer to sail to Europe on the *Queen Elizabeth II* and fly back on the Concorde. Sounded like a good deal to us, and we booked the trip. Off we went first class to Europe. It was quite the difference since Mama had traveled to Europe as a newlywed, but once again, Mama was a hit on the ship, telling her stories and laughing about life. Mama had a great "aura" that seemed to mesmerize people and make them feel happy.

King Juan Carlos and Queen Sophia at their residential palace in Spain,
presenting them with a flown Spanish flag to the moon aboard Apollo 14,
with Mama handing them the book *A Man on the Moon, Voyages of the
Apollo Astronauts*. The King and Queen were in attendance of the launch
of Apollo 14 in January 1971

An officer of the U.S. Embassy escorted us to the King and Queen's personal palace outside of Madrid. The official palace was in Madrid proper. When we first started organizing the trip, the royal son, Prince Felipe, was to accept the Spanish flag flown to the moon. We heard he was a space buff. I was excited, for he was single at the time, and so was I. Although he was a few years younger, I thought we would make a good match – for he was Catholic, I was Catholic, he was royalty, I was "space royalty." Why not? But then the King decided to accept the flag, and the Queen decided to join him. A joint audience with the royal couple was rare, and although honored, I was a bit disappointed not to meet my "prince charming." King Juan Carlos and Queen Sofia spoke perfect English, and instead of a few minutes of a meet and greet, we spent almost an hour with them. They were delightful.

At one point, Mama blurted out playfully, "It's good to be the King!"

Juan Carlos looked at her in a serious way, and playfully said, "It is."

For several years after Daddy's death, my mother and I were regularly traveling to Europe or someplace exotic. I was reliving the high lifestyle that I was exposed to as a teenager in Greece. Since Mama now had the means, we enjoyed luxury travel and dining. It was nice to be able to travel without a man in a way, for I could be myself and enjoy the moments with Mama, and she had a great time being in social circles. I considered Mama my best friend. We just enjoyed being around each other. It was a win-win, in our opinion. Our conversations flowed from serious to funny and were pleasant and interesting. Often times she would tell me about the books she was reading, for she could read three or four at a time. I used to ask her if she got confused with the plots, but she said "no" and that it was easy to pick up where she left off with each book. The only type books she did not read were grocery store romance novels. They bored her. Every now and then Mama would toss me a book saying I would enjoy it, and it would be anything from *The Celestine Prophecy* to the *Sweet Potato Queens' Book of Love*. There was a deep comfort level in knowing how each ticked. Our personalities complimented each other, and we were both patient in our travels together.

• • •

It was time to have an African adventure. We contacted Bert Klineburger, our friend from the hunting days, and he arranged for us to go to Zimbabwe. My goal was to hunt a leopard, and I had the perfect mount in mind for it. Before we left, I took out a rifle and would watch my two cats in the back yard. Playfully, and obviously without bullets, I would put them in my scope and follow them in the jungle island in my backyard. This seemed to horrify my friends, but at one Shikar-Safari meeting, Mrs. Cabela talked about women hunting on safaris and the need to practice with the rifle as much as possible. Since Daddy would not be there to hunt with me, I wanted to build my confidence with the gun on my own. The cats never seemed to mind.

In Africa, I shot several impalas for bait, a zebra, Egyptian geese, and a kudu. One evening while waiting for a leopard, I fell asleep. The guide nudged me and whispered in my ear, "Rosemary, the leopard is feeding at the bait." It was the most exciting words a man had ever spoken to me! Not "I love you," or "I want you to marry me," but "The leopard is feeding!" By the time I got into position with the rifle in my shoulder, the big cat was gone. No leopard. I returned to the campsite to my hut, which Mama and I shared, and Mama had a small candle burning for me. She had "kept the light on" in hopes, but no luck. I attributed my not getting a leopard to a "curse" that both Mandy and Michell had put on me. Neither wanted me to get one, and before I left, wished me bad luck on successfully collecting a leopard. The safari was a great adventure though, and I felt Daddy was with me in spirit. On the last night of the trip, it was my birthday. The witchdoctor from the local tribe brought the children from the village to sing me songs. It was an unforgettable, special evening. My African safari was all that I imagined it to be, minus the disappointment of the leopard, but the magical sunsets and the thrill of the hunt were amazing.

• • •

Kudu in Zimbabwe

Shikar-Safari meeting in Africa with cheetahs

At one point Mama was thinking of renting an apartment for a month or so in Venice. She wanted a place large enough to have the family over to come and go. I ordered brochures and rental catalogues. Mama reviewed them, and one evening after supper she handed me a large catalogue with apartments and homes throughout Italy. I first focused on the Venetian apartments, but they were small, and most had stairs with no elevators. She said she was not in good enough health to climb stairs every day, but asked if I saw anything else that hit my fancy. I slowly perused the book. Some homes were large but did not have a good "feel." Others were dumpy apartments in great cities but were not acceptable to Mama's style. Only one place hit me as a neat-looking villa called Rosa. It was 100 years old and pink. It had only three bedrooms but was spacious and had a big pool.

Mama did not say a word while I was looking through the book, and finally, I said, "Well, nothing looks like what you are looking for, but I like the looks of Villa Rosa."

She smiled and said, "That is the only one that hit me too." It was in a remote area outside of Rome in the Umbria region, south of Tuscany. It was too small and difficult to get to for a place for lots of people to come and go, but I had another birthday coming up in July.

As Mama and I pondered the place, she said, "Let's make it a birthday place for you, and we'll invite others."

We decided to invite my childhood friend, Cristi, and her Mama, Shirley, whom we'd met during the NASA days. I'd met Cristi when I was about 5 years old. Mama had sought out her family, who lived down the street. They had three girls, and Mama saw a potential playmate for me. Cristi said she remembered the exact day of our meeting and that I was wearing a dress with a poodle on it. Her mother, Shirley, had been married to Jim McQueen, who worked in the medical division of NASA and was studying germs that might come from space. He had three degrees. Jim was the one who made the medical call to pull Ken Mattingly from the Apollo 13 mission, since Ken had been exposed to the measles.

We also invited my friend Michell and her mama, Ada. Ada and Mama had become friends from being around us in college. We called them all

Villa Rosa outside of Poggio Mirteto, Italy

Three Mamas with our villa caretakers – Shirley (left), Ada (center), and Mama, with Guido (back) and Sammie (right)

Three daughters in Italy – Michell (left), me, and Cristi (right)

that night, and all enthusiastically said, "Let's do it! Since Cristi and her mom worked, we could go for only 10 days, but soon we were planning the trip for three mamas and three daughters to travel to Europe. The brochure mentioned that there was a caretaker who lived on the grounds but discreetly stayed in the distance.

We rented a Mercedes van and descended upon Rome, staying our first night in the Hassler Hotel, the same hotel at the top of the Spanish Steps where we had started the Roosa Dynasty in 1976. It was just as magical. We departed the next day and arrived in Poggio Mirteto. We could not pronounce it, so we called it Piggly Wiggly. I read the directions for how to get to the villa, but in Italy, the roads are confusing. We circled the foundation in the center of town about eight times looking for the correct turnoff but finally gave up. Mama said we should stop and call the discreet caretaker for assistance.

We pulled into a tiny café next to a fire station. Before you knew it, we had about six Italian GQ firemen coming to our rescue! We did not speak Italian, and they did not speak English, but the smiles were flashing. I realized the impact of six women on their own. Our caretaker, Guido, came and got us, and we followed him to the villa. It looked postcard-perfect — it had an arbor with grape vines, an inviting pool, typical Italian marble and tiles, and views that stretched for miles.

Mama's favorite song was *Mony Mony*, the Billy Idol version. We turned it on and danced for the fun of it. Guido was intrigued and introduced us to Sammie, his nephew, who also managed the house and grounds. Soon our discreet caretakers were coming to see us every evening, and we mentioned my birthday coming up on July 23. We also had the champagne flowing every night, and our two Italians would join us for supper when we were not out and about. We spent the days sightseeing or staying put relaxing. One day we drove to Assisi, the home of Saint Francis. We visited his sparse home with the peaceful gardens. While walking around the beautiful grounds, my thoughts went back to a nun that my parents had met years ago.

When Mama and Daddy had been stationed at Edwards Air Force Base, prior to his NASA selection, Mama told Stuart that she was going to invite the local nuns to the house for a barbecue. Daddy was a bit nervous.

He said, "Joan, you know that I like to drink beer when I grill, so what am I to do?"

"Drink one," she replied, "and offer them one, too! I doubt they will take it, but you can offer."

Daddy did, and they refused, but he drank his beer guilt-free while grilling. Daddy wasn't the only one drinking beer at Edwards. When Mama first arrived at Edwards Air Force Base — a fighter test pilot's dream — the women were invited for coffee by Glennis Yeager, the wife of base Commander, Chuck Yeager. Chuck had named the airplane that he broke the sound barrier with "Glamorous Glennis." Mama said the wives showed up with their hats and gloves, and then out walks Glennis and says, "I don't drink coffee," and popped open a beer. Daddy loved that line and used it for the rest of his life. But while at Edwards, Mama hosted the local visiting nuns, and one who bonded was Sister Ida. Daddy said Sister Ida had prayed for him on his trip to the moon and back. Daddy claimed Sister Ida had a hotline to God and would laugh that when she prayed, it probably went something like this:

"God?"

"Yes?"

"Sister Ida here; I need a miracle."

"Okay." And it would happen.

Other times when Daddy asked Sister Ida to pray about something, she would say, "No, can't do that one." And it didn't happen.

While in Assisi, something stirred in me about Sister Ida. I knew I had to track her down. She had been special to Daddy. Upon my return from Italy, after some searching, I did find Sister Ida in California with the Society Devoted to the Sacred Heart. I flew out to see her for the first time. She was terminally ill and didn't have long to live, but she radiated love — a pure love — God's love. She was a joy to be around and I could sense the "hotline." It had been several years since Daddy's death, but I felt his presence. The nuns had a private Mass for me in their residence, and the music they chose to play was *Amazing Grace* and *How Great Thou Art* — the

All aboard the Orient Express in Rome

Dining on the Orient Express

In the lobby of the Hotel Danieli in Venice, Italy

Reaching the tower after traversing a garden maze in Italy

two songs Daddy requested at his funeral. I do not know how they knew these were his favorite songs, but it moved me to tears, and I could not stop crying during the Mass. The Holy Spirit was strong, and I could feel that direct connection. We then had a beautiful lunch prepared by the Sisters. I took a bottle of champagne and had Sister Ida pop the cork, toasting, "To the Moon!" After our delightful afternoon, I never saw her again. She soon passed. I was grateful that I made it there in time.

• • •

Mama loved trains. It started when she was 7 and traveled by train from Tupelo to Saltillo. Mammy and Doc had put her on the train by herself. They knew she could handle it. Mama and I traveled on several trains together all over the world, including taking the Orient Express from Rome to Paris. The Orient Express was my first experience with luxury train travel. We boarded the deep, blue exterior cars through the bar car, and while dressing that morning, I put on a short red sundress with sunflowers and a brimmed straw hat with a sunflower in the back. The bartender was polishing glasses when he looked up and saw us walking past him. "Helloooo," he said, "My name is Alexander." Gotta love Italian men and their endless pursuit to flirt. The trip was extended between nights on the train and in hotels along the route, to make the journey an experience, not a destination. Although the cabins were small on the Orient Express, they were immaculate with plush fabric and burled wood with inlaid designs. There was not a fingerprint nor dust particle to be seen. For dinner, we dressed formally, and I wore a long black velvet gown. The dining car, etched with Lalique glass figures of nude women, had been the "interrogation" car used in the 1974 Agatha Christie movie, *Murder on the Orient Express*. White tablecloths and fine china made the cozy dining car elegant. For a nightcap, we headed to the bar car, and Mama said she would like a Brandy Alexander. I asked the bartender if he knew how to make one, and he pointed at his name tag and said, "I would hope so!" I could not help but laugh at his charms. We stopped in Venice and stayed at the same hotel, Hotel Danieli, where I was when I turned 13

About to board the Eastern Orient Express in Bangkok

Ending our train trip with an elephant ride in Chiang Mai, Thailand

years old. The memories flooded back, but this time Mama and I went and had lunch at the famous Harry's Bar that we by-passed years ago for my special pizza. Then our train trip proceeded through the Alps and eventually to Paris.

My mother enjoyed the train so much that a few years later she took the family for an overnight excursion on the Eastern Orient Express, boarding in Bangkok and ending in Chiang Mai. Once again we found ourselves in the bar car, this time being served by elegant Asian women in silk kimonos and glittering gold necklaces that looked like the temple tops in Thailand. We flew on to South Korea, then China, spending New Year's Eve in Hong Kong.

Another train experience was when Mama and I went to South Africa for a Shikar-Safari meeting. On that trip, Mama and I shared an entire half of a rail car on the Rovos Rail for a two-night trip beginning in Johannesburg and ending in Cape Town. The interesting part of this train trip was entering the station that was exclusively for the Rovos passengers. We walked in and were invited to have a glass of champagne and explore the polished coal-fed engine car that would start our journey. We did not sign in. We did not have tickets. The Rovos company just *knew* who we were. It was a paperless check-in. After we settled into our accommodations, a man in a snappy uniform was stationed at the back of the rail car and we were told that we could ask him for assistance 24 hours a day. The service was amazing. Mama and I were taken with the old-world elegance of the train, our suite's rich paisley fabrics, a full bed, and a bathroom with a tub. On the morning of the second day I took a bath with fizz balls while I looked out at the countryside that resembled West Texas. The terrain reminded me of our deer hunting days.

On the trip back, we took an overnight train, the Blue Train, from Cape Town to Johannesburg. It was more modern than the Rovos Rail with smaller cabins. It was just as luxurious though, and we found ourselves sitting in the cozy bar car for most of the trip. We did stop and tour the big hole in the ground where diamonds were discovered, a place called Kimberley. After learning how De Beers cornered the diamond market, we

Standing by the engine car of the Rovos Rail in Africa

Mama relaxing with a glass of wine on the Rovos Rail

strolled back to the train, and the staff had champagne in crystal flutes on silver trays for us enjoy. The train also had a gift shop on board, and besides diamonds, the man running it started telling me about the jewelry that was featured.

"This is tanzanite," he said, "in platinum." Showing me a three-stone ring.

"And this necklace is of a leopard head with diamonds around the nose and rubies for the eyes… and look, when you flip it over, it is the head of a cheetah with diamonds and emerald eyes," as he pulled it from the display cabinet. I admired it, for I had never seen anything like it.

"What are you wearing for dinner tonight?" he asked.

I replied slowly, "A leopard print dress, shorter in the front and longer in the back."

He replied, "Perfect, I will dress you for dinner in jewelry. This necklace will go great!"

Although stunned, I figured there was no place for me to go as the train sped through the night. It was like dressing for the Oscars, picking out the jewels for the formal evening.

• • •

Since I enjoyed hunting, Mama wanted me to become a member of Shikar-Safari. However, I needed another major hunt abroad to qualify. Instead of Africa, we booked a hunt in New Zealand. This time it was for a Himalayan tahr, which looks like a large goat with two horns that curve backwards. After a Harvard Business School class reunion in Australia, Mama and I headed down to Christchurch, the largest city in the South Island of New Zealand. The scenery was picture perfect with the coast nearby and the mountains not too far away. On the first day of the hunt, Mama was not feeling well, so I ventured out alone with my professional guide. We helicoptered into the "alps" in search of these elusive animals. As we climbed from one ridge to the other, I kept looking at serious harm if I slipped and fell off an embankment. My guide was used to the mountains, but I was from the flat country. Finally along the way, we saw a chamois, an antelope-type animal with two upright horns which curved slightly backwards at the tip. My professional hunter said to have a go. It was tricky in the steep mountains, but I braced myself in the rocks and terrain, tucked the rifle in my shoulder, looked through the scope, took my half breath, then squeezed the trigger. I got him with one-shot. I wish Daddy had been there to shake my hand. Towards dusk, we lucked upon a few Himalayan tahr, and I was able to get one, too. It was a successful hunt.

As we headed back, I was thinking about how blessed I was, being able to have such great adventures. I started pondering and reminiscing about my life and realized that I had traveled to fifty-plus countries and six continents — all but Antarctica. While in Christchurch, we could feel the arctic wind blowing across the land. It was a cold chill, and the wind never stopped. Little did I know that it foretold the winds of change that were coming for me.

Hunt in New Zealand with my chamois in the steep mountains

CHAPTER 12

Hurricane Katrina

Mama's health was slowly declining. The travel lessened, and since we were staying home more, I needed an intellectual project to keep me busy. Taking care of a parent is challenging, for the roles reverse, and it is hard not to experience burn-out — both physically and mentally. A balance is necessary for the caregiver too.

For years I had passed by William Carey University on the Coast, a small campus that overlooked the Gulf of Mexico. The main building was a large, welcoming rectangular structure with wooden floors and thick-paned windows that reflected the water. I knew the professor, Dr. Carol Jones, who headed a master of science program in industrial and organizational psychology at the school. Whenever I passed by the campus, I had felt the urge to call Dr. Jones. Then I ran into her at the Gulfport Yacht Club. Over a drink, she told me about the I/O program, which was a formal study of people in business — covering leadership, motivation, personality types, employee relations — basically how people function and think in organizations. The only catch was the program was underneath the umbrella of psychology, so to complete the 60-hour program, I would need to apply for a master's degree in psychology and take the GRE (Graduate Records Examination). I did and was accepted in to the program.

I had to laugh to myself about being in a psychology program, for Daddy — and the Apollo astronauts in general — were not fond of the psychologists at NASA and were always trying to outwit them. The astronauts were hot-shot pilots. Their decisions were based on skill and cunning, and they saw no need for psychoanalysis to determine whether they were good enough to fly in space. They believed that personality types were not as significant as talent and intelligence. And the astronauts used their intelligence to move them higher up the pyramid for selection.

During NASA's extensive physical and psychological exams, my father said he pegged what the psychologists were looking for in their answers: people, movement, and color – and a positive or optimistic story line. During one particular session with a NASA psychologist, Daddy was shown a black and white picture of a man getting out of bed and buckling his pants. In the bed was a half-naked woman, rustled sheets, and a cigarette ashtray to one side. A window showed a dark outside with curtains swaying. It was meant to be a very suggestive sexual image. The psychologist asked Daddy to tell him the story of what he saw in the scene.

"Oh, this is a great story…" my father started out.

As the psychologist looked at him stone-faced, he asked Daddy to continue.

"This is a newlywed couple in their first apartment. The curtains are a soothing shade of green that match the cotton sheets. The wife is pregnant with their first child, and she woke up in the middle of the night with a craving of vanilla ice cream with chocolate swirl."

"Continue," said the psychologist, looking a little puzzled but trying to not show it.

Daddy stated, "The husband is so much in love that he is getting out of bed to run down to the local convenience store to buy her some ice cream, for she has given up cigarettes, and he wants his wife to be happy."

Daddy looked at the psychologist with all seriousness, ready for the next photo. Pete Conrad (Apollo 12), also figured it out, and one time a psychologist held up a white sheet of paper and asked Pete to describe it. Pete told him it was the fair-skinned Lady Godiva on a big and beautiful white horse, with her long blonde hair flowing down her body, protecting her from a swirling snow storm — and that she was holding a white apple. The psychologist could not contain his surprised look and turned the sheet of paper around and stared at it.

"You see all that?!" asked the psychologist to Pete.

"Yep, sure do." Pete said seriously, not showing his gapped-tooth smile.

Although Daddy didn't cotton to psychologists, I enjoyed the camaraderie that I shared with my fellow students. I was the oldest in the group and at first thought perhaps I was too old to be in graduate school, but then Mama said to me, "You are going to get older anyway, might as well get older getting smarter." And with that, I didn't worry about it again. I enjoyed studying and pondering the theories and wound up with all A's in the program. In 2004, I graduated summa cum laude on Mama's 70th birthday. Mandy planned the party to celebrate both events, and we had strawberry cake and champagne.

It had taken me two and half years to complete my Master of Science in psychology, and it was not an easy program. In between taking care of Mama and studying, I would sometimes hit the town. My running buddies and I became known as "The Six Hot Chicks." It was not a self-proclaimed name, but one time while in Florida celebrating Tsh's (pronounced Tish, short for Patricia) birthday, we were invited to a party. As the six of us walked in one after the other, a guy on a couch said, "Look at all these chicks… and they are hot, too!" We laughed and had a great night. The name stuck.

• • •

2005 was an interesting, life-changing year. I was dating off and on, not seeming to find anyone to really connect with for a long-term relationship. Mama's health was also off and on, and by now she was permanently in a wheelchair. I was starting to feel like a lost soul without a clear direction.

My mornings consisted of waking up and spending about 30 minutes petting my two cats, which usually slept at the end of my queen-sized bed. I jokingly talked to them and would say… "Now that we have a quorum gathered, we can a hold a board of directors meeting…" They would look up at me and purr contentedly. However, this routine generally caused me to run late to Mama's house — and when I told her that I *had* to pet the cats,

Receiving my Master of Science in Psychology
from William Carey University

A night on the town
with friends at Beau
Rivage – Gail, me,
Barbara and Mary

Celebrating the holidays
with "The Hot Chicks" –
Tracy, Gail, me (on floor),
Mary, Barbara, Tsh

I could tell she would be irritated, but then laugh with a bit of sarcasm, "Oh yes, petting the cats takes priority." However, since she was a veterinarian's daughter, she knew the importance of animals in one's life, and for me it was the quiet time before the day began. No worries, no problems, just pure joy between a cat lover and her animals.

At Mama's house, I would always give Mama a kiss on the cheek. My father used to kiss my mother the first thing when he came in — a gesture that made an impression on me, for I thought it was the sweetest thing — so simple yet so meaningful. I wanted Mama to know that she was also a priority and appreciated. By now Mama needed additional care, so I would also visit with Mama's nighttime caretaker.

Then I'd see what Mama needed for the day. If errands needed to be run, I'd put her in the car and load up the wheelchair. Some days we would go to the Keesler Air Force Base commissary, loading up on provisions. Sometimes we would go to a doctor's appointment, but many days we would just sit at the house and visit. She loved to watch a soap opera, *The Young and the Restless*, and so I'd sit with her, and we would talk about the storyline and the characters. We had once met Eric Braeden, who played a character, Victor, in the show, in the Owner's Suite at the Indy 500 race. My Mama was thrilled and took a picture with him, and later the housekeeper asked if the photo was with a cut-out or really him. Even though Mama had met many famous people, to the housekeeper he was an untouchable celebrity.

After running errands or watching the soap opera, Mama would generally take a nap, and I would go through her mail, write checks, file papers – handle the general duties of managing her paperwork and affairs. Then she would get up, and we'd sit in the living room or outside by the pool and watch the golfers go by. I would start to get dinner ready, and if nothing was on TV, I would rent a movie. Generally, I would get a comedy, for Mama liked to laugh. We would have dinner and drink wine, or in Mama's case by now, water and wine. A friend had suggested mixing water with her wine to dilute the effects. I thought that idea was brilliant. Then we'd wind up the day, and I would clean up the dishes and put dinner away.

If there was a shift change with the sitters, we'd go through that routine and then settle in for the night.

I wanted to make sure that Mama's quality of life was not diminished, so after she was in bed, I'd light a candle or put on soft music, and we would talk as I sat on the couch in her bedroom. I had heard her stories many times but cherished hearing them again and again. I would also ponder life with her, and kept saying, "You know, I have done all those things that one says you should do to appreciate life… like look at a beautiful sunset, stop and smell the roses, tell people that you love them, and appreciate the little things in life." I would tell Mama that she was so lucky to have found a true love and to have had a successful and happy marriage. I'd wonder aloud why that was so elusive to me. She never had an answer, for deep down I felt that she did not want me to leave her. I was her companion, and although she had sitters, she had become dependent on her daughter for emotional support and social interaction.

When driving home one evening, I felt a strong sense that I had derailed my life and that I was "off-track." Career-wise, my life was on hold. But I kept saying to myself that God made only 10 commandments and that honoring thy mother and thy father was one of them. My mother had given birth to me, and I felt a need to take care of her since she had wanted a daughter so much. My life was her life now, and I was determined to make sure she was well cared for in her final years. If she wanted to go and do, by golly, we would go and make it happen.

The big trip planned for 2005 was a trip to China for a reunion with the Harvard Business School class. Mama had been four times previously to China and talked about its fascination. We had booked the Platinum American Express's offer of 2-for-1 first-class tickets. On a trip in the spring to take Mama to San Antonio for an astronauts' wives meeting, my friend Michell tagged along so that while Mama visited with the other wives from the NASA days, I would have a buddy. On the return trip from San Antonio to Houston, Mama out of the blue offered her seat on the China trip to Michell. Mama said she'd been to China and didn't feel as though she had the physical stamina for the trip. I was stunned, for Mama had not discussed it with me.

Michell answered excitedly, "Joan, my family has a trip planned for Europe this summer, but if I can make sure all the dates fit, heck yea, I'll go!" And off Michell and I went.

China was truly fascinating with its colorful pagodas, temples, and forbidden places. It was similar to Egypt in the fact that a highly developed civilization existed there thousands of years ago. The Great Wall itself was a feat in its day. Traveling with my OPM class was first-class too, and being back in the group and challenging each other intellectually while drinking champagne was fun. Being a political science major, I was fascinated with how capitalism and communism co-existed under the same government. At each tourist attraction we went to, someone was peddling a scarf, a watch, a CD, or some trinket. "One dollar, one dollar…" became the running line. Then one day while in Tiananmen Square in Beijing, the King and Queen of Belgium were visiting.

I said, "Hey, I've met them with the astronauts and cosmonauts…" and was trying to move my way toward their group when our guide said, "We must move out of the square, now!"

Michell and I started lingering, and our guide kept pushing the group along. "You do not understand; I can be thrown in jail for your not complying," the guide said frantically.

The Harvard group was trying to figure out where the brave Chinese had stood up to the tanks during the student protests of 1989. Then out of the blue, Chinese soldiers started marching in a solid line or "wall" toward us, pushing people out of the square and toward the Forbidden City. The tension in the air was palpable. Michell and I thought it was exciting and waited for them to approach. We felt something akin to foreign war journalists and had found our calling.

Smiling at each other and with the adrenaline flowing, I said, "For our next career, you take the pictures, and I'll write about it!"

• • •

After the China trip, I decided that if Mama could no longer travel as

Michell and me sitting on the Great Wall of China

Tiananmen Square with my Harvard Business School group

much, that I would go more on my own. In July 2005, I went down for the Shuttle launch's first flight since the Columbia re-entry tragedy. It had been two years since the Shuttle had flown, and as an astronaut's daughter, I felt this was another historic time in our space history that I should witness. I stayed in a rinky-dink hotel that was quite old and had a window unit as loud as a freight train, but I was there. NASA had a VIP bus tour that evening to view the Shuttle lit up at night, so I went down to the hotel restaurant and had some dinner by myself. I looked at the walls with old photos of astronauts and space launches and could just imagine if these walls could talk. The history and nostalgia were everywhere. Some of the old photos, aged and faded with time, showed celebrities of the day with the famous fly-boys. You could sense this was once a happenin' place with lots of pretty girls and the drinks flowing.

I went to the NASA bus pick-up, which then traveled to a newer hotel where most of the NASA personnel were staying. We learned that the tour would be delayed a couple of hours, so I got off the bus and went to the bar. I saw two guys drinking a Coors light, and I said, "Hey, that's a great beer! I used to sell it!"

One guy turned to me and said, "Are you Stu Roosa's daughter?"

I said, "Yes! How did you know?"

He answered, "There have only been a few astronauts who had distributorships, one being Stu Roosa, so if you are here and you used to sell it, I thought you must be an astronaut's daughter, and Stu came to mind since you look like him!"

As it turned out the guy was Ed White, the son of Astronaut Ed White, who died in the Apollo 1 fire.

I said, "I used to go to the elementary school that was named after your father!"

As we chatted, a girl came up and ordered a drink. I didn't instantly recognize her, but she heard us talking, and then said, "Rosemary? Ed White? I am Laura Shepard-Churchley — Alan Shepard's daughter!"

It was a small world, and I know our daddies had to help arrange it. The three of us just happened to be there on our own, and we became fast friends. It was an exciting evening, first seeing Laura and Ed, and then riding out to the launch pad to view the Shuttle all lit up by spotlights with the darkness of the night around like space.

We parked as close as NASA would allow, at the perimeter of the fence that encircled the launchpad and rocket. The crowd was respectfully excited, and all were taking pictures. Everyone was in awe. I could feel the gravity of the moment and was pleased that I was there. I thought about Mama and her days of coming to the Cape, and her witnessing every Apollo launch. There is just a feeling when looking at any rocket vehicle right before launch. Your mind wanders to what the astronauts are doing and thinking, too, for they have trained long and hard for their chance to ride that rocket. It moved me to stare so closely and intimately at this space vehicle, knowing the blood, sweat, and tears it took to get the program back up and running again. Also knowing that this intricate "being" would soon be spewing fire from the liquid oxygen and hydrogen mixture, hurtling a brave crew into space within minutes, caused me to pause and reflect. After Apollo 13, it was my father's crew that placed themselves on the launch pad after a delay. Now I was with the children of those brave men of spaceflight, and with the daughter of the Apollo 14 Commander. Though on this mission to return us back into space, the Commander was a woman, Eileen Collins. How far the space program had come.

It was very late when we returned to the hotels, and we had only a few hours to sleep before having to be up for the NASA bus to take us to the viewing area. The next morning, the new three amigos met up again to witness history in the making. We gathered hours before the actual launch time so that NASA could shut down the roads prior to take-off. We waited and waited, and then… the mission was scrubbed due to technical issues. The launch took off a week later, but I had to watch it on TV.

• • •

After the successful mission, I kept pondering my future. Daddy used to talk about leaving something for the next generation, so one day I stopped

"Return to Flight" Shuttle Mission – STS 114 – in 2005

off at an off-shoot campus of Tulane University near my house and asked if they needed any professors. They said they were always looking and to send in my resume and transcripts. I did and was called to teach Introduction to Psychology, beginning August 30, 2005.

It was hurricane season, and the Gulf had already seen several since the beginning of the season, which officially started in June. Hurricanes start out as tropical storms and are named alphabetically, beginning with A, and alternating between boys' and girls' names — a result of the equal opportunity movement. It used to be that storms were named only after girls, as in 1969 when Hurricane Camille devastated the Mississippi Gulf Coast. It was the worst storm in modern history, and my mother cried when she saw the devastation for the first time. She talked about how steps that once led to beautiful antebellum homes along the beach were the only thing that remained of those grand structures. Trees had been uprooted; boats had been tossed to shore, and unfortunately, lives were lost. My mother used to talk about how silly it was to stay for hurricanes, for it was one of the few monsters of Mother Nature that allowed for a day or two of warning. However, 2005 had already had ten tropical storms and four hurricanes, and getting ready for one is always a chore. Windows have to be boarded, water and provisions purchased, gas tanks filled, and evacuation plans implemented. We had a few scares that caused concern for us, but we had not yet had to evacuate due to predictions that they would not hit Mississippi.

We went about our daily routines, and I had the yard re-mulched, the carpets cleaned, and the house in order. I would go to Mama's every day as usual, and we talked about dodging a bullet with each passing storm. Then Hurricane Katrina started moving toward the United States. It started off the Coast of Africa in early August. It was heading straight to Florida. It passed over the bottom half of Florida as a Category 1, with sustained winds of approximately 75 mph. It weakened, but then came into the Gulf of Mexico and sat there. It gathered strength and was turning into a major hurricane. It was huge and ominous and predicted to hit New Orleans, not Mississippi. After being a bit weary of being on alert for previous storms and not having anything happen, this was the proverbial "cry wolf" scenario for most Mississippians. I had a bad feeling about it and debated with neighbors and family about whether to evacuate. Mama said she was going to wait it out at home. Moving Mama would not be easy. But as the days progressed, and this very large, well-defined hurricane started to engulf the entire Gulf, I started to get worried. On Friday night, Mama said she was not going anywhere. Her house had survived Hurricane Camille, and she was far enough from the beach to be okay.

New Orleans was in full-swing evacuation mode and had implemented a "contra-flow," which means that the incoming lanes into the city had been reversed, and only outgoing traffic was allowed. All lanes were used for a full-scale evacuation. People were filling up the Mississippi beach hotels, thinking it was far enough to the east of the predicted landfall. I went home that evening and watched the Weather Channel. On Saturday morning I got a call from Michell in Houston. The family was involved in the oil business. She told me her brother's company's private jet was flying into New Orleans to pick up friends, and she had reserved Mama and me two seats. Due to weight, balance, and size of plane, we would be allowed only our purses and a change of clothes - and nothing else. And we had to be there in three hours. It was impossible for several reasons — one was the contra-flow, another was that we needed to take more things, and finally, moving Mama required more time and effort.

I went to Mama's house that morning and tried to go through the routine, but my instincts were saying that we needed to evacuate. Mama seemed adamant about staying home, despite my reminders that she once said she would not stay for a hurricane. It was Saturday afternoon, and the storm was strengthening. Mama's sister and brother-in-law, Patti and Knox, said they were going to a friend's house that was off the beach and elevated. The news was warning that there were going to be strong winds and power outages. *Power outages*, that was it! I told Mama that at the very least there were going to be power outages, and she did not want to be in the heat without power for even a day or two. Air conditioning is a necessity in the South, particularly in the August heat when temperatures are regularly in the upper 90s. And with the humidity, the heat can feel like it's well into the 100s. This convinced Mama to prepare to leave, and I asked the sitter to prepare a bag, gather her medicines for a few days, and to batten down the hatches as best she could. We would leave in the morning.

I headed home to start preparing myself and to try and find us a place to stay. It was Saturday evening, August 27. I took out the atlas. Going west was out of the question. Many Coastians were heading north, so the hotels heading that way were full. I called as far as Atlanta, and there were no rooms. I kept looking at the map and thought the best way was to head due east. As I called for rooms along the I-10 corridor toward Orlando, I had no luck. Then I remembered seeing in a magazine a place called Rosemary Beach, about four hours away near Panama City, Florida. I called. I got a recorded message that said the office was open from Monday through Friday and to call back during working hours. I left a message and pleaded, saying that we were looking for a place to stay for a few days and that we were evacuating for Katrina. Not too long afterward, the phone rang. A kind young woman said she was calling from Rosemary Beach and that they were monitoring the phones, for they were receiving many calls from New Orleanians looking for places to stay. She told me about a couple of condos that were available, and I booked one. Bingo, we now had a place to stay. I started calling people to let them know where we were going, did my laundry, and started to pack. I moved my outside furniture into the garage, put in the plants, and packed up some photographs and insurance information. My house was built in 1990 on a small budget, and I thought that it would not sustain the high winds. I wondered if I would see it intact again but did not belabor the point.

Morning came, and I packed the car and called Mama and the sitter. The sitter was to change shifts that morning, but the other sitter called to say she was preparing for the storm and was not coming. I told the sitter I understood if she needed to go to her home, but she agreed to go with us, for we all thought it would be a quick trip. I got Mama's cat in a carrier, and we took my car back to my house and parked it in the garage. I put my two cats in another carrier, and we started for Rosemary Beach at high noon. We had the three of us, three cats, and a trunk with suitcases and a wheelchair. We got onto I-10, and then we saw the extent of the mass exodus from the area. The traffic was bumper to bumper. What would have been an hour's drive to Mobile, Alabama, took us over four hours. I don't think we ever got over 15 mph and sometimes were at a dead stop. It was a long trip, but we finally made it to Rosemary Beach just past 8 p.m. It was dark and rainy, but we were relieved to have a place to rest.

I got a call from a friend, Francisco, whom I had recently been out with on a first date. Francisco was a Venezuelan who had his U.S. permanent green card. We had met at a restaurant/bar called Bonefish Grill about two weeks prior to Katrina. My friend, Tsh, one of the Hot Chicks who was a tall blonde with big blue eyes, and I were going to a dive bar that evening to shoot some pool. I wanted to first have a drink at a nice, nearby place. We arrived at Bonefish Grill, and I saw my neighbor Steve. So we started chatting and having a drink together. I thought Francisco was handsome and nice but didn't think much of it. Tsh, who knew Francisco from the film industry, kept insisting that we go out, even if it was just to the movies. He called, and we saw *The 40-year-old Virgin*. I sneaked in a bottle of champagne, and by the end of the movie, we were laughing and smiling at each other.

I told Francisco where we were staying for the storm and he asked if I minded his calling again to check on us. "Please do," I said. As my head hit the pillow that night, I was praying hard that the Good Lord would wrap his hands around our homes and protect us from the hurricane. It was a dark night. As the wind blew and the rain fell around us, I kept thinking, "Twenty-four hours from now, it will all be over."

Hurricane Katrina hit Monday, August 29, 2005, squarely on the Mississippi Gulf Coast. The devastation was immense. I woke up trying to turn on the Weather Channel for news, but there was only a smattering. I was frustrated. But we were safe and sound in a beautiful refuge, so we ate and drank comfortably, just waiting on news about when we could return. But no clear news was coming in. Cell phone towers were out. A day went by, but we did not get much news other than that things were hit hard.

Then a levee broke in New Orleans, and the city flooded. Then the news started covering the rescue missions in New Orleans. Where was the news about Mississippi? Then my cell phone received a text message – a new form of communication - from a friend on the Mississippi Gulf Coast. It was bad news. Her home had suffered massive damage, and a tree had fallen on it.

Our land-line at Rosemary Beach started to ring the next day as more news spread among friends and family across the United States. But we knew no more than they did about our homes – we didn't know whether our houses had survived or not. All I knew from the weather reports was that Hurricane Katrina had stalled, with sustained winds of more than 125 mph, for more than seven hours over the Mississippi Gulf Coast. Finally, I saw a report from Bobby Mahoney, a colorful restaurant owner known for his corny jokes, but he was quite serious while talking to the reporter. He said he and his brother had stayed for the storm, and that they had to get to the second floor of the restaurant to escape the surge. Bobby was cut by broken glass on his behind, and his brother had been bitten by a venomous snake. A sinking feeling hit my gut. Then the sitter called for me as I was glued to the TV for more news. I had a phone call from Francisco. He had evacuated to Mobile, Alabama, but was back in Mississippi.

"Are you okay?" he asked. His voice, with its accent, was so kind and sweet. I told him we were worried about our homes. Francisco said he was able to obtain a special pass to go to the beach, for by now the National Guard was mobilizing to protect against looters. I gave him my mother's address, and he knew where I lived from our first and only date. He said he would check on the houses and call back.

In the interim, I called two of my brothers; one was living in Florida, and the other was in Huntsville, Alabama, for a week of meetings. I asked if they would go to Mississippi to help with the aftermath of Katrina and to check on our homes since I was with Mama. It was approaching the Labor Day weekend, and both said they had plans with their families that weekend. Another brother had gotten the news while he was deployed, and he was heading back to the U.S. to assist. He landed on Wednesday, and I expected him to start driving to the coast by Thursday. But he needed time to "decompress."

Francisco called. He had been to my home, and miraculously, it survived! Trees, fences, and roof shingles were scattered about, but it was in place with no major problems. I was in shock. My little house had survived the wrath of Mother Nature. Then I asked if he had been able to go to my mother's house, and I braced myself for his response, fearing the worst. It, too, had miraculously survived! But with trees, pots, shingles, and debris strewn around, it had suffered some roof damage, and there were leaks. He informed me that he and his son, Tino, had patched the leaks with blue tarps as best they could. I was touched. I had never met his son, but here were two men willing to help my mother in a time of need. I asked about his split-level home on the back bay.

He said, "I had over 14 feet of water in my home. Structurally it is there, but it is full of mud and standing water."

I felt bad for him, but he sounded upbeat. He had faith all would be well. Then he told me about the devastation on the Coast. It was like a bomb had gone off. Roads were full of holes, homes just gone – completely washed away. I had a hard time picturing "gone."

That Thursday night I fretted. What was I to do? How would I start the process of trying to get us back to our homes? The electricity was still off, and the water/sewage plants had been compromised. There was no clean drinking water. The Centers for Disease Control was issuing reports of condemning the entire Gulf Coast. On Friday morning, I told my mother that I was going to drive over to Mississippi for the day and that I would be back late that evening. I had to see and assess for myself. Then I could start making the necessary phone calls for the recovery. It was four hours there and four hours back… leaving me with a few hours to see for myself what had happened. My mother was reluctant for me to go, for we had only the one car, and she was concerned for my safety. I had a .38 revolver with me, and told her I would travel with it. She also knew I would use it properly if needed. By the time we finished the pros and cons, it was later than expected when I got on the road, around 10 a.m. I was planning on being back by 10 p.m. I assured her she would see me that evening.

As I started the drive over, I had no idea what to expect. As I drove through Alabama, some highway signs were twisted around. I thought, "Best that I fill up the gas tank." I found a truck stop and topped off the tank. The sky was sunny, but the air had a uneasy feel. As I proceeded, I saw signs of high winds — damaged trees and twisted - or gone - road signs. I finally made my way home. As I opened the door and started to walk around, the electricity came on! Hallelujah. I had not been there even 30 minutes when my land line phone rang. It was Francisco. He had called Rosemary Beach and my mother had told him I was heading this way. He said he had a jeep, a pass to the beach, and a secret place that had gas for refueling. He would be there shortly.

A feeling of relief came over me, and I called Mama to let her know that I was safe, about to go see her house, and then be on my way back to Rosemary Beach. As I looked around, I saw trees down; leaves everywhere, and it looked like a small tornado must have torn through the neighborhood, for some homes had more roof and yard damage than others. About then Francisco came to my door, smiling, handsome, with his brown hair blowing in the wind. Sure enough, he'd arrived in a red jeep, a 1943 Willis Jeep flat fender. He was Prince Charming coming to save the damsel in distress.

As I hopped into this open-air chariot, he said, "Be prepared; it is hard to see."

As we rounded a corner to head to the beach, there was an apartment complex that had an entire wall gone. It looked like a doll house. I could see the sink, closet, furniture, and a twin bed with the linens still on it. We came to the railroad crossing where the National Guard was already in place, telling us to stop and turn around. I showed them my driver's license, and Francisco showed him the pass to the beach. They hesitated but waved us on, giving a good stare that said we'd better not be there for looting or we would be in serious trouble.

As we hit the beach, we saw the force of the hurricane. The debris from the storm was everywhere. Where a McDonald's once stood, only the life-size cement clown was standing. As we neared my mother's street, the

homes that once stood majestically near the beachfront were no longer. Now I understood the term "gone." As we drove north on Southern Circle, where my mother's home was, the homes went from being gone, to kinda standing, to standing with a lot of damage. We pulled into her driveway. Besides obvious wind damage, it looked okay. I unlocked the front door. Since the electricity was still off in her neighborhood, the alarm was off. Then the heat hit me. The home had been sitting there since Monday without any air in the middle of summer and 90-degree temperatures. No flood water had come through, for the furniture had not been floating. All was in place. I looked out the back and saw a formal Queen Anne chair sitting on a green of the golf course. The screened-in back area was in shreds, as if someone had taken a razor blade and ripped through it effortlessly. The pool was murky, and we could not see the bottom. I could see why the CDC might be calling this area condemned, for this was now prime mosquito breeding grounds.

I was more worried about the space treasures in my mother's home. From the leaks in the roof, water had gotten into the house, and the carpets were soaking wet. In my old bedroom, there was a zebra skin on the bed, three elephant tusks under the bed, and a full lion's skin on the floor with the head posed in a "roar," its large, bone-breaking teeth bared in a snarl. My former room had turned into a trophy room of sorts, filled with animals my father had shot in Africa after the Apollo 14 mission.

My parents had extensively remodeled the home in 1984, adding two master bathrooms from their bedroom, which overlooked the pool. Off my mother's bathroom, behind a full-length glass mirror was a closet door, and behind that closet door was a room full of boxes of space items, along with a safe, shotguns, rifles, pistols, and family memorabilia. It was called the "safe-room," and it was fire proof. However, I just didn't know if it was flood proof. Since Francisco was barely in my life, I was not sure whether to tell him about this room, but I had no choice; those were the most precious and priceless items in the house. I pulled the mirror door away and unlocked the safe room. To my amazement, it was dry. Double hallelujah! I did not mess around too much in the room, relocked the door, pushed the mirror back, and continued around the house. Every room that had carpet was wet; thus, everything that was touching the floor was wet, too, including the lion skin. The heat was starting to become unbearable in the house, so I started gathering valuables that I could easily pack up and take back to my house for safekeeping.

As we loaded up the jeep, Francisco suggested we take one item to air out — the lion skin with the head in a growl. It was heavy, but we carried out this huge skin, which was now so wet and slick that the fur was wiping away. Francisco placed the head of the lion on the hood of the jeep like a large hood ornament, and we proceeded to drive around. As we hit the beach again, it was eerily deserted. Only essential personnel were allowed. Overhead were military helicopters. I thought that this must be what it feels like to be in a war zone.

My aunt and uncle's home was on the beach, and I asked Francisco to take me there. It was gone. Nothing was there but a cement floor and a debris-filled pool in the back. My heart sank. We continued along the beach for a few miles. Items were hanging from trees; wood was piled up from flattened homes, and even a large casino barge that featured a big-breasted mermaid on the front was sitting on top of what used to be a motel. Francisco and I were not saying a word, taking in the enormity of it all.

Finally, he said, "You can cry if you would like; it is okay."

I was too stunned to cry. My brain was in overload. It looked like a movie set that belonged in a horror film. Too hard to imagine it was all real.

As we drove this lion-adorned chariot to the safety of my home, I could not drive back to Rosemary Beach that night. There was too much to do to start the recovery. Francisco invited me to a friend's home for a cleaning-out-the-freezer dinner that night, so I called Mama and told her what we had seen and that I'd try to drive back in the next day or two. She had no choice but to sit tight, but I knew she was safe and comfortable. At dinner that night, Francisco and his pal Raymond talked about obtaining the bid to place concertina wire along the railroad tracks. Besides the jeep, Francisco had a Unimog, a rare "Tonka toy"-looking vehicle that was used as a tractor-truck by farmers in Germany after WWII. They were made by Mercedes-Benz around 1950. Francisco had bought one several years before for fun in the mud. It was powder blue, and just for kicks, the ball of the back hitch sported the top half of a Hulk plastic toy figure. Now the Unimog was being transformed with a device to hook up barbed wire so that it could be laid along the 20 miles or so of tracks that paralleled the beach about a half-mile from the shore. As Francisco and Raymond talked about gathering the forces — and gaining the okay from the state to proceed — my mind went back to Mama's house. In a few days, the mold would start to grow on the walls, like bacteria in a petri dish. It was a helpless feeling.

Mama told people where I was, and the phone rang with calls from concerned friends and family. I was patient with each one, explaining the situation again and again. There were things to do, though. It was like being in the center of a bicycle wheel, knowing that each spoke outward was a new project, and each one was equally important. But which spoke to traverse first? All needed to be done.

My neighbor Steve, the one who was with Francisco the day we met, was the director of the local ambulance service, AMR - American Medical Response. Steve's house was now hub to displaced high-ranking politicians, lawyers, and corporate people from AMR, which meant his house became a command post of sorts, but in the evening, it was party central. As day one and two passed, it became clear to me that there would be no leaving soon. What amazed me the most was how neighbor helped neighbor, and everyone pitched in with what they had to share, from a bottle of wine, to a good scotch, to sausage and steaks for the grill. It gave me faith in humanity. I called Mama and said there was no leaving until either more family or the cavalry arrived to help with her house.

Francisco got the bid to lay the wire along the tracks to help protect against looters while the National Guard monitored cross points of the roads. Then Francisco did another touching thing to help Mama. He pulled some of the crew laying wire to help yank the carpet from my mother's house. This abated the mold and saved the house from complete ruin. I kept calling insurance companies and repairmen, while finding a storage unit for Mama's household items. Francisco would stop by and check on me in the evenings, and we would wind up at Steve's house to talk about the day. At this point Francisco started looking pretty good to me, for he was kind, thoughtful, tall, dark, and handsome — with an accent to boot. He would regale me with the stories of his day — seeing lingerie or a stuffed toy up in the trees, and he would wonder who owned those items… for they once were part of a life and meant something. Now the world was upside down, and survival and recovery were all that were left.

Finally, after ten days had passed since the storm, my brother from overseas arrived with a married couple. They were expecting to camp out at my mother's house, but I offered them my home, which had air conditioning, comfortable beds, and a hot shower. While they worked on Mama's house, I knew I needed to return to Rosemary Beach, for Mama and the sitter had been alone for almost a week and needed a resupply of provisions. I kissed Francisco goodbye and headed back to Florida.

In the midst of all this chaos on the Gulf Coast, another kind gentleman came to Mama's rescue. It was her pharmacist, Jim Day, of Triplett-Day Drug Company. He had an old-fashioned malt shop and restaurant inside a general store and pharmacy. It was the town gathering spot for morning coffee and swapping of tales, and any "gossip" would be politely discussed in hushed tones. Mr. Day tracked us down in Florida and called me to let me know that he was worried about Mama's medicine supply, and for me to find a local pharmacy where he could call in her prescriptions. I was once again in awe of how folks took care of each other in our small towns.

After many weeks of being at Rosemary Beach, Mama needed to come home, for it was time to see her doctor. After writing a note of thanks in the guest book at our condo, we loaded up the cats and headed to my home. I gave Mama my downstairs master bedroom and moved upstairs. It was going to be a long haul.

Meeting Tom Hanks in Washington, D.C.

Francisco

CHAPTER 13

Trials and Tribulations

Prior to Hurricane Katrina, I had made plans to attend the IMAX premiere of *Magnificent Desolation*, to take place in Washington, D.C., in the fall of 2005. Co-produced and narrated by Tom Hanks, it was a documentary film about the thoughts and feelings of Apollo astronauts who walked on the moon. The premiere was being held at the Smithsonian Air & Space Museum. I decided to proceed as planned and asked Francisco if he would like to be my date to the event. He accepted and purchased a new black suit, a white shirt, and tie. Francisco produced commercials and films, so a movie premiere was right up his alley. He was very handsome dressed to the nines, for I had seen him only in jeans or casual clothes. We wound up walking down the red carpet into the museum.

I was chit-chatting and reminiscing with Jim Lovell about the Playboy Mansion when Jim said, "Oh, I guess we need to talk to some folks," and walked over to conduct an interview.

I imagined the reporters would be yelling, "Over here, over here!" in a frenzy, but they were quiet with their pen or microphone in hand and the cameras behind them. I did not realize the protocol was for the interviewees to approach them. So by the time we figured out the red-carpet walk, it was over! I asked Francisco to grab me a cosmopolitan martini, and we laughed that maybe we should go through the line again, but by now we were running into old astronaut friends and family.

We ran into the Lovell kids and Marilyn, as well as Laura Shepard-Churchley and Ed White - my amigos - so we gathered some appetizers and sat down to catch up. As we were chatting away, Jim came running over and said, "He's here, he's here - come on, Marilyn!"

"Who?" she asked.

"Tom Hanks," Jim replied.

I thought, "I want to meet Tom Hanks!" but Marilyn politely said she was visiting and that she would say hello later. So we stayed with Marilyn, one of Mama's good friends and a fellow astronaut's wife.

The IMAX 3-D movie was interesting and moving, and afterwards a woman from NASA said that Tom Hanks would meet privately with a small group and that he would not stay long. She escorted us to a roped-off area.

Although I was anxious to meet Tom Hanks, I said, "Wait!" She looked puzzled as I continued, "I must go find Laura and Ed. They will want to meet him, too!"

Soon Laura and Ed were on their way, and the woman from NASA commented as she held up the rope for us to walk under, "You Apollo children sure do look out for each other." It hit me that we were just as bonded as the astronauts and wives.

As recovery continued on the Gulf Coast, there was another storm brewing in the Roosa family. Mama's house was not coming along as planned, for after Katrina, Hurricane Rita hit the shores of Louisiana, near Texas. Rita was the seventeenth named storm of 2005, and the fifth major hurricane of the season. The contractor working on Mama's house moved from helping with homes in Mississippi to working on those in Louisiana and Texas.

Recovery was slow, and by this time my brother and his friends had left to return to their jobs. Mama kept her spirits up picking out fixtures and furniture. She was optimistic and invited Francisco, whose home was also in slow repair, to move in with us. He had been living in a FEMA trailer but was claustrophobic and allergic to the formaldehyde in the cabinets. He practically lived with us anyway, not wanting to go to his trailer in the evenings. Francisco and I fell in love. Mama enjoyed his three children

– Francesca, Tino, and Bella - coming by, and my little house seemed to accommodate all. The home was filled with laughter and warmth, despite the tragedies of Katrina.

• • •

Time was dragging on as we found repairmen. The entire coast had been wiped out, so finding reputable people to work took time. After a year and still slow progress on her home, Mama offered to upgrade my home with new carpet, flooring, appliances, and such. We enjoyed talking about new décor, for her tastes were exquisite and unique. I called it "classic contemporary." The plan was that I, and perhaps Francisco too, would move in with her after her home was finished, and the work would start on my home.

Then Mama decided to leave me her "rainy day" funds. The bulk of the funds were in New York City. She explained that the funds would provide immediate security upon her death. Mama said, "This money will give you some stability after I am gone and make life easier." She was trying to leave me her version of a "golden parachute." Mama called the investment company in Memphis in February 2006 and said she wanted her daughter to be the beneficiary on the account. The agent who handled her funds was not in that day, but the gentleman on the phone said he would send the papers. Mama also wanted to change her Will from 2002. Life had changed post-Katrina, and Mama wanted to change some things in her life, too.

My brothers and I were communicating, but not much. I was in a new relationship with Francisco, and life was busy with daily activities. Just after Katrina, Francisco and I started taking a few short trips together. We went to Guatemala for a wedding and to his mother's home in Venezuela. I enjoyed the new cultures. Having a handsome man order dinner in a foreign language is downright sexy. Francisco's family was different from mine, for I grew up in a stoic military family, and his family was just the opposite. Just talking about what to serve for dinner sounded like a heated argument in Spanish! In Venezuela, it is customary to hang artwork all over the walls, and not linearly like we mostly do in America. As I quietly observed the extreme variations in art from contemporary to classic from ceiling to floor at his mother's apartment, suddenly I felt a hand grab my arm tightly.

"What artwork do you like… the least?" Francisco's mother asked.

This was a tricky one. I did not know what to say but decided honesty was the best policy. I looked around and saw a contemporary piece with colors running down of yellow, red, black, and gray against a white background.

"I guess that I would have to say that one," I muttered.

"That one…" as she held my arm and looked at me with deep brown eyes… "is my favorite." Although she was opposite from my mother, we grew to like each other. I started calling her Mamacita Dos.

• • •

At home in Mississippi, Mama loved being around a social environment, and Francisco started calling her Mama Joan. Work continued on Mama's house, and as we were putting it back together, her home took on a different feel. Now going on two years since the storm, Mama's health was still off and on, but she was looking forward to attending an astronaut wives' gathering in mid-May 2007. The "original wives" as they called themselves, were the wives of those who were in The Program when their husbands went into space. It was a tight-knit, supportive group, and just as the men, they were bonded by their experiences together. The wives gathered every two years, with the previous one being in San Antonio when we were there with Michell. Unfortunately, Mama was not feeling well, and she went into the hospital in early May. I cancelled her trip. She suddenly seemed to be going down fast.

During the past few years as Mama would go in and out hospitals, I would be there to keep her spirits up. She loved to listen to rock and roll music, so I'd bring in a cassette/CD player and play her favorite song, *Mony, Mony,* or other good ol' dance tunes. I would get up and boogie, and sometimes felt embarrassed, but Mama would smile, and her eyes would move and bounce with me as if she were dancing, too. It was silly, but she enjoyed it. During her stays in the hospital, Francisco's kids would come by and play the guitar, do a few gymnastic moves, or just hold her hand and sing. Many times, we'd sing *You Are My Sunshine*... not her favorite, but we could all carry the tune.

Then one day her doctor told me to prepare for the worst, that her kidneys were failing. Mama looked frail. She was weakening. I asked the doctor if there was anything he could do.

He said, "I can put her on dialysis, but I don't recommend it."

This was it. If no more treatment, her body would shut down in a few days as the toxins built up in her body. As I went to bed that night, I prayed. Early the next morning I saw a candle that Mama had given me on a trip to Medjugorje, the place where the child, Vicka, saw the Virgin Mary. At the time Vicka allegedly saw the first apparition, the young girl claimed the Blessed Virgin Mary gave her a "prayer mission" to pray for the sick. The candle was round and blue, similar to how the earth had appeared to Daddy when he was flying into space — and that big blue marble he loved as a child. I took the candle with me and lit it in Mama's hospital room in a safe spot. The nurses did not object. It was the hardest day of my life, knowing if I did nothing, that in a few days she would be gone forever. The candle burned the entire day and into the evening. As the room got dark that night, I pulled a chair up to her bedside and gently held Mama's hand. She was pale but awake.

I got up close to her and lovingly looked her in the eyes. "Mama, it is time to make a decision, and I can't seem to make it. If you feel it is time, then Daddy is waiting for you on the other side, and it will be great. You have led a wonderful life, and God will welcome you into his Kingdom. But if you want to stay alive, then I need to know tonight, and you can go on dialysis. Either way, it needs to be your choice."

She tightened the grip on my hand as much as possible, and said in a weak voice, "I want to keep living."

I watched her fall asleep and went home to rest and feed the cats. It was approaching midnight when I crawled into bed, but I set my alarm for 3 a.m. The doctor tended to make his rounds early, from anywhere between 4 to 6 a.m. When the alarm rang, I dressed in a collared blue top with white pants. Casual but sharp. I was back by 4 a.m. Around 7 a.m., the doctor had not yet come by, and I was starting to panic that I'd missed him. Mama remained in a slumber-like state, but I needed to do something, and soon. I went to the nurse's station and asked to track down Dr. Lanier. He had gotten tied up with patients that morning, but then I saw him in the hallway. He knew me well from over the years.

"She wants to live!" I said to him. "Please start dialysis right away."

"What?" said the doctor.

"Ask her yourself!" I excitedly said.

He turned without a word and disappeared. After a few minutes he came back and directed the nurses to prepare Joan Roosa for dialysis. By 10 a.m. she was in dialysis, and that evening she was talking and telling a joke. It was a miracle. Daddy and God would wait. She had chosen to fight for her life and won. I breathed a sigh of relief and a prayer of thanks.

• • •

Mama's health since Daddy's death was like a wave; she would get sick, then recover. It was like she would go to the brink of death, look over to the other side, and then step back saying, "No, I am not ready." At one point when I was in graduate school, she became gravely ill. She was barely conscious. Last rites were administered. But her vital signs remained steady. I was hopeful. It was late one night, and the lights were low as I was reading one of my psychology books. The room was quiet except for the humming of the machine showing her vitals. Then I felt a presence. It stirred my soul. It was not human or threatening. I could not see anything, but I started praying really hard. It felt like an angel was in the room.

"Oh please, please… do not take her now! I know this is not my choice, but please, please, do not take her now… I am not ready!"

Then Mama stirred, and the feeling was gone. Mama bounced back.

Another time Mama had a close call when she started taking too much aspirin for a pain her in arm. Little did we know the aspirin was sticking in her esophagus and not going down into her stomach. The tiny pills wore a hole in the lining of her esophagus, and Mama started to bleed internally. At the crack of dawn, Mama called me, and her voice was weak. She barely said my name, when I said, "Hold on, Mama, I will be right there," as I jumped up and threw on some clothes, knowing something was terribly wrong. Her bedroom looked like a murder had taken place. Mama was throwing up blood. I called 9-1-1. The paramedics were so concerned they took her to the nearest hospital rather than Memorial, her usual hospital.

As the ER doctor immediately started pumping blood into her system, he said, "Next time you call right away if this happens! If you don't, I am going to personally kick your butt!" Mama meekly ribbed him for threatening to harm her rather than save her life. Last rites were administered then, too, but after a few days in ICU, she bounced back again.

In 2006, we took Mama on easy trips to keep her spirits up and wound up sailing on the *Queen Mary II* to Ireland for a Shikar-Safari meeting, and spent that Christmas in Sea Island, Georgia, at The Cloister. Mama's determination to live was strong, but her body grew weaker with every health scare. Now she had decided to live again and in May 2007 was progressing after dialysis; however, the doctors were keeping Mama in the hospital. My oldest brother flew in to check on the house and Mama. Francisco planned a trip to Oregon so that I could hunt a mountain lion, having missed the opportunity for a leopard in Africa. I debated whether to go, but my brother insisted Mama would be okay. Mama had stabilized. The roller coaster of her health was difficult to gauge, but life for a caregiver must continue and time off is necessary.

The plan was for me to hunt, then we would all meet up in Pebble Beach for the annual Shikar-Safari meeting. Even though I was not a member of the group, Mama had asked if I could attend in her place and have Francisco as her guest. The club agreed, and I started packing my hunting gear and borrowed Mama's .243 rifle. The hunt was in the spring, and it was hard to follow tracks since there was no snow. I refused to hunt with dogs, thinking it was not much of a challenge to tree a cat then shoot it. Hunting needed to be a fair chase. Our guide was young, and I was not sure of his skills. Francisco took his camera, and I took the rifle. The guide placed us in the open, with no blind, then played a recording of a wounded animal. The sound was awful. And the wooded area had been sheared by mass cuttings, leaving a "dead" feeling. We did not see much life other than an occasional bird. I figured the sound would at least attract a coyote. I asked the guide if we could find some other areas, and he reluctantly took us to a more wooded area.

As we were road hunting, slowly going down the dirt road, Francisco yelled, "Stop!"

We backed up a short bit, and there was a huge cougar print in the dirt. The adrenaline kicked in. I grabbed the rifle, and we jumped out, following the tracks. As we entered the deep woods, I was getting excited. Finally, I was going to have my big cat! Then the guide started to get very nervous and told us that he was once mauled by a mountain lion. He had been in some thick woods, and it came out of nowhere. He flinched and said we needed to go back into the open.

"What do you mean?" I said in frustration, "This area is perfect, and we know the animal is in there!" I was ready to shoot quickly. But soon our guide said he lost the tracks and headed to the truck. I knew we would not have this chance again. No leopard, no mountain lion.

As we drove to Pebble Beach, I recalled attending Shikar-Safari meetings off and on for almost 20 years. I was coming full circle. That first trip to Pebble Beach had changed the direction of my life when Daddy asked me to leave D.C., and this one was about to change it, too. My brother had been sitting with my mother while we were in Oregon. Something deep inside me felt this might be my last Shikar-Safari meeting, but not wanting to think such thoughts, I dismissed them. I had been nominated for membership, but rejected, with the thought being that I was not a serious hunter. It was the most painful rejection of my life, for this was a group that I enjoyed being around.

• • •

Back home, Francisco started recording videos of Mama for posterity. Some videos showed her under medication, some showed her better. However, at this point, what we wanted most for Mama was to get better, and she did.

As we nursed her back, she started saying, "When I get out of here, I want to go someplace where it is warm, beautiful, and there is a nice view."

Ahhh, the dream of a trip and traveling was keeping her going again. She was released from the hospital.

Before Mama had gone into the hospital in May, we had planned a trip to Venezuela for June 2007. Mama and I had purchased upgraded tickets, and Francisco had purchased tickets for himself and his three children. Mama had had a miraculous recovery, but now she was on dialysis three times a week. There was no good reason that Francisco should postpone the trip to his home country with his children, so off he went. One night shortly after Francisco left, Mama got a craving for soup and salad from a local restaurant. It was a small place that used to be a house, and was basically one room with funky paintings of New Orleans trumpet players, four-top tables, and a full-service bar. I ordered the food over the phone and then grabbed the car keys. When I arrived, the restaurant was busy, so I sat down on a bar stool and waited.

"Hey, Rosemary, what are you doing here?" It was Steve, my neighbor. He was sitting with an attorney, Don. Steve was still the head of the local ambulance service, AMR, and Don was an attorney for the organization. Don had also sued Gulf Coast Coors in the years past as a plaintiff attorney, and he had been brutal on my father during the trial. We were out-lawyered in that case and went from a settlement request of $250,000 to a jury awarding the plaintiff $1.2 million. It was a case that shocked the conscience of the court and was finally settled during appeal for $750,000.

I nodded at Don, and Steve asked me about Mama. I started telling him how she was missing a trip to Venezuela that would have satisfied her wish to see that beautiful vista and feel a cool breeze. Without a word, Steve grabbed his cell phone and went outside. I sat there awkwardly with Don and mumbled a few things, wondering why the food was taking so long. Then Steve walked back in and handed me a cocktail napkin with a name and number scribbled on it.

"Call this number when you get home," he said. "They are expecting your call. It will cost some money, but your Mama will get her wish."

The number was an air ambulance service based in Florida. I went home and talked to Mama about a trip. She said, "Let's go!" I checked with her doctors the next day, who gave the okay. "Just don't give her much water so that the fluid builds up," her doctor instructed.

After Mama's dialysis treatment, the jet showed up, and Mama was telling the crew how she was going to Margarita Island in Venezuela. When we landed, Francisco's sister had an ambulance ready and had ordered a hospital bed for the room. We arrived after dark, but the next morning, the shutters were opened to a gorgeous view of the water. A cool breeze started to drift on Mama's face. Life came back into Mama's veins, and we played *Mony, Mony*. She came back from the brink once again. Francisco recorded the visit, taking a few different angles and shots for his director/ film instincts kicked-in. Francisco's mother flew in, and our mothers got to meet each other. They both gave us their blessings. After a few days, it was time to return home for another dialysis treatment. When Francisco finally returned home, he found Mama sitting up on the side of the bed waving her arms to music while I danced.

It was amazing how much better Mama was feeling now, and in early August I asked Mama if she knew just how sick she had been in May.

"It was touch and go, Mama. You were very close to dying," I told her. She remembered it vaguely, but did say that she could feel the prayers.

She then looked at me with joy and love in her eyes, and said "Rosemary, just think of the adventure that I am about to take! This is going to be the greatest trip of all."

It was if to console and prepare me for her passing. She was ready, and actually looking forward to it. At that exact moment, we both felt at peace. I never brought it up again.

● ● ●

Mama moved back into her home on Southern Circle at the end of August 2007. Knowing the isolation and loneliness would be hard on Mama now that she was back into her house, I continued to be there for her. I started into the pre-Katrina routine of just spending time with her, taking care of her needs, and giving her as much quality of life as possible. Our mother/daughter love was deep. Each day was precious. All my life Mama had been my champion. Whenever I was doubtful, worried, or upset about something, she had a way of making things better with her words and care. Now it was my turn to do the same for her.

I asked friends to come by and visit, and one day Mandy came by while I was working in the office. Mandy went back into Mama's bedroom and said they had a nice talk, and that it was good to see "Mama Joan." I started to think of ways to make the house seem more lively and friendlier, so we threw Francisco's oldest daughter an engagement party. Mama had gotten her hair done the day of the party and was worn out, so people went to her bedroom, and Mama "held court." That gave me the idea to have another Halloween party in October. I asked Mama that if she approved, she could dress like a queen or royalty and stretch out on a lounge chair for comfort. She laughed at the idea and said to go ahead with the party plans. But Mama was getting weaker and weaker, and the dialysis three times a week was tedious. I kept trying to find a home dialysis machine and a nurse, but the area was still struggling from Katrina, and finding an independent qualified nurse was proving too difficult.

Toward late September, Mama went back into the hospital. I could tell the strain was getting to her with the continued poking and prodding. I made my usual visits with rock and roll music to keep her spirits up. Francisco's kids came by to cheer her up, too. Mama rebounded and returned home. The cycle of the health wave was continuing. I wrote a poem for the Halloween party invitation, and added a line that said, "Perhaps you might even see a ghost!" I felt a deep pang in my stomach at the line but put it out of my mind. Mama liked the poem. We made 100 copies, and I started to address the envelopes, but something told me to hold off.

Francisco and I would soon be moving in with Mama so that we could start the upgrades to my home. However, before doing that, he and I planned a trip to Cape Cod for the 50th birthday celebration of one of my Harvard classmates. Mama was getting tired of the dialysis, and sometimes it was a struggle to get her to go. But she would go, and life continued. Part of caring for a parent day-to-day is also taking breaks, so Francisco and I took our trip and left Mama with the sitters. Cape Cod was beautiful in the fall, and our hosts, Steve and Donna, had more champagne than anyone could drink. The house was party-till-ya-drop and it was nice to get away and reconnect with Harvard friends from around the world. Francisco and I planned a trip on our own to Nantucket and Martha's Vineyard after the birthday party.

While at Martha's Vineyard, I got a call late one night. It was from Mama's longtime sitter. Mama was not feeling well, and she thought Mama should go back into the hospital. I told her we would be on the first flight in the morning but to go ahead and call 9-1-1. We came home to find her in ICU. She was relieved to see me, and I tried my best to keep her going, but I could tell things were serious. I started talking about where our next trip should be and mentioned that there were cruise ships with dialysis machines. I said that Argentina would be nice, but she gave me a look that I had never seen before. It said, "It's not going to happen."

It scared me, and she was not talking much. After a couple of days, her heart rate was not coming down. I jokingly told her that Neil Armstrong would not be happy that she was using up all her heartbeats, for Neil had once told Mama that he believed a person had a certain number of heartbeats in life, and that he did not like using his up with exercise! He obviously was in great shape, but that's why Mama said she did not exercise — so that she did not deplete her heartbeats. I called and emailed my brothers, telling them they should consider flying in, but the oldest said he had been there in May and that he would be coming back for Christmas. The other two said they did not have time for their schedules were too busy.

Sunday came. I told Mama that I wanted to go to church later that evening and light her a candle. I turned to find the TV remote for a football game when Mama said, "Don't leave."

I turned back around and told her that I wasn't going anywhere anytime soon. ICU is strict on visitation times, but the nurses would let me linger.

A deacon, Dick Henderson, came by and asked if he could administer last rites. I told him to go ahead, but that Mama was probably a person to have received the most last rites without dying. He said this time I should be prepared for it. I could tell this time was different and said that my only wish was that she not die alone. It was my biggest worry. As the nurses came around for their duties, I could tell that I had pushed my time in ICU.

I told Mama I would be back after church, and she said "Rosemary..." but no more.

I kissed her on the check and said I would see her soon.

When I returned that evening after Mass, she was sleeping. The next morning came, and when I arrived for visitation, the nurses told me that they were transferring her to a room. Mama's vital signs had stabilized, although her heart rate was still up. I thought, "Once again the rebounder would be okay!" Mama was in and out of consciousness and could not talk. I kept telling her that this was a good sign that she was being moved into a room and that we would have her home soon.

I spent that Monday making her comfortable, and I was encouraged. As evening rolled on, a sitter was to take over for the night, but she did not return. Francisco joined me around 8 p.m. He asked if I wanted to go home and rest, but I told him I wanted to spend the night with Mama. He said he would stay, too.

The night nurse kept telling me that Mama was authorized for a morphine shot, but I snapped, "Do you see her wrist band? She is allergic to morphine! Do you want a patient who cannot talk to suffer from a medicine she is allergic to?"

The nurse said she did not want Mama to suffer and that is why she wanted to give her the morphine. She asked what type of pain medicine she normally took, and I told her Demerol. The nurse then called the doctor and came back and asked if she could give Mama Demerol.

The nurse was really pushing hard for the pain med, so I consented. After she gave Mama the shot, her heart started to act up, and the nurse called the emergency staff. I was asked to leave the room and told she was having a heart attack! The staff asked about resuscitation, but while I was reeling and trying to figure out what to do, Mama stabilized. Around midnight, the nurse offered me some scrubs and extra sheets. We made up the couch, and I finally fell asleep in Francisco's arms, physically exhausted and emotionally drained.

· · ·

At 5:15 a.m., the night nurse woke me up and said that Mama was dying. I had only a short time to say my last words. I was numb, "This can't be; she had come so far," I thought, but Francisco and I jumped up in a rush. He went to one side of the bed and I the other. We each took a hand and held each other's, forming a circle around Mama. The nurse had raised the bed so that Mama was sitting up. Her skin was pale, and her eyes were closed. Her mouth was open, and she was faintly breathing. We started telling Mama that it was okay to go and that we loved her, and what a glorious place that she was about to venture to! I started crying and looking around the room, for I had often prayed that when it was her time that Daddy would appear like out of the movie *Ghost*. I did not see his image, but the feeling that the Holy Spirit was present was strong. The angel that I once sensed was again among us. Francisco and I started to say *The Lord's Prayer*.

Just as we finished, Mama took her last breath. It was 5:30 a.m. on Tuesday, October 30, 2007. She did not die alone. As the tears continued down my face, we had sent her off with all our love and prayers. Mama was now physically gone from me. The last words that I had heard from her were my name. That gave me comfort.

The nurse came back in, said it was time to leave and asked which funeral home I wanted to call. Her matter-of-factness was astonishing to me, but Mama had been suffering. It was time for her to be at peace. It was still dark outside and too early to start calling people. I mentioned to Francisco that my neighbor Susan had given me a bottle of Veuve Clicquot for my birthday and that it was in the refrigerator. I said, "Why don't we go to the beach and pop the cork at sunrise? We'll toast to a beautiful Mama." So we went home and got a blanket, the bottle of champagne, and two painted Perrier-Jouet flutes. We went to an area of the beach that was not too far from her house. The sunrise was spectacular, and that's when I knew Daddy and she had been reunited. I felt the heavens rejoicing. Mama was departing on her endless adventure.

We had funeral planning to do, so we pulled back into the neighborhood. I saw Susan's light on at her house. I asked Francisco to please stop the car. As I walked to Susan's house, she looked up from the kitchen window, and I held up the bottle of champagne. She knew from this gesture that Mama had passed. She came to the door, and we made another toast to "Mama Joan!" Susan said she would help me get the word out. We came home, and I contacted my brothers, then Uncle Knox and Aunt Patti, and finally family friends. Francisco said we should rest for an hour or so, but soon my aunt and cousins came to the door. They were so comforting and started to help me plan the funeral.

My mother had been gone only six and a half hours, yet now I was looking at caskets and trying to make funeral arrangements. We knew that she would be buried with Daddy at Arlington, but since it would be difficult for local family and friends to make such a long journey, we decided to have a memorial service on the coast, with the funeral to follow in Washington. The local service would be Friday afternoon, giving time for my brothers to fly in. Since Mama loved the Gulfport Yacht Club on Friday nights, we'd have a cocktail and fried catfish reception that evening. Only my oldest brother flew in. The other two said they would wait for the service in Arlington.

At Arlington, the Old Post Chapel where my father's service had been held was booked until late in November, so we held a Mass at another church, then a shorter burial service at the graveside. Father Jim Julius, the former priest from the United States Retirement Home in Gulfport, agreed to fly up with us to assist in the Mass and graveside ceremony. I booked tickets for the three of us, Father Jim, Francisco, and me, and off we went.

We stayed at a hotel in Arlington off Route 50, not too far from the Iwo Jima Memorial. My mother had purchased an Omega Speedmaster watch like the astronauts wore in the Apollo program for whoever conducted her funeral. We presented the watch to Father Jim, who was a crusty ol' man and not what one would think of as priestly. He was almost caustic at times, and once said in a sermon that he was not fond of dogs or children. At the end of the sermon, he said, "Well, I guess dogs aren't so bad." That was just a front, though, and he knew our family well. Daddy, Mama, and I had started going to the chapel at the retirement home in the 1980s, and apparently Daddy went to Father Jim when he had some questions about his faith. Father Jim was proud that he had a signed and framed picture of Daddy in his home.

When we arrived at the Catholic church near Arlington Cemetery, Mama's casket was at the back of the church. The local priest said that the family should walk behind the casket as it was wheeled to the base of the altar, and then have a seat in the front pews. I waved to Francisco to walk with me. Francisco had been there when Mama died, and he should be there to walk with the family at her burial service. Just like at Daddy's funeral, friends were invited to conduct the readings and Responsorial Psalms, and the four children spoke.

Joan B. Roosa Funeral
Eulogy Comments by Rosemary Roosa
November 2007 for burial at Arlington Cemetery

My mother, Joan Roosa, was an original. She was an original rock & roller, an original wife, and when pushed by a reporter during Daddy's mission of what she did for a living… she answered, "I think original thoughts."

My mother was also my best friend. She understood me like no other, and was always so generous, kind, and loving. We shared a rare and wonderful mother/daughter bond. I was fortunate to be with her when she took her last breath – and although I will miss her somethin' fierce – I know she is in Heaven and making her presence known, like she did here on Earth.

When people think about my father, they look at him as the great adventurer – but it was my mother who was the true adventurer. As a little girl in Tupelo, Mississippi, going to grade school with Elvis Presley, she read a book in the 4th grade called Richard Halliburton's Book of Travels – and she knew right then that she wanted to travel the world.

After graduating from college, a group of friends took a map out and threw a dart at it, stating wherever it landed, they would move there. Well it almost landed in the water, but hit near Langley Air Force Base, Virginia. It was at Langley that Mama met Daddy, and he proceeded to woo her with his jet. Shortly after meeting, Mama told me the story how she was at a party with Daddy and some other pilots, and he said, "A real fighter pilot throws his glass into the fireplace when he finishes a drink." Without saying a word, Mama looked down at her glass and had about a swallow of champagne left, so she chugged it and hurled it right at the fireplace. She said Stuart was so shocked – but decided right then and there that he wanted to marry her.

And instead of taking what money they had and saving it on a first house, their honeymoon was a trip through Europe. They found their way around by a guide book that Daddy checked out of the library. He figured it was cheaper to pay the overdue fee than buy the book. And thus, their adventures together began. As us children came along, we hunted and fished and boated – and of course, traveled. Mama wound up traveling to almost every place listed in

Richard Halliburton's book, except for Mecca and Antarctica.

When my father died, I made Mama promise to live 10 more years. Well she did, and almost three more. I bet you Daddy's first words to her in Heaven were "'Bout time, Puddin'" But during her time here, she and I had many adventures together, and just last year we sailed to Europe on the Queen Mary. I will always remember Mama through our trips. She was her own person and one-of-kind - full of life, creativity, and vivaciousness.

When trying to figure out what to say about Mama today, I realized there is no good way to sum up Mama. I'm sure each of y'all have a "Joan Roosa" story that is fascinating and beautiful. So, we celebrate her life today, not her death, and take comfort that she is with Daddy, traveling the universe together. And if they check out a guide book, I'm sure God would not charge them an overdue fee.

Losing both my parents was not the worst of it. With disagreements about the family estate, my brothers and I are estranged. As of the writing of this book, the Roosa family holdings and assets are in litigation. I have wondered in disbelief how we could go to the moon and back in a decade, but yet, we cannot close an estate in over 10 years. As my family suffers through these trials and tribulations, I see only one answer: continue to love. Love in all forms is a powerful force.

CHAPTER 14

Moon Trees and Beyond

When my father retired from NASA, he wrote a letter to Deputy Administrator George Low. Daddy received a nice letter back saying he understood his leaving NASA, and George Low said, "I do not think we will see another Apollo in our lifetime." How prophetic that statement, because Stu Roosa did not see another deep space manned program before he died. The rise and fall of the Apollo program can in a way be compared to the Roosa family. We had formed a "dynasty" at the Hassler Hotel in Rome in 1976 and promised we would try to do great things together and pass them along. Now, the Roosa family is divided and conquered, never to "escape earth's atmosphere."

Yet another family emerged. Not one based on blood, but on the NASA family. The tight bonds of the Apollo program cannot be severed. There is a feeling of belonging to something great, something that was not achieved individually, but as a "family." It is inspiring to this day, and NASA shows what can be achieved with hard work and a team effort. Another family also emerged from good friends. The Six Hot Chicks still gather together to celebrate birthdays, share in the sorrow of losing parents, and support each other in good times and bad. And finally, Francisco's family, from his children to his sisters, cousins, aunts, and his mother. All have taken me under their wing. And I have my aunt and cousins on the coast, my Harvard Business School friends, and my community most of all. The Apollo children also share a strong bond.

With Harrison Ford as Master
of Ceremonies at the National
Aviation Hall of Fame

National Aviation Hall
of Fame Apollo 11 40th
anniversary tribute with
Dotty & Charlie Duke
and Zoe Dell Nutter

Meeting the one and
only Arnold Palmer at
National Aviation Hall
of Fame

In 2009, I received a call from Ed White, the son of the Apollo 1 astronaut. He said there were two big ceremonies planned. One was that his father was being inducted into the National Aviation Hall of Fame and that Neil Armstrong was going to do the honors. And the second was the 40th anniversary of Apollo 11 at the Smithsonian Air & Space Museum in Washington, D.C. Funds were tight, but Ed convinced me that I needed to attend both. It would be a whirlwind few days, but it was doable. I flew to Dayton, Ohio, and saw some old and familiar friends and faces. One friend was Zoe Dell Nutter, who had submitted me for membership in Shikar-Safari. Zoe Dell was on the board of the National Aviation Hall of Fame, and she wound up paying for my ticket and hotel room. The Nutters are a powerful name in Dayton, Ohio, and there are several buildings named after them, including the Wright State University Nutter Center. My room at the hotel was not just a room, but an entire suite that spanned half the hallway! It was meant for a party... but I was there alone, and thus, the bar and furnishings lay quiet that night. I could sense it had seen some wild nights, though. I arranged to have my hair done, and I dressed for the evening. Zoe Dell picked me up with her driver, and we proceeded to the event.

• • •

I had been to an event there with Zoe Dell a few years earlier in 2004 with my mother. Zoe Dell sat at Table #1 but was conducting politics with the federal and local politicians, so Mama and I were placed at Table #2. I thought about the time Mama and Daddy were placed at Table #1 with Miss Ima Hogg in Houston and Alan Shepard being impressed. That night, I ran into Laura Shepard-Churchley, who was at a table farther back. I had to chuckle to myself, for in my mind, she always "outranked" me, too. Nearby was Paul Tibbets, the man who dropped the atomic bomb at Hiroshima and who'd said words akin to "Oh my God, what have we done." The crowd was packed, and the Master of Ceremonies that evening was Harrison Ford, also a pilot. Even he seemed humbled about being in the room with *THE* pilots of the day. I met Harrison Ford, who was quiet and cordial. We snapped a picture, and I moved on. As the ceremonies progressed that night in 2004, the announcer said that Neil Armstrong was in the house. He was not speaking that night, but living not too far from Dayton, he was an honored guest. After the event, which was a tribute to the Wright Brothers & First Flight, the ceremony was closing. The crowd started to swoop upon Neil Armstrong. Mama was going to say hello to him, but he was quickly swallowed up in the crowd. She decided not to fight it and started walking away. Then out of the blue, a man's arm reached out and touched the back of her neck. She turned around to see Neil, and he said "Joan, how wonderful to see you here!" and gave her a big hug. I likened it to a salmon swimming upstream for him to reach Mama. But that is how strong the bond was for those who went through Apollo. It was a bond for life, and beyond.

• • •

Now I was back in 2009 without Mama, and Neil Armstrong was the main speaker. He was too surrounded for me to get to him, but knew I would see him the next day in D.C. for the 40th anniversary of his historic flight, Apollo 11. I met several other celebrities, including Arnold Palmer. With Francisco being the golf lover, I had to snap a picture with Arnold. The Master of Ceremonies this time was David Hartman from *Good Morning America*. I remember watching him on the morning show and thought how positive and likeable he was on TV. Later that evening in the hospitality suite, I got a chance to meet him. He was just as likeable in real life. He told me that he was going to travel with Neil Armstrong, Gene Cernan, and Jim Lovell for a world tour later that year, also in celebration of Apollo 11. He also told me how he had met my father in Oshkosh when they did a celebration to Apollo in 1994. David Hartman talked about how interesting my father's words were during the event. A few weeks later, he kindly sent me a video of the Oshkosh event, signed DH. In the video, my father explained what it was like when the explosion occurred on Apollo 13.

Daddy likened it to having a wing torn off your airplane, and then reaching for the emergency check-list on what to do. It was unprecedented.

The next morning it was off to D.C., with a stop in Atlanta. Francisco had managed an airline ticket for the D.C. festivities, and we were to meet at our hotel in Washington. He had booked a very early, less expensive flight. As I was hustling through the Atlanta airport, almost to my gate, I saw Francisco sleeping in a chair! He had gotten up so early that he had fallen asleep waiting on his connection and had missed the plane. Delta was understanding and put us both on the same flight for our nation's capital. Once there, the celebrations began again, and that evening was a spectacular event at the Kennedy Center.

The next evening, there was a large event at the Smithsonian Air & Space Museum. As Francisco and I entered the event, there were my pals, Laura and Ed, and once again the three amigos were together. It was the bonding of Apollo with the next generation. After a fitting tribute to the crew of Apollo 11 by the Master of Ceremonies, Neil deGrasse Tyson, Neil Armstrong gave an impressive and thoughtful speech. Afterward there were appetizers and cocktails, and we toured a gallery with an exhibit of the work of Alan Bean from Apollo 12, who was now a renowned artist. Alan Bean turned his space journey into painting the space images on canvas, often times using the tools he used on the moon and integrating parts of his suit in his works. As the event wound down, the three amigos decided it was champagne time at the Willard Hotel and to pop the cork to the moon. As we were leaving, the Smithsonian handed out goody bags full of pins, patches, and other commemorative items. Inside the bag was a tin container in a wrapped logo of the Apollo 40th tribute. It was a gift of Apollo 14 second generation moon tree seeds. Daddy was with us in spirit, and my heart felt the warmth of remembrance.

The next morning was also full of events, including a visit to the White House. As we toured the most famous mansion in the world, I paused in the East Room, where at the tender age of 7 years old, I had sat for a State Dinner. What a journey my life had been, thanks to Daddy. Although we did not meet President Obama, the crew of Apollo 11 was staying to do so.

Standing in between the first and last man to walk on the moon, Neil Armstrong (left) and Gene Cernan (right) with me in the center

Reminiscing about Apollo days with Walter Cronkite "And that's the way it is"

Francisco and me outside of White House

The health care initiative was in progress, and the President was too busy politicking to meet all the astronauts and families. Back at the hotel, there was a hospitality suite where they served lunch. I was in a festive mood and asked Francisco to purchase some wine to share. As we lounged there, slowly the group dispersed to rest for the evening events. Charlie Duke (Apollo 16) and Gene Cernan (Apollo 17) were to be on Neil Cavuto's program that afternoon, so Francisco and I turned on the TV to watch. Then Neil Armstrong and his family walked into the suite. I asked Neil how he liked meeting the President, and he just shrugged and smiled in a gentle way. Daddy used to say fame is fleeting, so I guess with the newer generation, the imprint and impact of Apollo was already diminishing.

Soon it was only Neil Armstrong, Francisco, and me in the hospitality suite. We sat around the TV on the sofa and chairs, making a triangle, with Neil at the top facing the TV. Francisco was left of the television and I to the right. We were watching Fox News, and Neil Cavuto introduced Charlie and Gene. The topic was the future of NASA and the space program.

As the back and forth rolled on, suddenly Cavuto interrupted and said, "Please wait a minute, for on this day, at this exact moment, Neil Armstrong was stepping out on the moon for the first time… so let's take a moment and pause."

For that second, as we sat in the room alone with the most famous man of Apollo, there was a feeling of accomplishment, achievement, pride in our country, and unity, just as it had been when he stepped foot on the moon 40 years ago. It was a heady pause. Francisco and I looked at Neil sitting between us, but we both knew the moment was too big for some trivial words. We wondered if Neil would say something, but he sat there quietly. No reason to boast or aggrandize the moment. That was Neil Armstrong.

In honor of the Apollo 14 40th anniversary in 2011, the Astronaut Scholarship Foundation near Cape Kennedy, Florida, hosted a first-of-its-kind fundraiser/dinner/tribute to the Apollo 14 crew. It was an intimate, $1,000-a-plate dinner, and was restricted to 50 people. It was held beneath a Saturn V rocket, one of three remaining rockets that had been built for Apollo 18, 19, and 20. In terms of rotation, my father would have likely been the Commander of Apollo 20, which would have had him walking on the moon by the mid-'70s. The event was all that I imagined it to be and more. Most of the Apollo astronauts attended, including Neil Armstrong. One of my Harvard Business School classmates flew in with his son, and I tried to introduce him to as many of his childhood heroes as possible. Apollo inspired children all over the world, and the group this night consisted mostly of businessmen in their 40s and 50s who wanted to be astronauts but wound up in different professions. Alan Shepard's daughter, Laura, and I gave a touching champagne toast to our fathers prior to the dinner, and then I shot a cork out of a champagne bottle and asked everyone to shout with me, "To the Moon!" The cork hit the corner of the room, and it set the mood for a memorable evening.

As we entered the Saturn V Center, guests walked by the Command Module of Apollo 14, *Kitty Hawk*, and took pictures with Edgar Mitchell — the only living crewmate from the mission — and Charlie Duke and Fred Haise, who were on the back-up crew. I looked in the capsule right before the photo and said "hello" to Daddy. At our table was a Swiss gentleman who was a pilot with Swiss Airlines. I was talking to the guests about what a busy week I was about to have, for not only did I have this event, but I was going back to Mississippi to plant a special tree — called a Moon Tree — with Fred Haise, Apollo 13 astronaut, at the new Infinity Science & Space Center near Stennis Space Center in Hancock County, Mississippi. Naturally, most wanted to know what a moon tree was. I explained about the tree seeds circling the moon, coming back to earth and being germinated, and how in my father's honor of his Apollo 14 mission, we were planting second-generation moon trees to keep the legacy alive.

I casually said to the Swiss pilot as I was cutting off a piece of filet mignon, "Let's plant a moon tree in Switzerland, too."

He said, "Fantastic! Let's do it!"

I was surprised with his positive response, for I wasn't sure how to do it, but we agreed to look into the possibilities. Also on that trip I had a conversation with Charlie Bolten, NASA Administrator and Shuttle astronaut, living in Washington, D.C. He was top dog at NASA, appointed

In front of the Apollo 14 Command Module with
Edgar Mitchell and Laura Shepard-Churchley

Apollo 14 40th anniversary with astronauts Al Worden of
Apollo 15 (left), Alan Bean of Apollo 12 (center by me), and
Neil Armstrong of Apollo 11 (right)

by Barack Obama. I showed Charlie the moon tree planted at the Kennedy Space Center and suggested we fly some moon tree seeds on the last Shuttle mission. He told me to get him the seeds right away. Going straight to the source is always good.

Francisco and I returned home to one of the coldest dips in temperature in several years. The moon tree planting at Infinity was still a "go," so we bundled up as warmly as we could and prepared to brave the elements. A good friend of mine, Mary Cracchiolo-Spain, wanted to ride with us, so we picked her up. As it turns out, the local paper, the *Sun Herald*, wrote a front-page article about the moon trees that hit the cover that morning, so she read the article to me as we drove toward Stennis, about a 45-minute drive along the scenic beach route, Highway 90. I was thinking of what I was going to say, and with the hectic week, for the first time I did not have my words written down.

I turned to Fred Haise and mentioned it, and he said, "Well then, as us pilots say, you will be flying by the seat of your pants!"

I talked about Ms. Gassett, Daddy's teacher back in Oklahoma, and how important it was to study hard in school. The moon tree ceremony was special, with hundreds of kids in attendance. Francisco's daughter, Bella, led the Pledge of Allegiance. The goal was to inspire the next generation to achieve great things in their lives by reaching for the stars in their own ways.

Arrangements were made to plant a moon tree at the Swiss Museum of Transport in Lucerne, Switzerland, thanks to the Swiss pilot, Lukas Viglietti, whom we met at the Apollo 14 40th anniversary. He had come through with his efforts. Beautiful dinners and presentations were conducted with other astronauts in attendance. Another moon tree was planted in Italy, thanks to Luigi Pizzimenti, at Parco Pineta near Milan. While in Italy, I told the story to Luigi about how on the day my Daddy died, we saw a streak going up into the sky. After planting the moon tree and taking pictures, at the end of the trip, Luigi presented Francisco and me with a photograph. It just so happened a streak was in the sky behind us. We had no clue at the time the photo was taken, but Daddy was giving his blessing and was once again there in spirit.

Planting a moon tree with Fred Haise of Apollo 13
at the Infinity Science Center in Mississippi

Moon tree planting in Switzerland with Lukas Viglietti - and Apollo
Astronaut Charlie Duke (far left), French Astronaut Jean-François Clervoy
(right of me), and Swiss Astronaut Claude Nicollier (far right)

Six months after the dinner at the Saturn V Center, we were back at the Cape, for on July 8, 2011, the last Shuttle mission was taking place. After 30 years of the Shuttle program, Atlantis was making its final ride. America was ending its program of putting U.S. astronauts into space on the International Space Station by our own vehicles. It was going to be up to the Russians now. At first our mortal enemy, they now were our friends in the space program. On board were some tiny seeds that had started their ancestry in deep space travel.

As the white smoke blasted outward from the start of the engines, the announcer's voice said, "All three engines up and running, and lift off... the final lift off of Atlantis on the shoulders of the Space Shuttle... America will continue the dream."

As Houston Mission Control took the helm, another announcer said, "Roger, roll, Atlantis! As the Space Shuttle spreads its wings one final time for the start of a sentimental journey..."

And with that, NASA ended the Shuttle program. The United States' space program had started out to beat the Russians, and now we would be dependent on them to get us into space.

Daddy's loving and guiding hand was with me that entire year for the 40th anniversary, for after speaking with Bo Bobko, an accomplished Shuttle astronaut who was head of the USA-side of ASE (Association of Space Explorers), Bo helped me present a moon tree to the Russian cosmonauts in Moscow for the 50th anniversary of Yuri Gagarin's flight. The theme for the conference was "He Invited Us All Into Space." I was back in Russia again, for the fourth time in my life. Finances were still tight, so I reached out to my Harvard class to ask if anyone had sky miles to share, and a classmate, Hersh Chadha, responded. Hersh, a superb photographer, was born in India but was now living in Dubai. Hersh wanted to have some of his nature photographs fly on the ISS - International Space Station. Hersh said he was inspired by Stu Roosa and wanted the astronauts to enjoy the beauty of earth while circling it. After carefully selecting a few photos, Hersh sent them to me. After presenting the moon tree to the cosmonauts, I presented the photographs to the U.S. representative in charge of the

American astronauts. Then the U.S. hit another snag in foreign relations and quit launching Americans into space by the Russian rockets. Negotiations slowed, and the photographs were put into storage. After arranging a dinner with the first Romanian cosmonaut, Dumitru Prunariu and Hersh, the Russia connection was reestablished. Hersh's photographs finally made it to the ISS in 2017 as the first permanent photo exhibition in space. Hersh was later invited to Star City with the cosmonauts to celebrate.

The Romanian cosmonaut, Dumitru, was also involved with the United Nations in Austria, and along the way, I was contacted by the U.S. Embassy in Vienna to plant a moon tree during the conference of the Peaceful Uses of Outer Space. We made the arrangements; my speech was written, and the expenses were paid by the United States government. My friend Michell and her mother said they would join us for the event, and they headed over early to Europe to celebrate Michell's 50th birthday. Two days before Francisco and I were to leave, we realized in all the bureaucracy, the paperwork for the tree had not been properly processed. The trip was canceled. It was very disappointing.

That trip was not meant to be, but another one soon appeared on the radar. The Association of Space Explorers was meeting in Saudi Arabia in 2012. Mama and Daddy had been there years before with another ASE trip, and Mama had talked about the culture. As the men gathered for meet-and-greets and space meetings, the wives were invited to other events and parties. Mama once described a party where the Saudi women arrived covered in the abaya, the traditional black "cloak." As the women took off their robes behind the public eye, Mama was stunned to see the beautiful Bulgari jewelry and exquisitely tailored clothes. Mama came back fascinated by the Muslim adventure, and now it was my turn to see this unique country.

It was decided to gift some of the precious moon tree seeds that flew on the last Shuttle mission. Prince Sultan, our host, had also flown on a Shuttle mission, so the tribute was fitting. After enjoying a camel ride and falcon show in the desert at sunset, the group went to a palace outside of Riyadh, and the men danced with swords. We toured "streets" that showed the history of Saudi Arabia like if we were on a movie set. We stayed in

Romanian Cosmonaut
Dumitru Prunariu

In Saudi Arabia
gifting Astronaut
Prince Sultan Shuttle/
Moon Tree seeds

Walter Anderson Museum of Art

Rosemary D. Roosa
Executive Director

510 Washington Ave.
Ocean Springs, MS 39564

(P) 228-872-3164   (F) 228-875-4494

rosemary@walterandersonmuseum.org
www.walterandersonmuseum.org

the ornate Ritz hotel, which had four bronze horses in the lobby rearing up on their hind legs. On the final evening, in an intricately decorated formal room, I presented the Prince with the beautifully framed seeds. I was grateful once again of what this small-town Mississippi girl was able to experience because of Daddy's mission to the moon.

Also in 2012, Francisco was working on a film shoot with a friend, Elaine Stevens. Elaine's father had been a local celebrity, having owned a successful nightclub, Gus Stevens, which hosted entertainers such as Jayne Mansfield and Elvis Presley. Elaine was now on the board of the Walter Anderson Museum of Art (WAMA), a beautiful fine art museum in nearby Ocean Springs. Ocean Springs is a quaint place with boutiques and restaurants. A local eccentric named Walter Anderson who lived from 1903 to 1965 was a prolific artist, writer, and nature lover. I had immediately connected with Anderson's work years earlier, as did many Southerners, and it was hard to find a home or office that did not have a print or pottery piece fashioned by Walter Anderson. Elaine explained that the museum was looking for an executive director. I had been teaching at Tulane off and on as an associate professor since 2005 after Katrina but was not teaching a psychology class that fall. I applied and got the job at WAMA. It was a treat to work around these lovely surroundings, and I felt it was a good place to plant a moon tree. Charlie Duke flew in for the dedication, and he regaled the crowd with tales of his time in the Apollo program. Children helped with the planting ceremony, and each placed some dirt around base of the tree. It was moving.

Mississippi, via film incentives, was becoming an attractive place to shoot movies and the like. *The Astronaut Wives Club* book was being converted into an ABC television series, and the Cocoa Beach scenes were being shot on our white sand beaches. Downtown Gulfport had several locations of shooting, including the Triplett Day Drug store, owned by the man (Mr. Day) who had tracked down Mama after Katrina. One day after work at the museum, I thought, "Mama was an astronaut's wife. I would like to meet these people!" and jumped in my Mercedes with its license tag: 2TMoon (To the Moon) and drove to downtown Gulfport. The quiet but sharp, petite woman producer/writer, Stephanie Savage, talked with me for

Toasting to the real astronaut wives with a bottle of champagne on the set of the ABC series *The Astronaut Wives Club*

a while. After an exchange, she kindly asked me if I would like a to have a cameo appearance. She gave me a couple of options. The grand finale was a Moon Ball, and that sounded like fun.

"Can I pop the cork on a bottle of champagne in honor of the real astronauts' wives?"

With no hesitation, she said, "Let's make it happen!" and wrote my three little words, "To the Moon!" in the script.

• • •

There are times when I really miss my parents. Sometimes I dream about them, and I say, "Oh, thank God, I thought you were *dead*! I am so happy to see you," and I start telling them about my life. And then I'll wake up and they are gone, but their spirit is not, nor is their love. There are times when they send me a sign. It generally comes out of the blue, and in my heart, I know it's from them. One day while working at the museum, I received an email from a gentleman named Christian Bourdeille in France, asking if I'd consider planting a moon tree at an observatory outside of Paris. The date for the planting was December 12, 2015. My father passed away on December 12, so I couldn't help but think it was a sign from Daddy. Francisco and I went, and it was magical in the City of Lights. There was also a sign from Mama, for a gentleman in the town where we were planting the tree was an Elvis-lover. When I told him my mother was from Tupelo and went to grade school with Elvis, the gentleman was more interested in that than he was in space and the moon tree!

In November 2016, the Astronaut Scholarship Foundation held a fundraiser at Cocoa Beach. This time they had the children of Apollo speak. The audience was packed, and we had several families represented from Neil Armstrong, Buzz Aldrin, Jim Lovell, Alan Shepard, and of course, Stu Roosa. It was fascinating to hear each other's stories, for we shared the same experiences but have not always had a chance to talk to each other about them. After the event, we, the Shepard girls, Rick Armstrong, and the Dukes made a champagne toast to the moon. Together, we ventured to those familiar sands of Cocoa Beach and popped the cork as high as it would travel. As we cheered "To the Moon!" I laughingly said, "It's trying to get into lunar orbit!" We talked privately about our lives and the moon, and we felt united as we smiled and reminisced about the "good ol' days" of Apollo. The generations were joined again.

During the solar eclipse in August 2017, we were invited to plant a moon tree at Pisgah National Forest in North Carolina. While there, we met a gentleman named Mr. Collins, who helped with satellite communications to Mission Control during Apollo. One communication allowed the astronauts' wives to talk to their husbands on the aircraft carrier after their fiery return to earth while the space capsule was picked up at sea. Small connections such as these show the reach of the Apollo program. My father said it took a cast of thousands to get him up there and back. Anyone who had a part feels a sense of accomplishment, and they should. The grower helping me with the moon trees recently recounted that a welder came to his farm, and as he was looking around, the welder saw the trees marked: Moon Trees. There was a visible change in the man's look. The welder recounted how he had a hand in putting the lunar module legs together, and he said it with pride and a sense of accomplishment. Now those same legs are sitting on the moon. Forever "frozen" in the non-atmospheric lunar landscape. On one particular lunar module, on the base of one of those spidery legs, is a plaque. It lists the names of the three men who journeyed there for nine days from January 31 to February 9, 1971 on Apollo 14. Engraved is the signatures of those men – Shepard, Mitchell, and Roosa. I hope to proudly carry on the Roosa name and inspire others.

What is it like to be a child of one of only a handful of men to go to the moon and back? Fascinating. And it is something I do not take for granted. My father's experience gave me many opportunities and adventures. "Life is an adventure" is my credo. But great things are generally inspired, so now is the time to focus on continuing the legacy of my father. The Moon Tree Foundation was officially formed, and in 2017, I resigned from the Walter Anderson Museum of Art after years at the helm and being the longest lasting director. The Moon Tree Foundation's purpose is to inspire interest in education, science, space, and conservation, as well as peace for all mankind. The motto is "Planting the Seeds of Inspiration." And we do it not because it is *hard*, but because it is *easy*.

There were vicious hurricanes in 2017, and unfortunately, one of the original moon trees planted at Kennedy Space Center in 1976 was destroyed by Hurricane Irma. However, this particular moon tree story has a happy ending, for as we celebrate the 50th anniversary in 2019 of the historic Apollo 11 flight in 1969, the Moon Tree Foundation is working with the Kennedy Space Center to plant a tree for each of the Apollo moon missions. The Moon Tree Garden will live for years as a tribute to Apollo and for all mankind to enjoy. During 2019 to 2022, for the 50th anniversaries of the Apollo moon missions, the Moon Tree Foundation's goal is to plant 50 trees in 50 locations. I have a feeling that Daddy's spirit will be there with each planting.

• • •

The moon has a special meaning. Since the dawn of time, humans have a wanted to fly, to slip the surly bonds of earth and to touch the sky. The Apollo program started as a space race to the moon, and it wound up being the greatest adventure of humankind. Soon there will be no more men walking this earth who have stepped on the moon. Those brave 24 men who traversed the unknown and took the ultimate risk of their lives should not be forgotten or read about in the books as ancient history. Their accomplishments should not be sullied by naysayers who claim that the moon visits were staged in a desert studio. Those 24 astronauts went there. They achieved. They conquered. And there are six American flags planted on the moon by those men.

Are all astronauts high achievers? You bet. Do they want to make a difference? Absolutely. They embody the competitive spirit, but in a "the sum is more than the parts" way. It is time for the United States to lead in space again. Although the requirements of an astronaut have changed from primarily fighter/test pilot to scientist/linguist, the same spirit of adventure is in all. Just as humans ventured from the cave to explore their surroundings, then ventured across the seas despite the fear of falling off the earth, we must continue to explore and venture into the unknown.

Some say there are alien beings out there. My father used to be asked this. His answer would be that although he did not experience or see anything, that space is too vast to not have another life form. I take another spin on it. What if we are the intelligent beings who are supposed to propagate the universe? NASA is working hard, as are most civilized nations today, to send satellites and rovers to places far away. The images that are sent back to earth are mind-boggling. Just as the Wright Brothers could not foresee what their first flight would lead to with the commercialization of aviation, my father felt that one day space travel should also be "ordinary" in a way. Daddy was a true pioneer in space flight, and he would have encouraged the commercializing of space.

• • •

Everyone probably has some type of connection with the moon, whether it be for lovers, for dreamers, or for doers. The moon is a beacon of hope. It is a source of inspiration. It needs to be conquered again. It will forever be a part of those who lived during the Apollo program. It is time for the new generation to experience an earth-uniting event.

Every time I look at the moon, I feel the spirit of my father and my mother. Sometimes the moon is a crescent; other times it is high in the sky and bright as a light — a beacon shining down on me saying, "All will be well." The moon and I are kindred spirits.

The moon is the ultimate sign of love. If we keep the faith, show kindness to one another, respect each other's views and perspectives, then love truly will show us the way. Next time a moonbeam is shining down, take it as a sign of love. And the next time a bottle of champagne is popped, be sure to cheer, "To the Moon!"

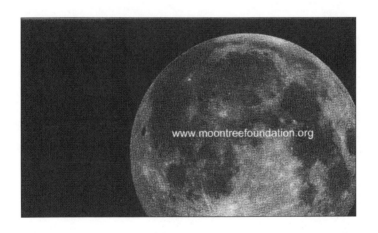

www.moontreefoundation.org

Walking down the red carpet as an Apollo astronaut's daughter, representing my parents at an Astronaut Scholarship Foundation event at Kennedy Space Center

ACKNOWLEDGEMENTS

Writing a book is a daunting process, particularly when it is about your own life. I started putting words to paper one summer when I was looking for a project, not knowing if it would be published. I just wanted to tell the story of my adventures in life, and the love of my parents and their impact on me. I would not have completed this book without the support of my wonderful partner, Francisco Gonzalez. His encouragement and support have been unwavering, and we have been going on 14 years together – a good number. After completing the chapters, the next step was to find an editor who could help me shape the stories into a flowing and consistent tone. This "God-send" was Karen Bryant. Her upbeat manner and "almost there" words kept me moving along.

I also want to thank MS University Press and Craig Gill who was patient with me as I worked on the chapters. His kind support and advice were invaluable. Thank you to Francis French who helped with technical aspects of the space flights. This book would not have been published without Neil White, creative director, and Sinclair Rishel, associate editor, at Nautilus Publishing Company, thank you for your good work. Other writers and editors who assisted me are Doug White (a fast reader with immediate input), Nancy McCaskey (a sweet friend with great commentary), and Billy Dugger (my neighbor who helped digitize the photographs). I also want to thank fellow international authors of Apollo books, Lukas Viglietti (my Swiss friend and moon tree advocate), Philippe Henarejos (a best-selling French author and champagne enthusiast), and Luigi Pizzimenti (whose love of all things Apollo is inspiring).

Thank you to my daughter Bella Gonzalez, who designed the cover and graphics, and whose personality and creativity will take her far in life; and to Tino Gonzalez and Francesca Wilson (and her rocket engine designing husband, Joel) and their wonderful children. And thanks to all of Francisco's family and cousins who have adopted me as part of their family, in particular, Maria Jones (Pitu) and Christina ("sis").

I want to acknowledge the steadfast friendship of my "Six Hot Chicks" – Tsh Hancock (BFF), Gail Kraemer Broussard, Tracy Byrd, Mary Cracchiolo Spain (board member of the Moon Tree Foundation), and special thanks to the beautiful Barbara Walker who provided photos. Thank you to Mandy Doyle and her husband, Greg, for the outstanding meals and conversation over the years; and to Michell Turkington and her husband, Scott, for their hospitality and support. And I could not have traveled without the care of my wonderful cat sitter, Pat Lesher, whose trust and friendship I value.

Thank you to the entire NASA family; Therrin Protze (who implemented the Moon Tree Garden at Kennedy Space Center); my Harvard Business School friends; and those who contributed to my book, with an especially big thank you to Apollo 16 Astronaut Charlie Duke and his wife, Dotty, whose love and support have been unwavering; Apollo 13 Astronaut Fred Haise, with whom I am pen-pals and sends daily NASA briefings; Billy Watkins, a fellow Mississippian and great friend; and to Lily Koppel, for her valuable feedback and input.

Finally, I would like to acknowledge the courageous crews of the Apollo missions and those 24 men who reached the moon. Their remarkable achievement truly is mankind's greatest adventure.

Made in the USA
Columbia, SC
14 January 2020